Praise for *In Search*

"It's hard to find someone who can keep their head in a level space as they research such a controversial and debated topic, but Richard Estep succeeds at this masterfully. In *In Search of Demons*, Richard examines horrific stories and lore from a place of curiosity and skepticism, something much needed when it comes to a subject heavily influenced by fearmongering and pop culture."

—**AMY BRUNI,** executive producer and host of Travel Channel's *Kindred Spirits* TV series

"Richard Estep doesn't take sides and he doesn't pull punches. If you want an honest look at demonic phenomena, this book is a must."

—**BRAD AND BARRY KLINGE,** hosts of Discovery Channel's *Ghost Lab* TV series

"Richard tackles this topic with his unbiased enthusiasm, scientific mindset, healthy skepticism, and openness to the unexplained through interviews with *regular* people like you and me, seasoned professionals and experts in the paranormal, and members of the Catholic Church's exorcism team….It is completely engrossing, thought provoking, and engaging."

—**HEATHER BLUMBERG,** star of *We Bought a Funeral Home* TV series

"Whether you are deeply religious or drawn towards the occult, Richard serves as a knowledgeable guide and interpreter to the realm of demons. With a methodical and considerate approach, he deciphers their tropes and treats claims of demonic encounters and expertise with fairness."

—**TOBIN LONG,** producer of *Haunted Hospitals, Paranormal 911,* and *Paranormal Night Shift* TV series

"Richard Estep takes you on a diabolical road trip to investigate the reality behind a subject that has piqued the public's interest and aroused their fears: demonic possession.…He thoroughly examines alternating viewpoints, all while maintaining objectivity. Every page leads you on an open-minded journey to answer the controversial questions about exorcisms and signs of demonic possession. Terror and intrigue await at every turn when *In Search of Demons*."

—**HEATHER TADDY,** paranormal investigator on *Paranormal State, Portals to Hell, Alien Highway,* and *Travel the Dead* TV series

"A spine-chilling journey into the most eerie manifestations of demonic influence. Juxtaposing skepticism with the unexplainable, Richard urges readers to question what lies beyond the surface."

—**JESSICA KNAPIK,** co-host of *What's Up Weirdo?* podcast

"*In Search of Demons* lifts a torch upon our passion for the ultimate evil. Citing work from renowned investigators, well-documented cases of hauntings, and discussing the need for the Devil himself, Richard Estep invites us to examine not just the existence of darker entities, but also that nature which lurks within each of us."

—**DUSTIN PARI,** paranormal investigator on *Ghost Hunters, Ghost Hunters International,* and other TV series

"Richard is both a seasoned writer and paranormal investigator, and he provides insights into his experiences and investigations involving purported encounters with demons.…Richard has carefully balanced personal experiences with detailed research and critical analysis. His balanced perspective offers readers a captivating journey into the world of demonic paranormal investigation. A must-read book."

—**PAUL STEVENSON,** editor of *Haunted Magazine*

IN SEARCH OF
DEMONS

© AliCottonphoto.com

About the Author

Richard Estep (Colorado) cofounded Boulder County Paranormal Research Society (BCPRS) with his wife, Laura, in 1999. He's the author of more than a dozen books detailing his most harrowing investigations, including *The Horrors of Fox Hollow Farm*. Visit him at RichardEstep.net.

IN SEARCH OF
DEMONS

Historic Cases & Firsthand Experiences
from Experts & Skeptics Alike

RICHARD ESTEP
Foreword by M. Belanger

LLEWELLYN
WOODBURY, MINNESOTA

FIRST EDITION
First Printing, 2024

Book design by Samantha Peterson
Cover design by Verlynda Pinckney
Photo provided by the author

Photography is used for illustrative purposes only. The persons depicted may not endorse or represent the book's subject.

Llewellyn Publications is a registered trademark of Llewellyn Worldwide Ltd.

Library of Congress Cataloging-in-Publication Data (Pending)
ISBN: 978-0-7387-7637-8

Llewellyn Publications
A Division of Llewellyn Worldwide Ltd.
2143 Wooddale Drive
Woodbury, MN 55125-2989
www.llewellyn.com

Printed in the United States of America

Other Books by Richard Estep

The Horrors of Fox Hollow Farm

For Bethany and Oliver,
With love on your wedding day
From, Uncle Richard

CONTENTS

Contents

FOREWORD

by M. Belanger

Demons are a divisive topic, particularly in the United States where they are wound up with fervently held religious beliefs. Finding reliable sources on the topic of demonology can be fraught, especially when many who present themselves as experts do so without ever questioning their own biases.

Enter Richard Estep.

A seasoned first responder, Richard Estep has cultivated a levelheaded pragmatism that he carries into his other personal calling: paranormal investigation. In thirty-five books (and counting), Estep recounts adventures seeking spirits in murder houses, abandoned prisons, and derelict hospitals, to name a few. One standout quality in all his books is how seamlessly he blends gripping storytelling with incisive reporting. When delving into a Richard Estep book, the reader is treated not only to a rollicking tale, but also to an exhaustively researched history lesson wrapped around an insightful meditation on human nature.

This book is no different.

It would be easy to write a book on demons that sensationalized the topic or pandered to one extreme belief or another. But Estep's goal here is not to dispense his own unquestioned beliefs, nor is it to put his opinion in the spotlight. Instead, Estep takes the role of an open-minded explorer eager to experience what the topic has to offer—and to share those experiences with the reader exactly as they are. With his cogent and lucid style coupled with a gentle and self-effacing humor, each chapter feels like a conversation shared between friends.

Traveling alongside Richard, we get to meet an all-star cast of interviewees from the world of paranormal media, each of whom has something to share on the topic of demons—both what demons are and why we continue to be so fascinated by them. Many names will be instantly recognizable to anyone interested in hauntings, spirits, and things that go bump in the night.

Robert Murch of the Talking Board Historical Society meets with Richard to discuss the widespread (and not entirely well-founded) belief that Ouija board use can lead to demonic possession. Jason Hawes, the titular ghost hunter of the hit series *Ghost Hunters* joins Richard between book signings to discuss how often he and his TAPS family have been called to investigate cases he felt were legitimately demonic (the answer will surprise you). Jeff Belanger, mountain climber, legend tripper, and occult consultant for television's *Ghost Adventures* offers his expert take on why demons appeal to us in the first place. Aaron Sagers, paranormal journalist with a focus on pop culture, chats with Richard about the media impact on modern demon beliefs, particularly how the 1973 blockbuster *The Exorcist* changed the landscape of belief for the past fifty years. Johnny Houser, caretaker of the infamous Villisca Axe Murder House, shares his harrowing personal experience with a dark force he believes to have been demonic.

In addition to this collection of scintillating figures, we'll meet a highly lauded stage magician, an ordained bishop from the Old Catholic Church, a psychiatrist, and even a witch. With each new interview, we are treated to another chapter representing Estep's own journey in search of demons. Some of the interviewees are believers, some are skeptics, many fall somewhere in the middle, but all have thought-provoking insights to offer on this frequently polarizing topic.

An avowed agnostic himself, Estep takes the role of the perfect stranger in each of his interviews. With an affable objectivity, he holds space for each person to share their unique point of view. When offering commentary, Richard is always quick to differentiate between fact, conjecture, and opinion, especially his own. This is one of the reasons why this book works so well. It presents a balanced and unbiased inquiry into a controversial topic.

Where most other people tackle the subject of demonology in order to promote their own beliefs, Richard Estep is here to learn along with the reader. He doesn't have an agenda beyond listening to what others think, taking some time to consider those thoughts, then faithfully articulating them in a way that leaves the ultimate interpretation up to the reader. And he manages to be incredibly entertaining while doing it.

Before you immerse yourself in this fascinating and sometimes spine-tingling journey, I want to end with a quote in Estep's own words, which I feel sums up the heart of this work:

"We need our ghosts. We need our gods. It may be that we also need our demons."

Turn the page to discover why.

M. Belanger
Author, *The Dictionary of Demons*

INTRODUCTION

It's a cold February night in southern England, and it's fair to say I'm just a little bit nervous. There's a chance I'm going to be sleeping with a demon.

Allow me to explain.

My name is Richard Estep. I've been a paranormal investigator for the past twenty-seven years, researching claims of ghostly goings-on across the United Kingdom and my adopted home, the United States.

When I first dipped my toes in the waters of the paranormal, it was the mid-1990s. There was no such thing as paranormal reality TV, other than the occasional documentary or local news segment around Halloween. Sure, there were plenty of horror movies, with *The Exorcist* leading the pack, and demons were mostly to be found on the silver screen or in the pages of books—primarily novels and fictional works.

In the decades since, the pop culture landscape has shifted dramatically with regard to the demonic, for reasons we'll explore in depth in this book. Living and working primarily in the United

States, one can hardly move in the paranormal community for claims of demons and demonic activity.

I've flown back across the Atlantic to the country of my birth in order to pursue a unique opportunity. The owners of a fifteenth-century English castle are giving me the keys and allowing me the run of the place for three complete days and nights. Simply that, in and of itself, is an offer I couldn't turn down; who *wouldn't* want to spend seventy-two hours living in a historic and reputedly haunted castle, exploring its mysteries and attempting to make contact with whatever it is that lurks within its walls?

What intrigues me most are the claims associated with one of the castle's bedchambers. According to local lore and legend, the room has long been cursed with a demonic infestation. In the sixteenth century, the lord of the castle was said to have been fascinated with the occult and black magic, and to have regularly conducted rituals of conjuration in an attempt to summon demons.

If you believe some of those stories, he was successful.

The demon is said to take on the form of a huge black dog, which likes to stare down terrified visitors with eyes that glow bright red. This spine-chilling beast emerges from the fireplace, the legend holds, although exactly what it does to those who encounter it has not been made clear.

British folklore refers to these spectral black "devil dogs" as *barghests*. According to the tradition, such demons are seen as harbingers of death, and their appearance is a prelude to a member of a nearby family dying.

Not for nothing are they referred to as Hellhounds or Dogs of Hell. They have even been enshrined in the wildly popular Dungeons & Dragons role-playing game.

Naturally, I aim to spend my nights at the castle sleeping in that specific room.

The author is holding what purports to be the diary of Father Raymond Bishop, one of the priests involved in the exorcism of Ronald Hunkeler that inspired the book and movie The Exorcist.

As I lie there in the darkness, waiting for something odd to happen (with just a hint of trepidation, I might add), my mind returns to the subject of demons in a broader sense.

It's now the twenty-first century, the year 2023. Humanity has sent astronauts to the moon and is preparing to send the first human mission to Mars. We have explored the outer reaches of our solar system and the depths of the earth's oceans. The internet and global telecommunications infrastructure allow nearly instantaneous connectivity between people living next door to one another, or on separate continents. The sum totality of our knowledge continues to grow at an exponential rate. Scientists make discovery after discovery in what can only be described as a golden age of science, technology, and innovation...

…and yet, there are still demons.

I mean this in a completely literal sense. The word *demon* has been used metaphorically, and sometimes in abstract terms. During the Prohibition era, supporters of the temperance movement referred to alcohol as "the demon drink." Today, those who have mental illness are sometimes spoken of as struggling with their demons.

Neither of those are the demons to which I refer. Although the subject of mental health and its potential connection with the demonic will be broached later on, the focus of this book, and the chain of thought that gave rise to it, is the fascination we still have with a concept that is thousands of years old—the idea that demonic entities could quite literally still live and move among us today, wreaking their own unique brand of havoc and misery upon the lives of innocents.

As physicists and other scientific researchers work diligently to unlock the most fundamental secrets of creation to offer up coherent hypotheses and theories to explain in detail the ways in which our world functions down to the smallest level, tens of millions of people remain convinced that forces of ancient evil still lurk among us. They believe demons interfere in the affairs of humanity, usually for the worse, and pose an extreme danger to those with whom they come into contact.

Although many atheists like to poke fun at this notion, belief in the demonic is widespread across the United States. It appears to be less so in the United Kingdom and other parts of the Western world, probably because it's a more secular country. Not only do I want to understand why that is, but I also want to assess the evidence for it. How much eyewitness testimony is there? What tangible proof might there be?

Introduction

As a card-carrying agnostic, I have no skin in this particular game. I don't come down hard on either side of the fence. Although I don't personally believe in demons, I also don't *not* believe in them. I remain open to the possibility that they might exist, but I am equally ready to accept that they may not.

The journey I undertake in this book is my attempt to answer that question, as clearly and succinctly as I can…and it really *was* an incredible journey. It would span the course of several years. In addition to the English castle, I visited the American heartland to personally experience one of the most notorious cases in the annals of modern psychic research—a case in which the family in question said they were tormented by a dark and malevolent entity that some claimed was a demon.

I sat down to speak with individuals who were highly knowledgeable and experienced with different facets of the subject. My list of interviewees ranged from hard-core skeptics to ardent believers, and those in between. Doctors, parapsychologists, demonologists, and exorcists; therapists, ghost hunters, authors, and more. I wanted to cover the theological, psychological, medical, and legal aspects of the demon question; I also talked to historians and pop culture experts in an attempt to place demons in their proper context. To that end, I also interviewed witches, priests, curators, and those who claimed to have had personal encounters with the demonic.

The journey we're about to embark on here will turn out to be one heck of a wild ride…one I will never forget for as long as I live. Every journey starts with a first step, and my search for demons would be no different.

So, Dear Reader, please turn the page and let's get started.

Richard Estep
Longmont, Colorado
January 1, 2024

one
DEMONIZED

It's difficult to assess the state of demonology in the United States without discussing the career of American demonologists Ed and Lorraine Warren. Even now, several years after their passing, the Warrens remain both controversial and polarizing figures. Some venerate and idolize them as pioneers and trailblazers—in no small part because of their dramatized representations in the Conjuring series of movies—whereas others decry them as frauds and charlatans. What cannot be denied is the enormous impact the duo had on the field of paranormal interest and demonology in particular—a legacy that continues to grow to this day. That makes them as good a starting point as any for us to consider the status of demons in present times.

The Warrens both hailed from Bridgeport, Connecticut. Born in 1926, Ed joined the Navy as a young man during the Second World War. Shortly before the war ended, he married a local girl named Lorraine Moran. Discharged from the service, Ed went to art school, developing his talent for painting. Ed's paintings were of sufficient quality that he was able to sell them to help pay the bills. Interested in ghosts and the paranormal from a young age, Ed often made haunted houses the subject of his paintings—this sometimes gave him a foot in the door, a way of getting the owner to allow himself and Lorraine inside the property to learn more about its haunting. As a young girl, Lorraine Warren saw halos surrounding other people. Describing herself as a clairvoyant medium, her approach to paranormal case research involved communicating with spirits and other supernatural entities…such as demons.

Both Ed and Lorraine were devout Catholics, which meant that a belief in the demonic was a key part of their worldview. Over the years, the Warrens claimed to have investigated thousands of claims of alleged paranormal activity and demonic infestation. These ranged from the relatively obscure to the world famous.

One of their best-known cases was what came to be called the Amityville Horror, thanks to the book of that name by author Jay Anson (along with the wildly successful Hollywood adaptation). The basis of the case began on November 13, 1974, in the affluent Long Island neighborhood of Amityville. Using a high-powered rifle, twenty-three-year-old Ronald "Butch" DeFeo Jr. shot his parents and four siblings dead in their home on Ocean Avenue. The DeFeos were all lying helpless in bed at the time of their deaths, presumably fast asleep. Butch DeFeo was the only credible suspect identified during the police investigation and was subsequently convicted and incarcerated for the murders.

In December 1975, the house was purchased by newlyweds George and Kathy Lutz, who moved in with their children. They failed to last a month, fleeing after living there for just twenty-eight days. The Lutzes told stories of diabolical forces being at work inside the residence, including swarms of flies and a demonic, red-eyed pig entity seen peering in at them from outside the windows.

Slime seeped from the walls. A phantom brass marching band was heard parading through the house. Kathy Lutz levitated above her bed. The list of phenomena reported by the Lutzes before they fled the house was staggeringly long.

In his memoir *As I Saw It: An Intrepid Reporter's Journey*, Emmy-winning journalist Marvin Scott recalled the night he spent with the Warrens at the Amityville house in March 1976. Neither the book nor the movie had come out at that time, some sixteen months after the murders took place. Having heard the stories of the house being demonically infested, Scott was understandably nervous.

In the early hours of the morning, right around the time Butch was killing his family members one by one, the reporter joined Lorraine Warren in one of the upstairs bedrooms in which two of the DeFeo children had been murdered in cold blood. Although nothing unusual happened to Scott, his cameraman grew short of breath on the stairs—in the very same place where Lorraine Warren said she was hit by something akin to "a torrent of water." He also felt a cold spot behind him; interesting, but not exactly proof of hard-core demonic infestation.

Were demonic powers really at work in Amityville? Marvin Scott maintained a sporadic correspondence with Butch DeFeo during his incarceration. In one of his letters, DeFeo addressed this question by stating, "There was no insanity. Only people talking to Weber [DeFeo's defense attorney] about books, about me being possessed…There was no demon. You know who the demon is. I am the demon."[1]

---

1. Learn more at https://pix11.com/news/local-news/long-island/i-am-the-demon-a-look-at-letters-amityville-horror-killer-ronald-defeo-sent-to-pix11s-marvin-scott/.

This seems like an open admission of fraud on DeFeo's part, yet it must also be borne in mind that the man changed his testimony about what happened on the night of the murders over and over again. Butch DeFeo was at best a completely unreliable source, and undeniably an outright liar.

Does this mean that the house in Amityville was not haunted, either by demons, dark spirits, or something else—was the whole thing a hoax? Some have maintained that it was. Others still swear it was genuine. Walking the middle ground, one of the Lutz children went on the record, stating that although many of the phenomena depicted in Anson's book and the movie were grossly exaggerated, the house really was haunted.

In an interview with the *Seattle Times*, Christopher Quaratino (Kathy Lutz's son) said that George Lutz had attempted to summon supernatural beings while living inside the house. "I don't know that I'd call it black magic, but it was…a way to call up spirits."[2]

In 2013, Christopher's brother, Danny Lutz, spoke out about his experiences at the house, claiming to have personally experienced violent paranormal phenomena there—and attributing the activity to demonic entities. Both George and Kathy Lutz are dead. Neither ever went back on their story about what had happened to them in Amityville.

Although none of the subsequent owners have experienced anything odd, for Ed and Lorraine Warren, there was no doubt that diabolical forces plagued the house on Ocean Avenue. Whereas two of the Lutz children had claimed their stepfather, George, had dabbled in occult practices and therefore caused the demonic activity in the house, Ed and Lorraine Warren believed the same was

---

2. Learn more at https://www.seattletimes.com/nation-world/ex-resident-of -house-debunks-much-of-amityville-horror/.

true of Ronald DeFeo—and that the demonic entity was at least partially responsible for causing the murders.

During a televised interview with his son-in-law, Tony Spera, Ed Warren recalled, "Lorraine and I do not back up the movie or the book. It was much more horrific than either."

He went on to add that six months prior to the murders, Mr. DeFeo had traveled to a shrine in Montreal, Canada, and upon his return, had brought with him an exorcist to say masses inside the house in Amityville. During the exorcism, Ed Warren claimed a wave of paranormal phenomena swept through the house, including the sound of phantom footsteps, candles being blown out, and doors opening and closing by themselves, and Ronald DeFeo Jr. ran out of the house, unwilling to stay for the duration of the ritual. Ed's implication is clear: demonic possession was to blame.

It's claimed that hundreds of years before, the Native Americans who lived on the land had placed their diseased, mentally ill, and dying in an enclosure that would come to be occupied by the DeFeo property's boathouse. "Demonic spirits are drawn to the suffering of human beings," explained Ed.

Interviewed in 2013 by Adam Pockross of *Yahoo*, Lorraine said, "Amityville was horrible, honey. It was absolutely horrible. It followed us right straight across the country…I will never go to the Amityville house ever again."[3]

Thanks to the 2014 film of the same name, a Raggedy Ann doll named Annabelle became instantly recognizable to the moviegoing public. Raggedy Ann has been a companion to children since the doll first hit the market in 1915. Annabelle was given to a twenty-eight-year-old woman in 1970, a gift from her mother that turned

---

3. Learn more at https://www.yahoo.com/entertainment/blogs/movie-talk/ghost-hunter-lorraine-warren-tells-us-one-haunted-050927065.

out to have very unanticipated consequences. It wasn't long before she realized that Annabelle had taken on a life of her own. No matter where she set the doll down, it would turn up somewhere else in her apartment, even when nobody had been around to move it.

Next came the handwritten messages begging for help. Scrawled on scraps of paper, they seemed to have materialized out of thin air. Matters escalated even further when the doll spontaneously developed what looked like bloodstains, with no apparent source.

How did Annabelle get her name? With the assistance of a psychic, the entity attached to the doll was identified as the spirit of a dead girl named Annabelle Higgins, who had died many years before in the area on which the apartment building had been constructed. While there was a certain logic to that story, it has long been a truism in the field of paranormal research that not everything that presents itself as a child really is…and indeed, may not necessarily even be human. Those who believe in demons often remark on their propensity to pose as children in order to evoke a sense of trust and lull their potential victims into a false sense of security.

Enter Ed and Lorraine, who told Annabelle's owner that the increasingly violent paranormal activity in her apartment—scratches were now being inflicted on her friends by an unseen force—was caused by a demon. The Annabelle Higgins story had been just that, they said…a story, a confidence trick played on them by the doll's demonic attachment. What was its purpose? To possess a living human being.

After an unsuccessful attempt at exorcism, the Warrens took the doll into their custody. While this was a relief for the nurse who had owned Annabelle, it caused problems for Ed and Lorraine, who recounted almost crashing their car on the drive home. Back at the Warrens' home, the doll was sealed in a glass-fronted case that bears the words *Warning. Positively do not open*. It remains there today, in the care of their son-in-law Tony Spera, who oversees the Warrens' collection of haunted artifacts and maintains awareness of their work.

One of the most fascinating aspects of the Annabelle case is the fact that it centers upon an inanimate object rather than a living person. There are conflicting beliefs as to whether this is a widespread occurrence, or even possible. There's little in the literature of the demonic to support or refute the idea. However, the concept of objects being haunted by the attached spirits of the dead is a common one. If this is indeed the case, then it's difficult to see why a demon—beings said to be far more powerful than garden-variety spirits—shouldn't be capable of doing the same thing.

The Warrens' profile increased dramatically upon the release of the first movie based on them and their works in 2013. *The Conjuring* was a surprise hit, which had the movie studio scrambling to make more movies set in what would become a shared universe.

For every fan of the movies and vocal supporter of their work, the Warrens garnered just as many detractors. One major point of contention concerned the extent to which their cases were fictionalized and dramatized, both in print and on the screen. The Conjuring movies are "based on" the Warrens' cases, which allows room for a certain degree of artistic license. Liberties have certainly been taken in all the films, yet that does not necessarily mean there isn't a kernel of truth (or more) to be found among the claims of demonic activity that the couple investigated.

Ed and Lorraine had been married for sixty-one years at the time of Ed's death in 2006, at the age of seventy-nine. Lorraine died thirteen years later, aged ninety-two. The Conjuring cinematic universe is now a multibillion-dollar blockbuster franchise, and one that shows no signs of slowing down.

Whether you're pro-Warrens or not, their impact on the public's perception of demons, possession, and demonic hauntings is undeniable. Now somewhat eclipsed by their onscreen dramatized personas, they nevertheless cast a long shadow over the subject of demonology in the United States in the twenty-first century.

For those of us living in North America, Europe, and the United Kingdom, it's a commonly held misconception that demons are an almost exclusively Western notion. Yet even the most cursory study of the belief systems of other cultures reveals that they are, in fact, a global phenomenon. This has been the case for thousands of years.

As a psychological concept, demons have always been exceptionally useful. It is in the basic nature of humanity to tell stories, and part of that process involves anthropomorphizing things that are greater than us. Humankind has always attributed personality and intelligence to the powers of creation, dividing them up into the forces of good and evil, the flip sides of the grand coin of life. The great divinity we like to think of as the ultimate eternal good is counterbalanced by the presence of evil malevolence. No matter what name is assigned to these opposing forces, each one of them has, by necessity, its foot soldiers…personifications of the supreme deities, tasked with interfering and intervening in human affairs.

There are the guardians of light—ethereals, celestial beings, divine messengers, angels—and set against them are the agents of darkness.

Fallen angels.

Djinn.

Demons.

The peoples of ancient Babylonia, Sumeria, and their neighboring cultures all believed in the existence of evil, inhuman spirits, and developed their own mystical frameworks to protect themselves from these supernatural predators. To them, the notion of being attacked or possessed by what would later come to be called demons was a very real and terrifying one.

The ancient Greeks believed in the daimon (or daemon), a type of supernatural being greater than a human, but also lacking the power of one of the gods in their pantheon—they were like gods, comparable in many ways, but tended to be lesser. The Greeks often attributed unexpected turns of fate to daimons, in the same way that we might term something an *act of God* today. The term was also used to describe the spirit or force that steered the destiny of great men and women. Most notably, while daimons were believed to be mysterious and unpredictable, they were more often considered good than they were evil.

Daimons were, however, a convenient thing on which to blame misfortune. If your horse turned mysteriously lame, an earthquake destroyed your home, or pestilence struck the settlement in which you lived, it wasn't unusual to scapegoat daimons for the calamity. It was an emotionally comforting way of explaining the seemingly inexplicable. Far more reassuring to pin a stroke of bad luck on the meddling of daimons than on the even more terrifying possibility that we might be living in a completely random, rudderless universe.

Over time, humanity's view of the daimons began to change, veering increasingly toward the negative. Some ancient civilizations saw them as the spirits of dead people, or trickster entities that did not have the best interests of the living at heart. It was possible for somebody to become an angry, usually meddlesome daimon after they had died, inflicting illness, injury, and ill luck upon the lives of men, women, and children.

The myths of antiquity are replete with nature spirits, such as satyrs, fauns, nymphs, and dryads, which were associated with woods, streams, rocks, and the wilds. Those beliefs persist today in the form of elementals, and there are those who connect them with the realm of demons.

For many people, the word *genie* conjures up mental images of Robin Williams in Disney's *Aladdin*. The notion of finding a magic lamp and rubbing it to gain three wishes has become embedded in popular culture. Yet the genie derives from the Arabic belief in djinn (or jinn), which were far from the friendly, comical animated character depicted in the film. These were similar to daimons, and while they could be aggressive and troublesome, they could also be helpful and benevolent when the mood took them. Still, they were a precursor to the demons that we refer to today, and they appear several times in the Qur'an. Djinn are said to live primarily in the deserts and wildernesses of the Eastern world, although lore holds that they may also be encountered in urban settings.

One similarity is that djinn could reportedly be conjured via a ritual, with the intent of having them perform the express bidding of their summoner—a form of psychic indenture. This usually entailed tasking the supernatural being with carrying out acts of mayhem and mischief, though they could also be given more mundane work, such as building structures or working the land. They were said to take on many different forms, including those of common animals such as dogs. This may explain why dogs are supposedly capable of seeing djinn, whereas human beings are not. Much like the Greek daimons, the djinn were not necessarily evil— they were capable of deciding for themselves whether their actions would be good or bad in nature.

Djinn are portrayed as being more alike human beings than they are unalike, and there are numerous stories of the two having sexual encounters and romantic relationships. They also have a natural lifespan, which ends in death. Belief in djinn remains widespread today throughout the Islamic world and nations that have Muslim population centers. Something that ties the djinn to the Western belief in demons is their reputation for possessing human beings. This requires them to be expelled by a *raqi*, an Islamic exorcist.

Demons have been part of the human worldview since time immemorial. No matter which mythos or religious belief system refers to them and their ilk, demons have been something on which humankind could pin its fears and uncertainties. They sow discord and confusion, forever up to mischief and spreading negativity and darkness wherever they go. Sometimes they act directly, meddling in the affairs of humans by causing tragedy and disease. At other times, demons are said to be the ultimate *agent provocateur*, inciting humans to perform deeds that engineer their own downfall.

Occult researcher Michelle Belanger believes that while demons aren't literally real, in the sense of them being individual entities with personalities and physical characteristics, they do exist in the sense of personifications for some of the darker aspects of our all-too-scary universe. It started out as a way for the earliest people to bring order to the chaos that surrounded them. Although the advancement of civilization has brought along great scientific progress, and with it a much deeper understanding of the universe, we still don't have all the answers. That goes a long way toward explaining why demons still have a place in our high-tech, AI-dominated twenty-first-century world.

For those of us living in the West, the word *demon* conjures up a very specific set of concepts, most prominently the iconography of the Catholic church—and thanks to a slew of Hollywood movies of varying scale and quality, images such as a lone priest heroically advancing upon a possessed person, brandishing a crucifix and attempting to case the demon out using God's power and the faith that accompanies it.

One would be hard-pressed to find somebody—even an atheist—who hasn't heard the story, taken from the Book of Mark, in which Jesus casts out the Legion of demons from a tormented and possessed man, driving them into a herd of two thousand swine, which then stampede to their deaths in a nearby lake, taking the demons along with them to their doom. Despite the long, multicultural skein of demonic lore running throughout all recorded human history, in the minds of many in the West, demons today are inextricably linked with Christianity. The reality is much broader and deeper than that.

Many believers refuse to even speak the name of a specific demon for fear that doing so will not only empower the entity, but it will also draw its attention. I have never been one of those people, as is evidenced by the adorable dog who sits at my feet as I write these words. Ten years old and incredibly sweet natured, Lilith is a rescue dog my wife and I adopted when she was five years old, when her first "family" decided she no longer fit in with their lifestyle. I can only assume they had little knowledge of demonology, as Lilith's namesake was a female demon reputed to kidnap and murder babes in the night. Indeed, at one point in time, protective charms designed to ward off Lilith's attentions were popular. In the Christian tradition, she was the first wife of Adam before being supplanted by Eve, although belief in her goes back much farther than the Bible.

At any rate, the baby-murdering flying succubus of demonic lore bears little resemblance to the floppy-eared, wag-tailed Lilith who pants happily at me from the window of my home office as I back my truck out of the driveway. I'm hitting the road. The first stop on my search for demons is to meet a man who will, I hope, provide me with deeper insight into the role demons have played throughout human history: folklorist, researcher, and consummate storyteller Jeff Belanger.

two
SYMPATHY FOR THE DEVIL

Journalist, author, folklorist, and podcaster Jeff Belanger has spent decades traveling the globe, running down stories of ghosts, cryptids, monsters…and demons. Belanger became so sufficiently accomplished at doing this that he was hired to be researcher for the popular television show *Ghost Adventures*, a role he still fulfills to this day.

If there's anyone who knows about the history of the Devil and his minions, it's Jeff.

"The idea of nonhuman, nonanimal entities has been around for a very long time," he begins. "The label *demon* adds a Christian veneer—to my mind at least. The fey folk, elementals, and so forth also fit that description, however. These entities are usually described as being evil, but that's also a label."

"Evil?"

"Yes. Think about an animal that's approaching you, growling, with its claws out. If it mauls you and eats you, is it evil—or is it just doing what an animal does? We call them evil because we're afraid."

Take the movie *Jaws*. It would be difficult to watch that particular film and conclude the great white shark is evil. It's simply doing what's in its nature. It's an eating machine, and the humans just happen to be in its path.

For Jeff's money, although the entities we like to call demons have been with us for millennia, matters really started to heat up in the Middle Ages, when artists that were funded by the church began to create images of demons. This is our classic image of them, with horns, tail, fangs, and claws. Their lord and master, the Devil himself, was portrayed rather differently. As a case in point, Jeff cites the example of a painted fresco dating to circa 550 AD. In it, the Devil is portrayed similarly to all the other angels, sitting on the left side of Jesus. Along with the classic angel wings, he also has a halo. He's also completely blue from head to toe—a world of difference from our present-day depictions.

Times change, and our beliefs change with them.

I point out that in some early religious texts, possession came not in the form of demons, but in unclean human spirits.

"The Devil and demons are not nearly as prominent in the Bible as many of us tend to think," Jeff goes on, warming to his theme. "In Judaism, we have the concept of the *dybbuk*—the spirit of a restless human that can attach itself to the living. In the Jewish equivalent of an exorcism, the intent is not to banish a demon...it's to split apart the living human and the dead spirit, then to cleanse and heal them both. That's not to say that exorcism of demons doesn't occur in Jewish tradition. It does...but dybbuks are not demons."

According to Jewish belief, dybbuks do not possess their host completely, totally subsuming their personality. They act as more of an aggressive, unwanted backseat driver, whose actions can be extremely unpleasant. The good news is that with preparation, perseverance, and sometimes enlisting the help of a good spirit, it is believed by many that a sufficiently pious rabbi can cast out a dybbuk from the possessed individual.

"Dybbuks attach to you because they're drawn to your energy," Jeff continues. "If you're prone to doing something negative, like hurting somebody or robbing a liquor store, then a spirit that did something like that in its own lifetime might latch on and go along for the ride…maybe even encouraging you to do it.

"However, in Judaism, this can work both ways. You can get help from a spirit if you're trying to lose weight, for example, or trying to write that book."

I look down at my ample waistline and at the laptop sitting open beside me. If there are any suitable spirits in the area that might be willing to help out with writing or weight loss, I certainly wouldn't say no.

"A spirit who dealt with one of these challenges in life might cling to you, help you through it, and then leave you pleasantly without any fuss. They're not always bad."

During the Middle Ages, the population was largely illiterate. Scripture was interpreted for them by representatives of the church. In order to really instill fear, however, words were no substitute for imagery. Although paintings of the Last Supper and the Crucifixion could be effective at capturing the imagination of parishioners, nothing compared to horrific, sometimes lurid pictures of the Devil and his demons tormenting the souls of the damned in Hell.

"People wanted to see this stuff for the same reason we go to see horror movies today," Jeff explains. "We like to be scared. We're drawn to dark imagery. If the *be really good and you'll go to*

Heaven message, which was intended to be the carrot, didn't get through to churchgoers, then here was the stick: hellfire and brimstone. These horrid beasts are what's waiting for you if you're bad.

"It's those artists from roughly 1300 to 1500 who really gave us demons," he continues. "They took the scariest things that they could think of, with bat wings and snakelike tongues, and it's no coincidence that this is the era when the Devil really rises to prominence. He becomes a figure to be reckoned with."

In order to show how our perception of the demonic has changed over the millennia, Jeff has set up a simple experiment prior to our interview. He used an AI to comb the internet, collect as many relevant images as it possibly could, and aggregate them into a picture. The search term he used was comprised of just two words: *The Devil*.

Now, we get to see the results. The picture is split into four quadrants, each with a broadly similar face and upper body. All four have horns. All have roughly textured, dark-colored skin with a tinge of red. One is grimacing, and a second smiles a toothy grin. The other two Devils have their mouths closed. One wears a demonic-looking suit and tie, whereas the remaining three have ridged, scaly flesh. All four have glowing red eyes.

These four pictures are the sum total of *centuries* worth of artists, all painting their interpretations of the Devil and telling us that this is what he looks like. This encompasses everything from *Dante's Inferno* to the TV show *Lucifer*, which portrays its titular character as a suave yet sometimes sulfuric Brit. It's a world away from the blue angelic version of the Dark One from 550 AD.

"The suave, charismatic version is a byproduct of the movies and TV," Jeff says. "This version is the more convincing of the two aspects, because he's alluring and deals primarily in temptation. It's no coincidence that among the Puritans of days gone by, stories of incubi and succubi were so prevalent."

An incubus is a male demon that is wont to engage in sex with a living person. A succubus is the female version.

"Some of the Puritans had sexual dreams, sometimes centered around people they knew. Friends and neighbors. Then they'd wake up, and they'd have to justify to themselves how their 'good and pure' Christian selves would *never* countenance such a thing. The demons were a convenient explanation for them to use as scapegoats for the products of their repressed subconscious. Far more palatable to believe that you have been targeted by demonic forces than that you're sexually repressed and frustrated—particularly when the local priest tells you that you could be damned for it."

Fast-forward to the present day, and demons are still being scapegoated. We're all familiar with the phrase "the Devil made me do it," which has been uttered by criminals seeking to justify or deflect responsibility for their crimes. The concept was popularized in the movie *The Devil Made Me Do It*, the third entry in the Conjuring series. It's based on a 1981 murder case in the small town of Brookfield, Connecticut, in which a man stabbed his landlord to death. The self-styled demonologists Ed and Lorraine Warren were involved with the case. Ed claimed the killer had been possessed by several demons at the time of the murder. This resulted in the case becoming a sensation, not least because it seemed as if the notion of demonic possession would be tested before the law. It was touted by some as putting the Devil himself on trial in the courtroom.

Predictably, the judge was having none of it, refusing to allow the claim of possession as a defense against murder charges. Satan never did get his day in court.

"Had the judge allowed it to go forward," Belanger shakes his head, "would there be a murder suspect in the entire country who wouldn't say *the Devil made ME do it too?*"

A precedent would have been set, which would clog up the legal system in tens of thousands of cases.

"Besides," he goes on, "they're not *wrong*."

That has my attention. It sounds as if Jeff's advocating for the defense. "I'm sorry?"

Belanger explains that over the years, he has interviewed countless prison guards and wardens, many of whom have made the same point. A number of the murderers they guard aren't necessarily awful people—although it would justifiably seem that way to the families of their victims. Prior to the one defining moment of their lives, these were ordinary men and women, the sort of people who might be your friend or neighbor. The big difference is that in the matter of a few moments—sometimes seconds—they made a horrible choice. Under similar circumstances, other people would have kept their cool. They did not, and the consequences landed them in prison. They killed somebody, and now they have to serve their sentence for it.

"Did the Devil really make them do it?" he muses. "I bet that *they* would say so. In some cases, they may not have the slightest recollection of committing the murder. They took another human life in an absolute blind rage, and ended up with, *Oh my God, what have I done?*"

There are shades of this with the so-called Amityville Horror, the infamous familicide turned alleged haunting. It, too, spawned a hugely successful movie franchise after the Warrens claimed demons were behind it all. Convicted murderer Butch DeFeo ultimately confessed from prison that there was only one demon at work in the Amityville murders—and that demon was him.

The interest in demons has never been higher. To what does Jeff Belanger attribute their continual presence in our consciousness? While researching his most recent book *The Fright Before*

Christmas, he was struck by the presence of these dark, monstrous beings from generations past still holding strong in our lives today.

"We are collectively summoning them from the folklore of our past, because we *need* them for reasons of our own. In the case of dark entities and Christmas, they bring balance to a holiday that just got too saccharine sweet for many of us to stomach. Christmas became far too commercial, and the weird antidote to that is Krampus and his ilk."

Arising from Germanic folklore, Krampus is defined by the *Encyclopedia Britannica* as "a half-goat, half-demon monster" and "the devilish companion of St. Nicholas." When he isn't punishing unruly children by hitting them with sticks, Krampus is either eating them or dragging them down into the depths of Hell.

"Creatures this dark and scary are here to meet our emotional and psychological needs, whether we realize it or not." Continuing in the Yuletide vein, Jeff jumps to the undisputed classic of all holiday stories: *A Christmas Carol* by Charles Dickens. "Ebenezer Scrooge has to go through Hell himself in order to be redeemed. He's facing the ghosts of Christmas past, present, and future, but it's not a stretch to say that in them, Scrooge is facing his own demons."

It's an astute point, and one I have never considered before. *A Christmas Carol* is unabashedly a morality tale, albeit one festooned with seasonal trimmings, but Jeff's right. At its core, it's every bit as much a tale about a man facing and conquering his demons as Stephen King's *The Shining* is.

"Scrooge's exorcism was ultimately successful, but it took the power of Christmas and the help of an old friend—Jacob Marley—in order to make it happen."

"So, what is the primary role that demons play in our world today?" I ask, steering the subject into the twenty-first century.

"Scapegoats," Jeff replies without hesitation. "They're the ultimate scapegoat, something to pin our fears on…but there's also a certain catharsis in defeating them. Are you familiar with what David Bowie said about demons?"

I shake my head. Jeff gives me the quote.

What I like my music to do to me is to awaken the ghosts inside of me. Not the DEMONS, you understand…but the ghosts.

There are parallels with Jeff's own creative process. When he researches reported hauntings and demonic cases for *Ghost Adventures*, Jeff gathers as much information and eyewitness testimony as possible, submits it to the production, and it's out of his hands. When he's writing a book, things are somewhat different. They become personal.

"When I get inspired to work on a creative project, it haunts me…in a metaphorical way. Here's an example. I got a vague idea to write about the monsters and ghosts of Christmas. I thought *that'd be cool* and I let it sit and percolate in my brain for a while. A few days later, I caught myself thinking, *Oh, we could show a lot of the old Krampus postcards*, and then again, *I've gotta include Belsnickel.*"

Belsnickel is a neanderthal-like hybrid of Santa Claus and Krampus, and one who also possesses demonic overtones in certain depictions.

"Weeks go by, and I keep thinking about it, and thinking about it. At some point, I become convinced that if I don't act on this gestating idea, those ghosts *will* turn into demons. They will grow angrier and angrier, and they won't leave me alone until I get the equivalent of an exorcism…and that exorcism, of course, is to write the book. Once it's written, those words and ideas are out of me and down on the page, the exorcism is complete, and the demons will leave me because they got what they wanted."

It's quite the analogy, and while Jeff obviously isn't dealing with the type of demons I'm searching for, it illustrates beautifully why creative people are sometimes beset by a strange type of possession...not by dark spirits, but by ideas demanding to be given both form and life.

He's given me a lot of food for thought. Yet despite his years of research, Jeff has yet to come into contact with something he would consider demonic in the literal sense. Now that I've been educated in the place that demons and the Devil have played throughout history, it's time for me to visit a man who believes he *has* encountered the literal thing: a demonic entity that, he says, left him physically injured and psychologically scarred.

For that, I have to drive five hundred fifty miles east and visit the scene of one of the most brutal mass murders in Iowa's history: the Villisca Axe Murders.

three
BURNED

According to the 1910 census, 2,039 people called Villisca home. In 2023, that number has almost halved. Although it's technically considered a city, this rural settlement in southwestern Iowa is really more of a town. It has that small-town feel so characteristic of the American Midwest. In addition to farming, Villisca was a popular stop on the railroad, which was the primary means of long-distance transportation in the early twentieth century. The heyday of the motorcar was right around the corner, but plenty of Americans still rode the rails, both for work and for pleasure, and it is believed by many criminologists that the man responsible for committing one of the most horrific crimes in the history of Iowa—if not the entire country—rode them as well.

On the night of June 9 and the early morning hours of June 10, 1912, an intruder broke into the home of J. B. Moore and his family on E. 2nd Street. The Moores—Josiah and wife, Sara, plus four children—were joined by two girls who were friends of the family, the Stillinger sisters. All were fast asleep in their beds when the killer struck. Using an axe taken from the barn, the unidentified perpetrator went from room to room in the small two-story house, bludgeoning each of his victims to death with the flat head of the axe. The attack was so sudden, so unexpected, that there was no opportunity to fight back in any meaningful way.

Mr. and Mrs. Moore died in the second-floor master bedroom. So vicious were the repeated axe blows that they left gouges in the ceiling on the backswing, traces of which can still be seen today. A few feet down the hall, all four of the Moore children shared a room. Each died of massive blunt force trauma to the head.

Last, in the downstairs bedroom usually occupied by the Moores' daughter, Ina and Lena Stillinger were murdered.

The bodies were discovered the following morning, after the alert was raised by a neighbor named Mary Peckham. She became concerned when the house remained dark and still even as the sun climbed higher in the sky. Like most people with farmyard animals, the Moores were early risers to take care of their needs. Each was dead in bed, their faces covered with bloodstained clothing. All the drapes were drawn. The mirrors were covered, as if the killer could not stand to see himself after the fact.

In the subsequent whirlwind of accusation and recrimination that constituted the police investigation, several suspects were identified; one confessed (only to recant later), but nobody was ever convicted of the crime. Indeed, to this day, the Villisca Axe Murders remain one of the great unsolved homicide cases of the twentieth century, with various theories competing for who did it…and why.

One of the principal suspects was a priest named Reverend Lyn George Kelly, a "holy man" with some rather disturbing peccadilloes. These included soliciting young women to undress for him. He was later caught red-handed peeping in windows and attempting to watch women undress. He had a documented history of mental instability and psychosis, which caused him to be institutionalized. Kelly had the means, the motive, and the opportunity to commit the murders. He attended the same church as the Moores did on the night of their deaths and was staying in town with a local priest, a man who didn't keep particularly close tabs on Kelly's movements. He was left-handed, just as the killer had been, and when police officers watched him chop wood while in jail, he proved to have a surprisingly strong axe swing. Kelly fled Villisca early on the morning of the murders, never to return.

Then there is the matter of the confession. His story changed many times, depending on his audience, ranging from flat denials of guilt—Kelly having heard the murders taking place when he was outside the house—to having used "detective skills" gained in his native Great Britain to uncover the identity of the killer. In the days after the murders, no matter how much legal trouble he managed to find himself in, Kelly would not shut up about the murders in Villisca. After a forceful interrogation under conditions that would not be allowed today, he confessed to having been in the grip of a force he could not understand while taking a late-night walk through the streets of Villisca. A voice in his head egged him on to murder, Kelly said, instructing him to "slay utterly."

Kelly attributed the homicidal impulses he felt to be directed by God. He claimed to have followed a mysterious shadow onto the Moores' property. After taking an axe from the woodpile, Kelly said that he made entry into the home and murdered everybody inside, one by one, in a series of what he referred to as "blood sacrifices" to the Lord.

His confession is an inversion of the classic "the Devil made me do it" defense. Yet his story kept changing, and the inconsistencies in Kelly's statements make it difficult to know what to believe. He went on to blame the mysterious shadow for causing him to massacre the Moores and their two houseguests. If there was any truth to his at least partially coerced confession, whose was the voice telling Kelly to slay utterly—and what was the elusive shadow he said attracted him to the house in the first place?

The phrase "slay utterly" comes from the Bible, specifically Ezekiel 9:6, which instructs, *Slay utterly old and young, both maids and little children and women.* It's not surprising that a potentially psychotic preacher would express homicidal rage in the form of scripture, yet there are those who believe Kelly—if he was truly guilty—was influenced not by his God, but by a demon masquerading as God.

After his first trial ended in a hung jury, Kelly was tried a second time…and acquitted. Nobody was ever convicted of the murders, which remain unsolved to this date. Villisca scholars debate the identity of the killer. Some still believe Kelly was the guilty man. Others adhere to the hypothesis that a transient serial killer committed the murders, traveling across the country by railroad and leaving a slew of axe slayings in his wake.

In the aftermath of the crime, the Moore house became a home for many tenants. By all accounts, few of them experienced anything strange while living there. Matters changed after the house was purchased and renovated. After several TV appearances, it soon became a beacon for ghost hunters and paranormal enthusiasts, who flocked to Villisca from across the United States and all around the world, hoping to connect with its spirits.

Some of them will never get over the experience.

In recent years, some visitors claim to have encountered the ghost of Reverend Kelly in the barn adjacent to the Moore house. Far more disturbing are the reports of a demonic entity infesting the basement, and it is these accounts that lead me to travel to Villisca to visit the house in person. In my capacity as a paranormal researcher, I investigated the house extensively while researching my book *A Nightmare in Villisca*, and I continued to return after its publication. As part of the process, I stayed in the Moore house for several days and nights. While I was there, I interviewed a number of eyewitnesses who experienced dark and disturbing phenomena.

Documentary filmmakers Seth and Jesse Alne found the house to be paranormally active from the moment they stepped across the threshold. It began with the sound of voices speaking conversationally from somewhere over their heads, the noise carrying through the air vent set into the floor of the children's room. When the brothers went to check, they found the house to be completely empty, both upstairs and down.

Seth Alne equates the Moore house with a psychic sponge, its walls and rafters having soaked up energy from the evil deeds that took place there. Although paranormal investigators report interacting with a range of spirits inside the house, including children and adults, Seth believes there is a single dark entity resident, which is playing the parts of all the spirits encountered there.

Seth's brother Jesse, along with two colleagues, saw a shadowy figure inside the house. The being had glowing red eyes, glowering at them from the attic doorway. The entity exerted a strange freezing effect on all three of them, rooting them to the spot and rendering them incapable of moving a muscle, other than to breathe.

One of Jesse's companions began to cry. The dark entity slithered across the floor like an oversized snake, reared up, and hissed in Jesse's face.

"What was this thing?" I asked Seth during our interview, hanging on his every word. He believes it to be the inhuman entity behind all the paranormal activity inside the home. In contrast with those who attribute the haunting to the axe murders, Alne thinks the slithering creature predates the events of 1912 and was the evil force that drove Reverend Kelly to slay the Moores and the two Stillinger girls as they slept in their beds. To it belonged the voice Kelly heard in his head, the shadow seen by the itinerant priest as he walked the streets of Villisca that fateful night.

Jesse Alne encountered the entity again in the cellar. Sitting in the near darkness, he conducted a solo vigil in the hopes of gathering more evidence. It wasn't long before he noticed wisps of dark smoke emerging from the cellar wall. Smoky tendrils drifted toward him and began to wrap around his legs, in the same way a boa constrictor coils itself around its prey.

Horrified at the experience, the terrified Jesse could only watch as the nebulous creature rose in front of him. When it reached his eyeline, its face transformed into that of a stern woman—yet this was no human woman.

By the time Seth helped his brother out of the cellar, Jesse was experiencing visual flashes of what can only be described as Hell itself, seeing screaming and tormented souls being cast into lakes of fire by demonic creatures. Everybody present could see that Jesse had turned as white as a sheet, plainly horrified by what he was experiencing. Seth decided the best thing to do was get Jesse away from the murder house. Helping his brother across the front yard and out into the street, Seth began to pray over him, calling upon God for protection. Finally, after what must have seemed like an eternity, Jesse slowly returned to a semblance of his normal self.

Nevertheless, the experience scarred him. Even now, it takes no effort on Jesse's part to call up the awful things he saw and experienced that day. For his part, Seth has no hesitation in describing the experience as demonic in nature. "It wants to cause fear. Anything could happen in that house…including murder. This thing at Villisca, it likes to put on a show. It'll tell you whatever it is you want to hear. It messes with people."

Our conversation ended with a warning from Seth to me.

"You gotta know what you're doing, if you're going to go to that house. It's not something to joke around with."

And here I am, sitting on the porch of the Moore residence, reading a book and soaking in the peace and quiet. It's a glorious Sunday morning, bright and sunny. I have an appointment with Johnny Houser, caretaker of what is now known as the Villisca Axe Murder House. Houser lives in what used to be the home of Mary Peckham. He has had his own share of unnerving experiences, both in his own home and in that of the Moores, which is just a stone's throw from his house. The two homes are separated by just a few feet of grass.

We're old friends and do that awkward half handshake, half hug men sometimes feel obligated to do in order to show their affection for one another. "Go on in," Houser tells me. "I've got a couple of chores to do, then I'll be right over."

Unlocking the door, I step into the kitchen. The house has that expectant hush that reminds visitors something terrible once happened here, something that still echoes down the years to the present day. The house is essentially a living time capsule, circa the early 1900s, as if a century-old piece of Midwest American life was somehow frozen in amber. Climbing the narrow stairs, the steps creak with each thud from my boots. Directly to my left is the master bedroom, where Josiah and Sara Moore were murdered. Next to the bed is a dresser, its mirror covered with a cloth, just as it was on the night of the murders. Framed photographs of the couple adorn the walls, looking back at me with the austere, expressionless look so common in photographs from that period.

Chapter Three

Following along the hallway, I pass the open door to the attic. The floor is covered with toys, gifts from well-wishers who have visited the house. I don't go inside. The nails protruding from the roof are hazardous to a guy my height. I peek into the children's room, where an assortment of beds and cribs occupies most of the space. There's the closet door, which has been known to open and close itself, even when there's no airflow in the house. More toys. I look at framed pictures of the children, trying not to think about what happened to those four innocent souls in this room.

Nothing moves. There's not even the sound of phantom footsteps that were witnessed the last time I was here. Retracing my steps, I head back downstairs, passing from the kitchen into the living room. The only other doorway leading off from here is the bedroom in which Lena and Ina Stillinger were killed. It's small, containing a bed, dresser, and chair. It too is festooned with toys. If it weren't for the atmosphere, which is so thick you could almost cut it with a knife, then one would have no idea of its awful history.

I take a seat in the living room and wait. A few minutes later, Johnny enters and sits next to me. We spend a few minutes catching up, and then get to the point of my visit: Johnny Houser's encounter with the demonic.

Johnny grew up, attended church regularly, and knew scripture off by heart. As a young man, he swung the other way spiritually, rejecting the Christian values he'd been raised with. Looking back, he thinks this may have been the typical rebellious behavior many teenagers engage in, rejecting authority in general and the beliefs of their parents in particular. He became interested in the philosophy of Wicca and other belief systems, before finally coming full circle and returning to Christianity. He no longer goes to church, but he still believes in the tenets and guiding principles of the Christian faith.

"At the heart of it all is love, and I try to live my life by that," he muses, which is really all he needs to say. He's also an unabashed believer in the demonic. "A demon's ultimate goal is to destroy your enemy—God, and those who believe in him. That's why they don't possess atheists. It's much more fun for them to target believers, and ruin their lives, than it is to go after nonbelievers."

It's an interesting point, and one I haven't thought of before. If Johnny's right, then as an agnostic, I ought to be safe…but I'm not willing to count my chickens just yet. I've heard too many stories about those who wandered blithely into these murky waters having bad things happen to them. I resolve to stay open-minded but also to keep my guard up.

Which brings our conversation to the house we're now sitting in, and the killings that took place here. Who does Johnny think was the guilty man?

"When you look at all the subjects and compare them, Kelly has the most check marks against his name," he says, before talking about the black shadow the disgraced priest claims influenced him to commit the murders. "It takes a lot of nerve to walk into a house full of strangers, carrying an axe."

"Especially when you're a short and relatively puny guy."

"Right. The part of his account that talks about him following the shadow to this house, seems a lot like he was led by something, or controlled by something. Whether that's a demon, or just some nasty nonhuman entity, I'm not entirely sure. Whatever it was, it saw that Kelly was unstable, latched on to him, and exploited him." There are times when something similar has happened to Johnny himself, times when he feels inexplicably confused and zoned out. The only answer, much as it was with Jesse Alne, is for him to get out of the house as quickly as possible, and to stay away until the condition passes.

A shadowy human-shaped entity is still seen inside the house to this day. Houser is convinced that whatever this entity may be, it was here long before the murders in 1912. He takes care to describe the figure not as a *him*, but as an *it*. While the Villisca entity is, in his view, not necessarily a demon, he tells me that what he encountered in the basement of an ordinary-looking house in the Midwest more than likely is.

Johnny knew that the house had a reputation for dark paranormal activity, with numerous reports of individuals being scratched while there. Stepping through the front door, he developed what he can only describe as a "vile, filthy, sick feeling." Doing his best to ignore it, he made his way down the steep and narrow steps to the basement. On the bare concrete floor, occult sigils had been crudely covered over with black paint. He was aware of stories circulating concerning occult rituals having taken place within the house and, in what proved to be an unwise decision, elected to try religious provocation. Standing directly on top of the chalk symbol, Johnny cleared his throat and addressed the empty basement.

"In the name of Jesus Christ, do *something*."

Searing pain suddenly shot up the back of one of Johnny's legs. Rolling up his pant leg, he found a reddened patch of skin about the size of a tennis ball that was somehow denuded of hair. Unbelievably, the hairs around the new bald spot were singed. Johnny could smell the burning. Shocked but unwilling to back down, he went back upstairs and decided on a new approach. Aware that there was a church and Catholic school in town, Johnny left the house and came back an hour later armed with as many crucifixes, St. Michael medallions, and containers of holy water as he could carry. In terms of spiritual warfare, it was time to call in the heavy artillery.

Better armed, Johnny went back to the house along with a couple of friends. He set one of the vials of holy water down in the basement, then set about investigating the house. The following morning, Johnny went back to retrieve his bottle. Picking it up, he was shocked to find that it was empty. All the water was gone. The seal was unbroken.

"When I got home, I felt out of sorts for about two months," he recalls, shaking his head. Johnny's then-wife told him that sometimes, for no apparent reason, she would notice him glaring at her in such a way that she felt as if he wanted to kill her. Johnny felt nothing of the kind, and he had no recollection of acting that way. He still doesn't.

One day, a good friend of his arrived at Johnny's house and knocked on the door. Johnny walked out to meet him and slammed the door in his face without a word. Once again, he could not explain why he behaved in that way. He became a recluse, developing an aggressive attitude. He began snapping at people who did nothing to deserve it. Those versed in the field of demonology might recognize this behavior as potential signs of attachment or oppression, indications that a dark entity may have attached itself to a person and begun influencing not just their moods but their actions as well.

Even more alarming, Johnny opened a kitchen drawer one night and caught sight of the wine bottle corkscrew sitting in there. From out of nowhere, he suddenly envisioned picking it up and jamming it into a family member's eyeball. Yet again, there was no rhyme or reason behind this that he could see. As quickly as the vision came, it dissipated, leaving Johnny equally bemused and alarmed at what was happening to his mind.

There seemed to be just one answer to his quandary. Johnny went back to church, attending regularly for three days each week for the space of a year. The sense of relief he felt after returning to church was palpable and immediate. Before long, he was back to his happy-go-lucky old self.

"Something tried to get a hold of me, but couldn't finish it, thank God."

Due to a combination of his experiences and beliefs, Johnny has no problem believing demons exist in our twenty-first-century world. He briefly expressed an interest in learning more about them to an Episcopalian priest, who gestured to Johnny's children and told him, "Don't. They will come after not just you, but your loved ones as well. They will ruin your life. *Don't do it.*"

Johnny heeded the priest's advice. At the time of this writing, he remains clear of the dark influence from the house, and he is determined to stay well away from anything he suspects may be demonic.

I, on the other hand, am not that smart.

After giving him one last hug and a handshake, I say goodbye to Johnny and hit the road. My destination: the house he's just warned me about.

After all, I'm thinking, with no idea of what I might be getting myself into, *how bad can it really be?*

four
INFESTATION

As an agnostic, am I personally in any danger of being possessed? Conventional wisdom holds that, generally speaking, one has to be a person of religious faith (to some degree) to become susceptible to possession. Yet not everybody thinks so.

Interviewed in 2020 by *Esquire* magazine, Dr. Richard Gallagher told journalist Adrienne Westenfeld that anybody who is involved with the practices of Satanism, witchcraft, or the occult could be at risk.[4] Although I have friends who are practicing witches (and wonderful people to boot), I don't believe I qualify on that account, but Dr. Gallagher goes on to add, "It doesn't in any way depend on a particular religious tradition, nor does it even depend on a person's belief or disbelief in God. It's not going to happen to your average atheist of goodwill, but if somebody has no religious belief and they've turned to evil, in some ways, they're in a worse condition because they don't know how to get help. I've met people with

_____

4. Learn more at https://www.esquire.com/entertainment/books/a34226478 /dr-richard-gallagher-demonic-possession-expert-isnt-trying-to-convince-you/.

completely agnostic or atheistic beliefs who somehow dabbled in the occult, then found themselves way in over their heads."

As I pull up outside the ordinary-looking house, which sits on an ordinary street in what seems like a fairly ordinary neighborhood, I'm thinking about some of the worrisome claims made about this place…particularly the history of demonic attacks said to have taken place here. At least one former resident of the home engaged in occult practices of some form, as is evidenced by the presence of magical symbols that were found and hastily painted over. Locking up my truck and walking hesitantly from the sidewalk toward the front door, I'm asking myself whether spending time inside the house that put the literal fear of God into Johnny Houser and so many others constitutes as "dabbling in the occult."

I'm about to find out.

Although I'm an experienced paranormal field researcher, I have never before set out with the express purpose of investigating a demonic haunting. That's why I've made a point of consulting with Steve Higgins, author of *The Rational Demonologist's Handbook* and creator of the United Kingdom's popular paranormal website Higgypop. I like Steve's no-nonsense, no-drama approach to the subject at hand.

Steve prefers the term *paranormal researcher* to *investigator*. It's an important distinction, in that he focuses much of his attention on tracking trends within the paranormal community. I tend to think of him as being something akin to an analyst, monitoring the ebb and flow of beliefs and behaviors among the great mass of people who are involved with the realm of the unexplained. As such, he's had his eye on the growing interest in demons over the past few years.

Steve published a particularly intriguing article on November 13, 2023. The survey of one thousand respondents revealed that an overwhelming majority of them believed there was too much focus on the demonic taking place on reality television.[5] More than half of those polled also felt that adding a demonologist to the cast of a show negatively impacted its credibility. Could this perhaps be an indicator that even paranormal enthusiasts are starting to feel *demoned out*, for want of a better term…or are they simply questioning the way in which the subject is approached?

"I think that fascination with demons is going from strength to strength, and it will keep growing stronger over the next few years," Steve tells me. "Indeed, there are people who think researching demons is the real future of ghost hunting. I think there's a separation, however: not everybody who goes out and ghost hunts regularly is a fan of paranormal television, and many of them see those shows as a source of entertainment, rather than being genuine research."

In other words, not all field investigators buy into the existence of demons, no matter what they might see on TV. It's important to note that not *every* paranormal reality show has gone down the demon route. *Ghost Hunters* is a notable exception, as is Britain's longest-running paranormal show *Most Haunted*, which, despite having had demonologists as part of the cast, rarely, if ever, seems to encounter demonic hauntings.

Raised Catholic, Steve studied religion in high school and came to believe that other faiths were no less valid than the one he'd been raised with. As to the question of whether demons truly do exist or not, Steve tells me he has a hard time separating the concept of a demonic entity from that of a ghost that happens to be evil. This may reflect the fact that he hails from the United Kingdom, where

---

5. Learn more at https://www.higgypop.com/news/demons-are-overdone/.

a belief in the traditional fire-and-brimstone demon is less widespread than it is in the United States.

"Going back to the end of the nineteenth century, the Society of Psychical Research launched a massive study on ghost sightings," Steve explains, referring to an 1894 census. "What was remarkable was that so many of the apparitions reported were of *living people*...not the dead. This suggests that at that point of time, when people saw something unexplained, the cultural norm was for them to see the ghost of somebody who was still alive. That was a common trend. Elsewhere throughout history there have been similar trends with ladies in white and headless horsemen. With the passage of time, these types of sightings have aged out of our collective psyche."

"And demons have jumped right in to fill the spot," I conclude, seeing where Steve's train of thought is heading.

"Exactly," he nods, "demons are the next step in our cultural interpretation of a phenomenon we don't fully understand. The same thing has happened with UFOs and faeries, to give just two examples."

Steve is exactly right. During the 1940s and 1950s, when UFOs first gained mass awareness, those who claimed to have contacted the inhabitants of flying saucers said that they came from the moon, Mars, or Venus. Then humanity sent probes and spacecraft to those places, only to discover no signs of life. Lo and behold, the saucer occupants now claimed to have come from farther afield in the solar system. Once again, we sent probes out, discovered inhospitable conditions and no evidence of extraterrestrial civilizations...and contactees started to be told that UFOs were coming from planets orbiting around other stars. The appearance of the phenomenon changed to keep one step ahead of humanity's perception of the world around it. Why wouldn't ghosts and demons do the same thing?

"Demons and angels are a manifestation of our current way of thinking," Steve tells me. "They're a kind of anomaly that filters through from somewhere into our reality. Our brains can't see them properly, so what we do see is the best interpretation of that phenomenon."

I'm curious as to what other trending beliefs Steve has identified among those who spend their time searching for demons.

"A fairly common warning is to be cautious of what appears to be the spirits of children, because it's said that sometimes these are demons in disguise, pretending to be the spirit of a child," he says. I've personally come across this line of thought in numerous haunted locations, so it doesn't come as a great surprise to me that Steve is also seeing it at a macro level. But then Steve flips the script. "But if that's true, how can we rule out the opposite: that what appears to be a *demon* isn't in fact the spirit of a child that's also just pretending to be a demon?"

Steve's logic makes total sense to me. All things being equal, why would one explanation—the demon masquerading as a child, versus a child masquerading as a demon—be more likely than the other?

"If I was dead, roleplaying demons sounds like a lot of fun. I'd certainly be up for giving it a try," he chuckles.

The possibility of human spirits masquerading as demons is one that will emerge again later in my search for demons, when we'll learn about the case of a haunted property in the Hollywood Hills.

I'm interested in how Steve categorizes a demonic haunting. His response is that it's very difficult to do, particularly when compared with something such as a poltergeist case. "If you write down the characteristics of supposedly demonic and poltergeist cases side by side and compare them, they're almost impossible to distinguish from one another. Both are mischievous; can be attached to a place, person, or object; they can be transitory in nature, coming and going. Each can be violent and aggressive once they escalate. It's difficult to objectively differentiate a poltergeist haunting from what people call a demonic infestation."

That's very much worth keeping in mind as I investigate the house that will become my temporary home for several nights. Some, such as Johnny Houser, have labeled it a demonic haunting. Others think the driving force behind it was either an aggressive poltergeist or an egregore, a manufactured thought form. It's going to be a challenge figuring out exactly what is going on, and Steve has given me a timely reminder to keep an open mind and to beware classifying the situation prematurely...

...and with that, it's time for me to step inside and get started.

Despite its mundane facade, as I punch in the entry code on the keypad that opens the front door, I'm reminded of the saying that appearances can be deceptive. The door swings open with a sinister creak that seems appropriate, given the place's reputation... though it's nothing a little WD-40 wouldn't fix.

It looks like one of a hundred American family residences I've visited. There's a conjoined living and dining room, behind which is a reasonably sized kitchen and a door leading out to the backyard. Upstairs are three bedrooms and a bathroom. I know there's also a basement, which I plan to leave until last to investigate.

While I wait for my fellow investigators to arrive, I walk through the house, familiarizing myself with its layout. Nothing seems particularly off-putting, let alone dark or demonic. The living room couch looks comfortable enough that I could stretch out on it and go to sleep.

Of course, it's early in the day, and bright sunlight is streaming in through the windows. Things will probably look a lot different in a few hours' time, once night has fallen.

Although I'm bringing in several colleagues to help investigate the house, I also want to spend a little time soloing it. Sitting on the couch, I get the shock of my life when I look up to see a young boy's face staring at me through the living room window. My heart rate doubles in a split second. The boy slowly backs away. Getting up and going over to the window, I part the blinds and see a family of eight standing tentatively on the street outside, their expressions a mixture of excitement and fear. An elderly lady slowly makes the sign of the cross while saying what I'm pretty sure is a prayer of protection. The boy was the only one whose curiosity got the better of him to such an extent that he set foot on the property itself. The seven adults are all acting as though there's an invisible force field between them and the house, pointing at the empty windows and speaking excitedly to one another but never leaving the sidewalk.

Such is the reputation of the house.

Leaving the family to their harmless sightseeing, I make a cup of tea in the kitchen and settle down on the couch again. After a few minutes, I hear what sounds like footsteps walking around upstairs. I know the house is empty, having searched it inside and out and made sure that all the doors are locked and the windows securely fastened. For the second time today, my pulse quickens as I climb the stairs up to the second floor to investigate. No sooner has my foot hit the first step than the sounds above me stop. The nursery, bathroom, and bedrooms are all just as they were on my initial walkthrough. Nothing is out of place. I play the sound back on my voice recorder. It's rhythmic, like the sound of somebody walking across floorboards. Could it be an animal, such as a raccoon? Potentially, though there's no trace of one.

Over the space of several noncontiguous days spent in the house, I get to know it and its foibles well. I soon learn which creaks are made by the structure settling in the evening, the natural contractures that accompany temperature changes. Not everything can be so easily explained away. Some knocks and apparent footsteps in empty rooms have me scratching my head.

In the basement, a large patch of black paint indicates the spot at which somebody has attempted to cover up occult sigils that were marked out on the concrete floor. A local paranormal investigator was kind enough to supply me with photographs of the symbols in question. I send them to occult researcher Michelle Belanger, who tells me that in her expert opinion, whoever drew them has been practicing rituals in the house intended to conjure up dark entities.

"This wasn't done by an experienced practitioner," Michelle tells me during our consultation. "This looks like the work of a dabbler, not a pro…somebody who read a few things, maybe browsed a few websites, and threw together some half-baked hotchpotch of what they thought was workable dark magic."

In other words, it's as if somebody watched a few episodes of a TV medical drama and then decided to try their hand at brain surgery.

This alleged conjuration attempt took place years after the first major outbreak of paranormal activity in the house, so it can't be held responsible for the initial aggressive haunting. Yet a logbook left in the house for visitors to record their experiences suggests that it is still actively haunted. For every entry that states nothing happened and the visitor slept peacefully through the night, there are entries like the following:

The toilet flushed on its own. (Both toilets in the house are manual, not automatic.)

Heard steps coming up from the (empty) basement.

Toy moved itself in the nursery. Items seem to move around regularly inside the house, with toys making particularly attractive trigger objects. This happens on all floors and rooms, not just the upstairs nursery.

Doors have a habit of opening and closing by themselves. During an investigation, I carefully check to see how well each door is seated in its frame. Sometimes, stepping on a certain floorboard can cause vibration sufficient to pop a loose door open. In *this* house, however, there are documented incidents of eyewitnesses seeing the door handles physically turn before the door opened. That's much harder to explain away.

A number of those who stayed overnight suffered from nightmares, with a common theme being eyes peering from the darkness. One woman woke up screaming for her mother. Another noted that her husband lucidly dreamed about the pair of them as they slept inside the house.

Just as Johnny Houser experienced, other visitors said they suffered scratches and burns on their skin. One guest had their ankle grabbed by an unseen hand.

One particularly sinister entry states that the best-known ghost associated with the house isn't actually here at all. Instead, the unidentified author claims, something is masquerading as it. They sign off with:

If you hear your name called in the middle of the night—LEAVE. Trust me...

Despite the warnings, the knocks, and the footsteps, there's little evidence of demonic activity to be found during my time in the house. Yet not everything is quiet, either. I'm sitting in the living room with two seasoned fellow investigators, Rob and Sarah, early one evening. We're just hanging out and talking about our plan of attack for investigating later tonight when Rob suddenly leaps out of his chair as though he's been given an electric shock.

He insists that a cold, child-sized hand has just touched him on the small of his back…beneath his shirt. I've spent time in a lot of haunted places with Rob. He isn't easily shaken. This unexpected brush with *something* inside the house has most definitely unnerved him, and I suspect he'll be sleeping with one eye open from now on.

A different group of investigators joins me for my next night in the house. We run through some spirit box and EVP sessions. Most of the communications we receive are profane, with a few choice cuss words thrown my way, or salacious and sexually explicit comments directed at female members of the team. I begin to suspect we're dealing with an all-too-human communicator, rather than something demonic, though I can't say for sure. Then I'm given reason to look at things in a different light when not just one but two psychic medium friends of mine contact me with a stark warning.

Independently of one another—they have never met or spoken—each tells me I need to be wary, because a malevolent entity associated with the location I'm investigating has taken a sudden interest in me. It's worth pointing out that neither psychic knows the name of this location, let alone its dark reputation. Yet each describes a very tall, thin, human-shaped figure with sticklike dimensions, eerily long fingers that resemble claws, and glowing red eyes.

The entity, I'm told, is trying to attach itself to me, and it means me harm.

Now, I do believe in coincidence. By the same token, I find it hard to believe that two people, living on opposite sides of the Atlantic, would suddenly pull something like this out of thin air at the same time while I'm investigating a location that's said to be demonically infested. By my standards at least, that's stretching the bounds of coincidence too far.

Ever since an encounter with something negative that hitch-hiked back to my home from an investigation, I've made a habit of engaging in psychic protection whenever I leave a supposedly haunted place. As we wrap up our investigation, I stand in the street outside the residence and clear myself, envisioning a cascade of white light coming down from above, entering my head and washing out all traces of negativity and darkness that may have permeated me during my stay. It's the early hours of the morning, and the normally busy street is now quiet and still.

After hugging Erin and Mike, my investigative partners, we all get into our separate vehicles and hit the road. It's a long drive back to Colorado, and I haven't gotten more than a few miles out of town when my phone rings. It's Erin. She has quite a story to tell me. They hadn't driven far before realizing they had left some food in the refrigerator. Not wanting to leave their trash for others to pick up, they turned around and went back.

The house is empty and dark when they get back, just as expected. Mike punched in the code and went inside, closing the front door behind him. Somewhere inside the house, most likely upstairs, a door slammed shut. Unfazed, Mike went through the living room toward the kitchen...only to have the light switch itself on in there, right in front of his eyes.

That's something that would stop even the most experienced investigator in their tracks. Wasting no time, Mike pulled the left-over food from the fridge and threw it in the trash. Then he turned off the light and went back to the car.

It's only when he got into the driver's seat that his wife asked him why he had gone upstairs. Except, of course, he hadn't. Now it's Erin's turn to be puzzled, because she had very clearly seen the bedroom light switch on and then, a few seconds later, go off again.

At no point had her husband ever gone up there.

I'm impressed with what I think was the house's last word to us. It turns out that I might be wrong. A few hours before sunrise, I'm heading westbound on the interstate when I suddenly lose control of my truck. The rear end fishtails. I turn into it as best I can, letting my foot off the gas pedal. My heart is pounding in my chest, and I have visions of wrecking out, but luckily, I'm able to guide my vehicle to the side of the road. It's four o'clock in the morning and I'm in the middle of nowhere. Population: me, and a couple of curious deer. Putting on the parking brake, I climb out of the cab, more than a little shaken. There's a strong smell of burnt rubber and a huge plume of dust that makes me cough.

My rear driver's side tire is shredded. Not flat: destroyed. Tatters of torn rubber are attached to the wheel's frame. I was doing the post limit of seventy-five miles per hour when it blew. The tires are new, with a little less than five thousand miles on them. They're a quality brand, one with a sterling safety record.

It's bitterly cold, with a howling wind blowing across the flats, and I'm stranded here at the side of the interstate. Trucks and cars zoom by.

Turning back to my damaged truck, I can't help but wonder if this is just one of those apparently unlucky but actually random occurrences, or whether the bad energy of the house has somehow rubbed off on me, and whatever haunts the place is having a laugh at my expense. More worrying still, have I gotten on something's bad side?

I ask my two psychic friends, Stephen and MJ, for guidance, and also consult again with Michelle Belanger. The advice across the board is to protect myself from whatever may have tried to attach itself to me at that house. Whether it's a demon, a wraith (as MJ believes it to be), or simply a vengeful human spirit, if it truly was responsible for my accident, I can't afford to take any chances. When I arrive home, my wife spends ten minutes clearing me with an enormous stick of burning sage while I stand in my driveway. I catch glimpses of bemused neighbors peeking out from behind curtains. Who knows what they make of this odd-looking ritual? Yet if it works, I couldn't care less.

Once I get inside, I fuss my pets and then run a hot bath into which I dump half a packet of Himalayan salt. Many in the paranormal community believe that salt baths can help cleanse that psychic aura and remove negative influences. I'm certainly happy to give it a shot, and while I soak, I reflect on the case in its entirety.

My mind keeps going back to MJ's description of the entity she believed was stalking me at the house. In her own words, *What I saw certainly was not human and never has been. Like this, but slimmer and way creepier…and about seven feet tall, with extreme red eyes.*

I've investigated more claims of hauntings than I can remember over the years, yet virtually none of them sound even remotely like this. The words *not human and never has been* keep running through my brain.

If it's not human, and never has been…what does that leave?

five
"I AM THE DEMON!"

Are all demons bad? That sounds like an obvious, if not borderline ridiculous question, but sometimes those can yield the most interesting answers. This possibility is very much on my mind as I sit down to talk with Karen A. Dahlman.

In addition to being an author, Karen is a registered art psychotherapist and licensed professional counselor, with a list of credentials and qualifications that would take up their own paragraph if I listed them here. Suffice it to say that she's an expert in her field and has the documentation and experience to back it up.

She also has one of the most bizarre and unexpected encounters with an alleged demon I've ever heard.

As a therapist, Karen specializes in the treatment of dissociative identity disorder, or DID. This condition was once more commonly known as multiple personality disorder. Those who have this disorder appear to have two or more separate and discrete personalities within them, and tend to jump back and forth between them, sometimes at an extremely fast rate. The personalities can be as unique as different characters in a book or a movie, ranging from children to old adults, males and females, each with characteristics that are distinct to them. As each different personality comes to the fore, the voice and mannerisms of the DID sufferer change, sometimes quite drastically.

The condition can arise in response to a deeply traumatizing event, particularly those sustained during childhood. DID is often born out of extreme physical, emotional, or sexual abuse. While often uncomfortable and difficult to live with, it may serve as a protective mechanism to help the sufferer avoid being retraumatized by those memories.

"DID is basically the mind saying, *How can I control this?*" Karen explains. "What it does is dissociate the personality, splitting off into one or more *alters*—alternative personalities. There can be a host of up to a hundred or more alters, though usually the number is significantly less than that."

Typically, it is an alter that bears the burden of the most horrific abuse that was endured by the patient, sparing the original personality from some of that pain and suffering. Alters can continue to spawn, often speaking in their own distinctive voices and idioms. It is not unknown for alternative personalities to adopt different dialects and even entirely different languages. Their mannerisms are also unique to each alter; it truly seems like dealing with an entirely separate personality. There are males, females, adults, children, and the elderly, all in one person.

There can be baffling side effects associated with DID. Karen recalls the time when one of her patients, while painting a picture during a therapeutic art session, spontaneously developed what appeared to be cigarette burns running along the length of her arm. Such burns had been part of the abuse the patient had suffered leading up to developing DID, and they were now recurring whenever the primary alter dominated her mind. This ties in with cases of exorcism in which welts and other traumatic injuries, including the appearance of symbols and words, materialize on the possessed individual's skin. Could the mechanism behind the two types of injury pattern be the same?

"The subconscious mind really *is* that powerful," Karen affirms. "Similar things happen during past-life regression. Patients take on the characteristics of wounds and trauma they suffered during those past lives."

She points out that it doesn't matter whether these past-life experiences, or the possessions some of the afflicted individuals believe they are undergoing, are truly, objectively real...it only matters that they themselves believe it. In the cases of possession, past-life regression, and DID, it is not uncommon for the patient's entire demeanor and their vital signs—blood pressure, heart rate, respiratory rate, and more—to change once the new personality hops into the driving seat.

This brings us to the case of a lady to whom Karen has given the pseudonym of MaryAnne. During the 1990s, Karen was working on an inpatient lockdown unit at a large hospital. Diagnosed with DID after enduring appalling abuse at a younger age, MaryAnne was nonetheless responding well to art therapy. As the sessions progressed, the number of times she felt compelled to cut herself with a razor or knife began to diminish. She felt compelled to take her own life less and less frequently. Karen was encouraged to see that MaryAnne's numerous personalities clashed with one another less often, seeming to come to something of a livable detente. All the indicators a therapist would look for in assessing somebody like MaryAnne were trending in a positive direction.

The next step was to supplement the group sessions with individual, personalized therapy sessions with just Karen and MaryAnne working together twice a week. Sessions began with Karen encouraging any of the alters who wanted to work with art materials to come forward and be creative. This often turned out to be the younger childlike personalities. MaryAnne's voice instantly changed, becoming the high-pitched excitable tone of a little boy or girl.

During one such session, the child alter was rudely thrust aside during the middle of an art session, and a completely new personality barged its way in. Without warning, MaryAnne leaped onto her chair, towering over the shocked therapist. In a deep, masculine voice that was equally raspy and belligerent, the new alter growled, *"I AM THE DEMON!"*

Unwilling to show fear, Karen maintained a calm affect and maintained eye contact with the self-professed demon. What followed was a stream of profanities that would have made a Marine blush. Seemingly unfazed, Karen just sat through the tirade and let the storm blow itself out.

"Some alters want to make you afraid, or to shock you," she explains. "If they perceive weakness, you're empowering them, and that's a bad place to be. They want you to be on edge, to feel some of the pain and torment they are personally suffering. They're coming at you from a place of pain, with the intent of having you share it."

Once the "demon" stopped for a moment to take a breath, Karen told it that she would indeed be willing to listen to its story, but only on the condition that it sat down and ceased acting aggressively.

"I'm not gonna talk to *you*!" the demon spat back.

Karen folded her arms and sat there in silence. After a moment, the demon alter disappeared, and MaryAnne was back. She was far from okay; emotionally exhausted and sobbing, she said to Karen, "I know that *he* must have been here."

"He was," Karen confirmed.

MaryAnne knew of Demon's existence, but Karen had never encountered this particular alter before.

"Did he do anything bad?" MaryAnne asked, trembling.

"I told him that he needs to sit in his place if he thinks we're going to make any progress together," Karen told her.

The rest of the session became focused on self-care for Mary-Anne. In Karen's experience, once the most dominant alter comes to light—this was the first time Demon had made an appearance—it is sometimes prone to harming the primary personality. Karen feared that Demon would take charge again and begin cutting MaryAnne.

Why had one of her alters assumed a demonic mantle? Mary-Anne had been raised in a deeply religious family environment and had been subjected to brutal ritualistic abuse during her formative years. Part of the abuse involved an authority figure telling her that she was impure, and that the demon possessing her needed to be exorcised. The method of supposed "exorcism" was sexual in nature.

Between sessions, Karen pondered on how best she might handle the situation with Demon. After giving the matter much thought, she decided that when Demon emerged again in a future session, she was going to tell it a story. The next time MaryAnne sat down to draw and paint, the same thing happened: a young child alter was ejected and in came Demon, screaming that he was going to kill Karen.

"Look," Karen said, gesturing to the chair in front of her. "I am going to listen to you, but you have to obey the rules. That means you sit down and don't interrupt while I tell you a story...a story about a demon."

Reluctantly, Demon sat down, and Karen began to spin a tale about a demon called Daemon, a name that harkens back to the sometimes inspirational divine spirits of ancient times. The story centered upon a little girl who "had horrible things" happen to her as a child, Karen went on, and suffered awfully until the wonderful and kind Daemon stepped up to protect her.

"Daemon shielded the little girl from all the bad things that had been inflicted on her," Karen said, noting that the apparently disinterested Demon was watching her from the corner of its eye when it thought she wasn't looking. Carefully avoiding clinical terms such as *abuse*, the therapist created a fairy tale in which the demon assumed the role not of a tormentor, but of a *protector*. She took care to spell the entity's name to Demon as D-A-E-M-O-N, which she hoped would separate it in MaryAnne's mind from the malevolent demons she had been told possessed her when she was a child.

Karen was essentially trying to flip the script, turning a negative into a positive...a positive that would hopefully be of benefit to MaryAnne whenever Demon was in charge.

"Do you know anybody with a name like that?" Karen asked.

After a pause, Demon grunted, "I've been spelling my name wrong."

Bingo.

"You have," she agreed.

That was the turning point. Demon—now renamed Daemon—continued to come through in future sessions. Its behavior had significantly changed, however. Daemon started to work *with* the children and other alters, rather than against them. All wasn't exactly sweetness and light. Daemon would still sometimes cut MaryAnne on bad days, but this happened far less often. The Daemon alter had adopted an attitude of cooperation rather than one of dominance and intimidation. Perhaps most telling of all, when this particular alter completed a piece of artwork by itself, it would sign the picture *Daemon*—adding the *A* made all the difference.

Fortunately, MaryAnne became a success story. She was eventually released from the hospital facility and began to pick up the threads of her life once more. Daemon never went away—in some cases, such alters never do—but this is one of the few instances I could find in which a purported demon switched from being a tormentor to an ally.

Of course, there are other hypotheses out there. There are those who hold the view that in cases of DID, what's truly at work isn't a disease process or illness; rather, it is a case of demonic oppression or possession, with each alternate personality actually being a spirit attachment rather than a construct of the patient's own mind. Obviously, this isn't a commonly held view among members of the psychiatric and medical community, and it depends on one's own belief system. It isn't rooted in science or evidence-based clinical medicine. Still, the possibility intrigues me, and it's one I will revisit in more detail down the road, when my quest takes me to a small town in Iowa and the scene of a controversial exorcism from the 1920s.

Karen isn't an adherent of this particular hypothesis, and she doesn't believe that Demon was *actually* a demon. If it had been, it wouldn't have done a complete about-face once it was told the story of Daemon. Demons are evil and never have the best interests of their victims and hosts at heart. MaryAnne continued to improve, partly because of Daemon's help. This isn't suggestive of what we think of as demonic behavior.

Nevertheless, it has me wondering just how many cases of alleged demonic possession throughout history could actually be attributed to cases of DID—and how many of them had tragic outcomes, because there was nobody around to change the paradigm and flip the demon into a daemon. If MaryAnne had lived a hundred years ago or more, her case of apparent possession would almost certainly have placed her in the hands of the church or in the unfortunately named lunatic asylums. She would not have received the care and therapy she so desperately needed.

The thought is a disconcerting one, to say the least, and I have a difficult time shaking it as I head for the next stop on my search for demons.

six
THE GHOST HUNTER

Jason Hawes has been seeking spirits for decades. Starring in the hit TV show *Ghost Hunters*, the success of which helped usher in a tsunami of ghost hunting shows that continues to this day, Jason and his colleagues from the group he started, The Atlantic Paranormal Society (TAPS), have traveled across the United States and overseas to investigate claims of ghosts and hauntings. His children are also involved with what he describes simply as "the search for truth." Each brings their own unique skillset to the table to such an extent that for the Hawes, paranormal investigation really is the family business.

There are currently sixteen seasons of *Ghost Hunters*, and Jason is busier than ever, continuing to work in the plumbing field and attending numerous paranormal events each year. He was kind enough to take a little time out of his schedule to share his own perspective on the subject of demons.

It might be tempting to dismiss Jason's perspective as being biased in the direction of disbelief, so I ask him a little about his upbringing and spiritual beliefs. Jason was born into and raised in a Roman Catholic family. Until the age of eighteen, he went to church and studied catechism. His career as a ghost hunter brought him into contact with a variety of religious organizations and he investigated numerous cases of purported possession or demonic hauntings.

"I believe in a higher power," Hawes explains, "but I don't follow the whole God versus the Devil approach."

His beliefs essentially fall under the category "spiritual but not religious."

Jason is known for being forthright and speaking his mind, and this interview was to be no exception. It's a sunny morning with just a hint of fall chill in the air. We've both spent the previous evening investigating an abandoned asylum, and now we're sitting in the basement of a supposedly haunted schoolhouse, signing books and autographs at a public event. We're interrupted by a constant stream of attendees, most of whom want to meet Jason and get their picture taken with him, to which he willingly obliges. Between visits, the ghost hunter reflects on his career in the paranormal field.

Ghost Hunters first aired on October 6, 2004. In the nineteen years the show has been on the air, it is notable for just how few allegedly demonic cases the TAPS team encountered during their travels. Admittedly, there were some dark and aggressive hauntings featured on the show, but as for demons—they are notable for their absence. This sets *Ghost Hunters* apart from many other shows, some of which reached a stage where they were encountering a demon of the week.

"There are a number of religious organizations that bring us in to investigate," Jason begins, getting as comfortable as possible on a plastic classroom chair. "They send preliminary reports of allegedly demonic cases, and 99.9 percent of the time, upon further investigation, they turn out to have nothing at all to do with demons and there's no possession going on."

That's particularly interesting. If they're not demonic, as the referring agencies seem to think they are, what's really going on?

"Many of them turn out to be very religious individuals. In fact, I've never encountered somebody who's not religious who came to believe they are possessed. That simply doesn't fall within their belief system." He begins checking the explanations off on his fingers. "Some are overly medicated; others are undermedicated. Sadly, some are *self*-medicated."

One of the first things Jason and his fellow investigators do when they make a site visit is to assess the contents of the reporting party's library and movie collection. Are there lots of paranormally themed books and movies, indicating a deep fascination with the subject? While owning a copy of *The Exorcist* or *Rosemary's Baby* doesn't necessarily mean a client has nothing paranormal going on, it does indicate an interest in the realm of ghosts and possibly demons.

"We try to ascertain their basis for believing that they're becoming possessed, or afflicted with a demon haunting," Hawes goes on. "Most of Hollywood's output makes it seem as if all these hauntings are demonic in nature."

He's correct. For every feel-good movie such as *Ghost* or *Casper*, there are ten *Exorcists* or *Conjurings*. Not that such movies can't be entertaining, but they definitely paint a distorted picture of reality—one skewed heavily toward the dark side of the paranormal.

"Now, I'm a firm believer in both human *and* inhuman haunts," Jason clarifies. "If you're a miserable person in life, you're also going to be a miserable person *after* life. Just because someone's aggressive and mean, doesn't make them demonic. That said, I do believe there are things out there that have never walked the earth in human form, but I'm not going to sit here and say that they're *demons*."

Why not? Because in Jason Hawes' view, the term *demon* has very specific religious connotations.

"I believe in a higher power," he goes on, "and I also believe that there's a negative side to that. All too often, however, we see the word *demon* used as a selling feature, something meant to boost ratings or sell movie tickets."

I want to know whether Jason has ever seen anything that might genuinely fit the bill.

"TAPS has investigated cases in which people were speaking languages other than their own, sometimes languages that haven't been commonly spoken in thousands of years. Where did they learn to do that? It's not easy to tell whether that's coming in from somewhere else or not."

He points out that *nonhuman* is a very broad term. An ant fits that description. So would a shark, a lion, or even an extraterrestrial, if you happen to believe in such things. Hawes doesn't completely discount the possibility of animal hauntings, and if they were indeed to happen, it's worth remembering that quite a number of animals happen to bite, claw, and scratch. There's a wealth of anecdotal evidence regarding human ghosts slapping, shoving, and pushing people. Why couldn't a spirit animal do something similar? Anyone who's ever shared their home with a cat could wince at that particular possibility.

"Let's look at this frankly," Jason says. "If there's a demonic entity that has lived for thousands upon thousands of years, it would be naive to think that we would have the ability to stop it simply by throwing out some religious provocation. I've witnessed a number of these rituals, and while I don't think there's any one single religion that is the *only* faith for this, I do think that having a strong faith in what they're saying can sometimes push these things away. However, there's no single specific religious scripture somebody can preach that will get rid of these entities."

Our topic of conversation turns to spiritual protection.

"The capacity for self-protection comes from inside us. I have never gone into a haunted location with, say, holy water, a rabbit's foot, or some kind of protective object, because if it were to be taken away, I would be rendered vulnerable. It's within all of us to protect ourselves, and that's something that can never be taken from us."

"Belief is immensely powerful," I agree, raising the subject of the placebo effect. Our genuine, profound belief in something, whether good or bad, can have strong, tangible effects in the material world.

"There are no actual professionals in this field," Hawes qualifies, "just people like us who are trying to figure it all out. But if somebody calls in me and my team, and let's say we were to come into the case with strong religious beliefs—including demons, angels, and so forth—you're much more likely to accept what I say about those scratches being demonic in nature."

This is why it's so important for those who reach out for what they suspect may be a haunting or possession to carefully vet the individuals they allow into their lives and into their homes. Every single human being who ever lived views the world through their own individual set of beliefs and biases. It's vital that we don't impose them on others.

It's well known that Jason has been a plumber for many years. "Assuming that you call me in and ask me whether your toilet is broken, if I then tell you that it is, you're likely to take me at my word because many people don't know the first thing about toilets. It behooves you to always consider the source."

Jason's absolutely right. It's wise to ask oneself, Who is this person I've brought into my home? Are they accredited? Do they have references? What are their biases, their level of training and education, and perhaps, most importantly of all, do they have an agenda?

"It's similar to going to the doctor when you're sick," I agree. "Firstly, we tell the doctor our signs and symptoms, then answer their questions. They'll draw labs for analysis and assess the situation. A key component of the ethics medical professionals are supposed to adhere to centers upon objectivity. Evidence-based medicine means that patients should be treated according to best practice guidelines. Those guidelines, in turn, are based on data culled from scientific studies. Although some, if not all, of those studies have flaws, the insight they provide is preferable to hunches and beliefs."

Also worth remembering is that physicians are far from perfect themselves, and that's why seeking a second medical opinion can often be valuable. When it comes to assessing the potential for a haunting or possession, not all demonologists or investigators are necessarily open to asking advice themselves. Consulting with another trusted researcher, particularly one who approaches the subject from a different perspective, might raise the possibility that what at first seems demonic might actually be something entirely different. As the old saying goes, when you're holding a hammer, there's a tendency for every problem to look like a nail.

Another problem is when the prospect of financial gain enters the picture. "I've seen cases in which somebody says, *Let me sell you this special candle, or trinket, to push these dark things out of your life,*" Jason recalls. In multiple cases, he has encountered unscrupulous individuals working in the paranormal field who are trying to push a demonic agenda in order to profit financially from the fears and insecurities of others.

Follow the money is a common axiom in law enforcement and is something the savvy paranormal investigator also bears in mind. Is there profit to be made or some other form of gain to be had by claiming that demons are at work?

TAPS does not ask for or accept money for its investigative services. In Jason's view, "The rich, the poor, and everybody in between can all have paranormal problems. I'm never going to help only those people who could afford to pay for our services, so we don't charge anybody." Charging a fee to investigate a potential haunting is unethical, and so is doing the same for looking into an allegedly demonic case.

We take a break so that Jason can sign a few autographs before picking up the conversation again.

"Many of the supposedly demonic cases I've looked into had a psychological cause," he recalls. "No matter what we find, the client's belief was often so strong, they refused to accept any other explanation than that a dark or negative entity was causing them harm. Sometimes, they'd slip and stumble down the stairs and insist that they were pushed. They would accidentally catch themselves on a sharp corner, and scratch themselves, but believe that the scratch was an attack on them. Our cameras have even found clients scratching themselves with hangnails while they slept, only to wake up in terror that they were demonically attacked because they had scratches across their skin. Investigating what people think are demonic cases can sometimes be opening up a real can of worms."

He refers back to cases in which clients went sleepwalking without knowing it, receiving injuries from bumping into objects and surfaces along the way. Medications such as Ambien are notorious for causing such behavior, all of it unknown by the person to whom it is prescribed. There are documented cases in which people taking the drug unknowingly spent thousands of dollars shopping on the internet, bit themselves until they bled, had sex with strangers, and even beat themselves insensible—all without having the slightest idea of what was going on. It is easy to see how somebody who believed they were plagued by a demon might jump to the conclusion that the malevolent entity was responsible for it all, rather than an innocent-seeming sleeping pill.

Jason Hawes was prescribed Ambien himself at one point of his life. He was warned about its potential side effects by his friend Meat Loaf, the much-loved singer.

"Be careful of that stuff, Jay," the rock icon cautioned him. "One time I woke up in a bar with a bill for drinks. I was still wearing my pajamas!"

If there's one thing I'll remember forever about our interview, it's the image of a pajama-clad Meat Loaf sitting on a barstool, drinking the night away with strangers—and not remembering a minute of it. Although that might seem comical, the risks of taking this kind of medication are very real, and it should only be considered after a thorough consultation with one's physician. Ambien and its pharmacological siblings are responsible for more than one misconstrued "demonic nocturnal attack."

"If you're told that a demon is responsible for attacking you in your sleep, and if that fits your frame of reference, you will most likely believe it…especially when you don't remember a thing about the episode," Hawes tells me. "We've also learned that some of those who call us for help just *want* their place to be haunted. Whether it's a negative haunting, demonic, or a plain and simple ghost, doesn't necessarily matter to them. Those darker explanations bring notoriety, however, and that's very appealing to some people.

"I'm not there primarily to be their friend," the ghost hunter sums up. "If they call me, I'm there to help out and to try to figure out what's really going on. I'm not just going to tell them what they want to hear simply to make them happy. I owe them an honest answer, and that's what they're going to get."

I'm curious to learn where he stands on the matter of demonic possession. Is this a real phenomenon, something that he's encountered in the decades he has spent investigating the paranormal? We come straight back to the matter of belief.

"Those who take on the characteristics of possession seem to always be those who believe in the possibility," Hawes reflects. "Have you ever seen a nonreligious person become possessed?"

I shake my head. This is something I'll explore further as my search for demons goes on.

"The Catholic Church has been experiencing a decline in membership and started raising the topic of possessions more often. Why did they do that? It was an attempt to reach younger generations, I think, to get them to believe that demons were real, and the church was doing battle with them. To think: *This sounds pretty cool, let me get involved.*"

A 2018 *Reuters* article by Philip Pullella highlighted the increased demand for exorcisms by members of the Roman Catholic Church, as evidenced by an exorcism course attended by two hundred priests. It's intriguing to note that, two years before the Covid-19 pandemic sent much of society into lockdown, one of the options for exorcism taught on the course involved doing it remotely by telephone—in other words, this course was training exorcists to serve the Zoom generation.

One of the exorcists quoted in Pullella's article claimed to have performed the ritual more than fifty times in a thirty-month period. Considering the very real risks that can accompany exorcisms, one reassuring point held that exorcisms were only to be performed "after doctors are unable to explain the behavior of a person deemed to be demonically possessed."

"You've been investigating claims of demonic hauntings for a long time now, Jason," I point out. "Have you ever encountered even a single one you thought was genuinely a demon?"

"Genuine possession—no. However, I have found cases in which people were able to do things that were completely new to them, such as speaking in tongues. However, the mind is an incredible instrument, and it has surprising abilities."

I ask him whether many of us in the paranormal community jump too quickly to demons and the demonic as an explanation for whatever it is we're investigating.

"Demons sell," he states flatly. "There are people out there looking for their fifteen minutes of fame, who are all too willing to effectively sell their souls to TV production companies in order to get on TV. They'll say whatever they're asked to say. Those production companies, in turn, are trying to put out what they think will get the most bang for their buck. On *Ghost Hunters*, we've never been pushed to go that way.

"Demons *do* sell, but the fact of the matter is, they're hurting the next generation, because we have younger people growing up and believing that there are all these demonic hauntings and possessions going on, when really, there aren't. What's great for the TV and movie industry really sucks for real-life investigations. I really hope this changes in the future."

Jason's tone implies a lack of faith that things will change.

"People need to get back to keeping it real," the seasoned ghost hunter concludes. It isn't lost on me that the numerous autographs he has signed for fans during our interview all bear that same message: *Keep it real*.

It's a sentiment I can totally get behind. As our interview wraps up, I can't help pondering the fact that if someone with as many years spent in the field as Jason Hawes has never encountered a genuine demonic case—or at least, is firmly convinced that he hasn't—then such instances would have to be much rarer than many people think.

Having covered the skeptical perspective in some detail, I decide it's time for me to hop over the other side of the fence...and consult a real-life exorcist.

seven
AN EXORCIST'S PERSPECTIVE

On the day of my interview with Bishop Bryan Oullette, I don't know quite what to expect. I begin by explaining my reasons for writing *In Search of Demons* and explained that, while I don't follow any traditional belief system, I'm open to learning more about all of them—particularly as it pertained to the subject of demons and demonology.

"This is a phenomenon that is dealt with differently by cultures all around the world," he begins. "It's a consistent part of the human experience, one that has been with us for thousands of years. At the same time, our awareness of that experience has evolved over time, and some long-held beliefs that go back this far don't always keep up with progress in other areas, such as science."

That's a very progressive approach to take, and I'm delighted to hear it coming from a bishop of the Old Catholic Church. He tells me to call him Bryan, rather than Bishop, and answers my questions in a thoughtful, relaxed manner.

I've just gotten back from the movies, and before the main feature (Christopher Nolan's *Oppenheimer*), there was a trailer for another *Exorcist* sequel, this one called *The Exorcist: Believer*. I ask whether movies such as this are feeding the increased call for exorcisms.

"There is definitely a higher demand, but there are multiple contributing factors to that. The most pervasive part of that is paranormal television. It also seems that every year, we have to tick another notch off the list of exorcism films, not least because the Catholic ritual is very dramatic, and that's good material for Hollywood. The reality of it all is quite different, and more mundane than people realize."

Bryan points out that some religious faiths have identified evil not as a monster lurking in the darkness, but rather, the dark side of human nature.

"We are essentially monkeys with very sophisticated brains," he continues. "Primates are some of the most violent, destructive animals on the planet. Giving primates a *brain* is an almost perfect recipe for creating evil."

So, it's as simple as that—humans are capable of evil, and we're the worst thing that's out there?

"There *are* metaphysical things going on that can't be ignored," the bishop clarifies, "but this phenomenon we're dealing with doesn't have to be completely divorced from science, as some people think it should be."

I started out by telling Bryan I'm an agnostic. To my surprise, he tells me that it puts me in a good position to study the field of demonology, by helping me analyze the evidence objectively.

"Bias is a pitfall for many people. It's difficult for many people who are in the field to maintain objectivity, me included, and that's necessary in order for us to help people, which is what we're ultimately setting out to do. The goal isn't to *play with demons* or to put on some grand display, or to prove their existence. We're here to help those who believe they are having a spiritual problem."

This seems like an enlightened perspective to take, in my opinion. Based on everything I've learned about religion, the entire point is to care for those who need help, no matter which belief system you follow. (Admittedly, there are a few rare exceptions to this rule.)

"Think of it like a doctor trying to cure an illness," the exorcist goes on. "If he or she has their mind made up at the outset, if they can't remain objective, the patient could be misdiagnosed, mistreated…or even die. The same is true for an exorcist. We have to maintain that balanced approach. Exorcists no longer live in a time when ancient, medieval concepts apply."

I have to admit, this is not what I expected to hear from an exorcist. If I was speaking to a representative of the more traditional Catholic Church, I may not be hearing it at all. The ritual of exorcism is steeped in history. Whatever else it may be, "modern" it most certainly is not. Bryan freely admits that what he's telling me is purely *his* approach, and that it often disappoints people, because it's pragmatic and practical, rather than dramatic.

This leads me to the question I'm asking every single interviewee for this book: does Bishop Bryan Oullette believe in the literal existence of demons?

"Objectively, within the range of human experience, they *do* exist," he replies after giving the matter a moment's thought. "However, once we step *outside* the range of human experience, they are something completely different than what we expect them to be.

"The term *psyche* comes from the Greek word for soul, and from here we derive the term *psychology*. To the modern person, psychology is a common field of study. Every university offers a psychology degree, and indeed, I have one myself. To the ancient mind, there was no difference between the world of the mind and that of the spirit. Today, when we talk about the spiritual world, we're referring to a nonphysical dimension that's meant to be somewhere out there; a place that's inaccessible to us as physical beings. To the ancients, however, that separation didn't exist. They saw the spiritual world as being the world within the human mind."

All very interesting, I think, but how does this relate to demons?

"In order to understand the subject of noncorporeal creatures, we have to bear in mind that they evolved out of ancient societies that did not distinguish between the thoughts in the brain and the spiritual world. To them, the external physical world was seen as being a shared experienced, and the internal workings of the mind were regarded as being the spiritual realm—the place where we could commune with God.

"Carl Jung and others formulated what became the field of psychology based upon *archetypes*. When we're dealing with something such as *evil*, it's too intangible a concept. The brain objectifies and personifies it into something more understandable, and projects it out into something that's meaningful to it."

And *voilà*, we have our notion of the Devil and demons, as Bryan explains.

"The brain is creating a sophisticated archetype of that evil, and it's something that can be experienced and perceived by others. That's how we can tell the difference between psychosis and an actual manifestation of evil, by the way; the difference between those who experience hallucinations or delusions and somebody having a genuine demonic encounter is that the latter can be experienced by other individuals who are in the same room."

As a practicing paramedic, I have been responsible for attending many patients who believed they were being plagued by demons, evil spirits, and, in some cases, none other than Satan himself. Some have claimed that none other than Jesus Christ was in the back of the ambulance with us, and in one notable case, I cared for a patient who was utterly convinced she was being tormented by the urban legend Bloody Mary. In none of those cases did I experience anything to suggest that another being or intelligence was *actually* present at the time; nothing to suggest that these unfortunate individuals were being plagued by anything other than constructs of their own minds. (In the interest of balance, I should add that I have spoken with a number of medical providers who are convinced their patients *were* being influenced by something external, something dark and malign that they were unable or unwilling to name.)

I pause, taking a moment to parse what Bryan has told me so far. If I understand correctly, in his perspective, demons are a sort of collective consensus many people agree upon with regard to a certain type of evil. *Demon* is a label we've given this particular brand of darkness.

"Thinking back to some of the earliest animistic or shamanistic religions, which were dominant on Earth for thousands of years… they saw the universe having independent characteristics that could be interacted with. In that view, everything is sentient. Everything has a spirit—not just people, but also animals, trees, even rocks and crystals. That's why they were seen as being objects of power. Our belief in this has been passed down from one generation to the next, as part of our spiritual and physical evolution. Carl Jung called this *the collective unconscious*. Others refer to it as *the Akashic Records*. Whatever you want to call this, it's a database in our DNA that we can access incorporeally via our own minds. Some people are very good at doing this. Others are quite detached from it, being more comfortable in the physical world than the spiritual.

"When a culture exists that has been taught to disregard the internal world, dismissing it as fiction, and raised to believe that the only true reality is that which is outside of them, people begin moving away from these spiritual principles en masse. That means they're unable to properly interact with these things when they do show up. Just because you're ignoring them [demons, spirits, and other archetypes], it doesn't mean they'll simply go away. Suppressing and repressing what's going on usually results in some kind of pathology—in other words, a demonic event. Psychology and medicine don't really have a vocabulary to properly describe things such as these, which is why they tend to fall into the realm of religion."

That's a lot to digest, and one of the last things I would expect to hear from a bishop and an exorcist. Yet no matter what we believe—and I for one am still not sure what I believe—it does have its own inherent logic.

"Every religion today has its own variation of the evil spirit. Christianity has fallen angels and demons. Islam has the djinn. Even Buddhism has its equivalent."

Bryan is correct. Although the Buddhist worldview on demons doesn't align with those of the religions previously mentioned, it does recognize the existence of nature spirits, something more akin to what the Western world thinks of as elementals. They are seen more as trickster entities and other lower levels of spirit form, beings to be pitied rather than feared. Crucially, they are capable of progressing spiritually in the same way that human beings can, elevating themselves to higher realms should they so choose.

The closest thing that Buddhism has to a demon is Mara, the Lord of Death, the personification of everything that is bad and negative in human nature—the impulses and behaviors that ought to be beneath us. Buddhism conceives evil as continually springing from the baser emotions such as greed and hatred, and the "demon" Mara represents that spiritual darkness in archetypal form.

Why are claims of demonic activity increasing? According to Bryan, it's because society is failing to deal with that negativity in an active way. Humans have always been experts of repressing their inner demons, rather than confronting them, and many would argue that the twenty-first century has seen a huge increase in entitlement and selfishness…a trend that only continues to grow.

"Fewer people have spiritual connections today," Bryan opines. "They don't think they're necessary. Society tells us that it's just superstition, and as a mass we're moving away from faith. This ignores the fact that human beings are *wired* for religion. Traditionalists maintain that moving away from God gives the Devil the opportunity to move in and fill that gap, yet even that explanation is archetypal. A more objective explanation is that, because we are no longer fostering our own internal spiritual reality, it manifests instead in a destructive and pathological manner—in other words, demons."

In Bryan's view, demons are an externalized manifestation of internal human experiences. That isn't to say that they aren't "real" to him. He sees it as a tangible shared experience, an objective reality that is very different from a mass psychosis or delusion.

"I have *seen* demons manifest in front of me during exorcisms," he recalls. "Other people present in the room saw them too. I saw them affect electronic equipment. Since we were children, we were taught that the internal world is imaginary, when in actuality, it's very much the opposite. Our external world is built upon the foundation of our inner spiritual world. Few people understand just how powerful the human mind truly is."

In a nutshell, according to Bryan, demons aren't mysterious monsters hiding in the darkness. They exist as creations of our own internal mental and spiritual processes. This is very much not the story one would hear in a Bible study class—which isn't to say it doesn't hold some validity. After all, why should this be any harder to accept than *the Devil is a fallen angel who surrounds himself with evil minions*?

I raise the point that has come up several times during my discussions for this book. Is it possible for those who don't believe in demons to become possessed? A number of my interviewees say it doesn't happen, but that doesn't fit with Bryan's experience.

"I've definitely seen it happen a number of times," he tells me. "I have helped them eliminate the problem, and as a result, they tended to become Christians. It is *exceptionally* rare, however. There's a certain psychic protection that comes with not involving oneself with these archetypes, which can be dangerous. This can sometimes be seen with method actors who allow a TV or movie role to completely consume them; they actually *become* the identity, the character they are playing, and that can have tragic consequences. As a generality, atheists tend not to have much time or use for these archetypes, so they aren't at any risk of being subsumed by them."

That being said, simply because somebody is atheist or agnostic, does not mean they are not spiritual. Belief in a specific religion or faith is not necessary to engage in practical magic or occultism. The darker aspects once again expose them to the archetypes of demons and negative spirits.

Those who believe in angels and demons can benefit from that belief or be harmed by them, depending on a multitude of factors. There are safe archetypes and dangerous ones—the benevolent and the malevolent kind, respectively.

"Some people like to flirt with the most dangerous types, such as demons," Bryan goes on. "You have to intentionally engage with them first in order to be harmed by that interaction. Engaging in behavior that connects you to those archetypes tends to draw them in closer to you, and that is how possession can happen."

I ask Bryan his views regarding two infamous reports of possession: the 1928 Earling, Iowa case, and the 1949 St. Louis exorcism, both of which we'll cover in detail shortly. If the multiple eyewitness accounts documented in each of those cases are to be believed, then a range of phenomena took place that were objectively real.

"The physical aspects of these cases need their own recognition," the bishop says. "They needed to be dealt with according to the archetype in question—and in these cases, that meant an exorcism."

I'm curious regarding the process Bryan and his colleagues follow in order to determine whether an exorcism is warranted when somebody comes to them for help.

"A psychological and medical evaluation is required first," he begins, "in order to rule out those factors as potential causes. Although when somebody is having a demonic experience, there is always some form of psychological distress and anxiety, the subject needs to be cleared by a psychiatrist before I'm willing to step in. There may even be a degree of dissociation going on. We have to be very astute in evaluating such cases, to determine how pervasive the possession is. For example, is the person functional in most other aspects of their life? Does the problem have an acute onset, or is it chronic? We search for more mundane explanations before looking more closely at the mysterious ones.

"We're looking for things that are consistently unexplainable in medical and psychological terms. For example, how would it be the case that somebody who barely made it through high school can suddenly speak in ancient Aramaic? A person who has never spoken this dead language before in their lives suddenly becomes fluent when they're in a stuporous state. That's very suggestive of possession."

Fluency is definitely a key point here. Simply typing the word *Aramaic* into YouTube brings up a host of video lessons on how to speak it. It's one thing to memorize a few words and phrases from an online tutorial; it's something else entirely to be able to converse in the long-forgotten tongue. Bryan and his colleagues must always consider fraud as a possible explanation. Those who are trying to deceive them rarely go to the trouble of studying an ancient language for hours upon end in order to become truly proficient.

"Bryan, have you ever seen a possessed individual levitate, or do something that violates the laws of physics as we currently understand them?"

"Yes," he responds without hesitation. "I have. Although I haven't seen a person float on up to the ceiling, as they do in the movies, I have seen them rise above the surface of their bed by several inches."

I make a note to follow up on that. One of the future stops in my search for demons will involve a world-class illusionist. I want to know if it's possible for a skilled stage magician to fake something like that, for purposes known only to themselves. Of course, I'm also confident that Bryan has been doing this long enough that he would be able to tell if somebody was trying to pull the wool over his eyes.

"There was absolutely nothing underneath them at the time," he goes on, as though anticipating my question. "We pushed the person back down onto the bed, and *something* pushed them back upward again. It was necessary for us to dedicate four people to hold that single person down, one assigned to each limb. That was the only way to stop them from floating. It's a very rare phenomenon, however, and few cases are that clear-cut."

"Then what are some more common indicators?" I want to know.

"Scratches and symbols that spontaneously appear on their skin—under circumstances in which the person who's the focus is most definitely not doing it to themselves. My colleagues and I pay very close attention. On one episode of a TV show I appeared on, we all saw these scratches appearing on the client's body. This looked very convincing, at first, but there was a lot going on to distract us at that time, not least the cameras continually rolling. We truly believed that we were seeing physical manifestations of the demonic attacks that she [the client] had been reporting…but it was only when we were able to review the footage, it became apparent that the scratches were inflicted by a human being."

No demon or aggressive spirit was involved.

Far more impressive, in Bryan's view, is when marks appear on the skin when that person is restrained, thereby ruling out self-inflicted injuries.

"I've seen symbols appear on somebody's abdomen while their arms and legs were being controlled," he continues. "True demonic possession always seems to follow the same protocol. There's rarely much in the way of variation. One simple thing to try is giving the person in question a pastoral blessing. There isn't any harm in that, but if they react adversely to the blessing or the holy water, then we find it a little more compelling."

"How often are exorcisms successful?" I ask. I'm curious as to how frequently they achieve the desired effect—freeing the afflicted person of their symptoms—as opposed to either doing nothing at all, or even making things worse.

"When we're dealing with genuine demonic activity, then exorcism tends to be *very* effective…often, one or two sessions can eliminate the problem entirely. But, if what's going on is really the manifestation of a person's own trauma, then it can take months or even years to liberate them. A prerequisite for somebody to undergo the rite of exorcism is for them to first come to terms with their trauma. Under those circumstances, the client needs to be working with a conventional therapist in order to address those issues, at the same time they're receiving pastoral care from us.

"Sometimes, people believe we're exploiting mentally ill people by performing these supposedly aggressive rituals on them—but all we're doing is praying, and often prayer is completely sufficient."

Bryan recalls a case of alleged demonic possession he was called upon to deal with several years prior. The client believed that they were possessed by a demon, but although the family knew *something* was wrong with their loved one, his family refused to accept that possibility. The man had been living with a great deal of unresolved guilt, primarily because of certain sexual urges he found to be repugnant. Although he had never acted on those desires, they nonetheless caused him a great deal of strife and inner turmoil.

To address this deep-seated issue, Bryan offered to hear the man's confession and then offer absolution. The two men sat down in a private room and the client began to unburden himself to the priest. As the man spoke, Bryan listened intently, noting that his voice and accent changed as he started to confess his sins. It was as if somebody completely different was now speaking through the man's mouth. The confession soon devolved into the confessor repeating a single word over and over again, a word that originated from a language Bryan's client had never spoken or studied until that moment.

Bryan proceeded to perform a minor rite of exorcism, which seemed to restore a sufficient amount of the man's faculties that he was able to complete the confession. At its conclusion, he was granted the absolution he so desperately wanted. Afterward, the man walked back into his old life as if nothing had ever happened. The twin factors of exorcism and absolution had succeeded in resolving all his problems, and no hint of possession ever reared its head again.

That isn't to say that all was sunshine and roses. There were still deep psychological issues that needed to be addressed, but those required the help of a trained counselor, not a member of the clergy. The last time Bryan spoke with him, the man had progressed further along the road to healing via more conventional means.

Wrapping up our conversation, I thank Bryan, and we say our goodbyes. I keep thinking about the final client Bryan exorcised, and the potential coexistence of demonic possession and other issues. I've heard tell of a similar case, which took place in the American Midwest almost one hundred years ago.

My discussion with Bishop Oullette has prompted me to want to learn more about the infamous Earling case. Although it has long been overshadowed by the exorcism that took place in St. Louis twenty years later (events on which the novel and subsequent movie *The Exorcist* were based), the story of what happened in small-town Iowa back in the 1920s is every bit as fascinating. It's time for me to hit the road to take a personal deep dive into the case.

My destination will be a church and the remnants of a convent in which, if the stories are true, a major battle between the forces of light and darkness once took place. I can't help but wonder what traces, if any, may still linger there today.

It's time to go and find out.

eight
HELL IN EARLING

It's a hot summer morning when I take the interstate on-ramp, heading north. After passing through Council Bluffs, Iowa, historically renowned for being the eastern terminus of the Transcontinental Railroad, the highway eventually gives way to rolling countryside, serviced by a series of smaller roads. I slow down, being careful to obey the speed limit as I pass through a series of rural towns. Here in Shelby County, families are out picnicking in the parks, enjoying the seasonably good weather. It's an idyllic day, one for which the subject of my research trip seems grossly inappropriate.

County Road M16 takes me to a town that few non-Iowans know exists. It's a beautiful place, with clean streets bordered by houses of neatly manicured lawns and what seems like a great sense of community. I park on the main street, near to the town's brewery, bar, and grill, just outside a building I can only assume is a former slaughterhouse—faded exterior lettering declares that there's "butchering Mon, Tue, and Wed."

Main Street slopes uphill to a huge water tower, emblazoned with the name of the town: Earling. According to the most recent census, fewer than four hundred people live here. That number hasn't changed much since the town was founded in 1882. It's safe to say that, despite its picturesque charm, the existence of Earling would be unremarkable were it not for the events that took place there in the latter half of 1928.

The town's website acknowledges this by listing Earling's centerpiece, St. Joseph Catholic Church, as a "must-see for visitors."[6] I'm in complete agreement. Walking up the hill, I locate the church at the intersection of Main Street and Second Street. It's a huge brick structure with a towering steeple that's visible from all over town. As I approach the church, I find myself wondering how different the atmosphere would have felt ninety-five years ago, when it is said that all Hell quite literally broke loose inside the building next door: a Franciscan convent that was the scene of one of the most remarkable documented exorcisms in the history of the United States—if not the world.

Most of the information that is publicly available on the Earling case comes from the text *Begone, Satan!* by Reverend Carl Vogl, a German account published in 1935 and translated into English by Celestine Kapsner. Vogl was not present personally at the exorcism but was given access to documentation and permitted to interview eyewitnesses and direct participants. His "star witness" was Reverend Joseph Steiger, who served as an assistant to the exorcist himself, a fifty-eight-year-old Capuchin monk named Father Theophilus Riesinger.

Father Riesinger shared his own perspective of events with fellow churchman Frederick J. Bunse in 1934. Whereas Vogl's account

---

6. Learn more at https://www.exploreshelbycounty.com/earling.html.

gained widespread popularity over the years following its publication, earning itself a broad readership and garnering great interest, Bunse never published his and Riesinger's version of events. Even today, it remains exceptionally difficult to get hold of. Readers wanting to form their own opinion can find translated excerpts in *The Penguin Book of Exorcisms*, edited by Joseph P. Laycock, which contains flashes of insight that are missing from *Begone, Satan!* Bunse, too, chose to give Emma a pseudonym: Mary.

A number of factors regarding the case remain murky and opaque. Much of it involves the early life of its principal, who has been referred to by the name Anna Ecklund in writing, an attempt to protect her anonymity, but whose real name is believed to have been Emma Schmid (sometimes spelled Schmidt) or possibly a variation thereof. Born in 1882, Emma aspired to be a nun when she grew up. Perhaps this is what made her a tempting target for possession.

Little is known of Emma's mother, but by all accounts, her father Jacob seems to have been a vile excuse for a human being—profane, cruel, and lascivious. There are claims that he tried to force himself on his daughter sexually; when Emma spurned his incestuous advances, Jacob's lover, Minnie or Mina (who was also Emma's aunt, according to some accounts), cursed her niece at his behest. Auntie had a reputation for practicing witchcraft—which if true would have put her at odds with the rest of her community—and supposedly worked "dark magic" on a meal Emma unknowingly ate. Matters went rapidly downhill from there.

The man who would ultimately confront Emma's possession head-on, Theophilus Riesinger, was a remarkable individual. Born in Bavaria, he emigrated to the United States, ultimately taking up residence in Milwaukee and devoting his life to the church. He began "casting out devils" relatively late in his life, performing his first exorcism at the age of forty, and went on to become a respected and sought-after authority on the subject. This is not how the case of Emma Schmid came to his attention, however; as a girl, Emma was one of Father Riesinger's own penitents, a member of his congregation who came to him regularly to make her confession. As such, Riesinger had the opportunity to observe her behavior over the course of several years prior to his direct involvement as an exorcist. He noticed no signs of her leading anything other than a normal and virtuous lifestyle in accord with her Christian faith—until 1908, when the first symptoms of what he suspected was demonic possession kicked in.

Looking at the list of those symptoms today, especially through a clinical lens, it is tempting to simply dismiss them as manifestations of mental illness. Emma began to hear voices in her head, voices that taunted her and tried to goad her into doing things that ran directly against her personal values. She began to field a hatred toward religious iconography and holy artifacts, things that until that point had been sources of comfort to her. Emma struggled with the urge to smash up the church in which she worshiped and to physically assault its representatives. Doctors were consulted and returned a clean bill of health.

In determining whether an exorcism is appropriate or not, one of the principal red flags is the presence of capabilities that cannot be explained away in conventional terms. Foremost would be behavior that cannot be ascribed to seizures, psychiatric illness, drug intoxication, or even plain and simple playacting. (A great many individuals have been accused of claiming to be possessed purely to gain attention, and sometimes this does turn out to be the case.) While it is entirely possible that Emma Schmid was doing the same thing, it wasn't long before things started to happen that defied such a simple explanation. This included the ability for her to comprehend languages to which she had never even been exposed, let alone learned how to speak or understand. Far stranger attributes would soon develop.

Emma was around forty-six years old at the time of the 1928 exorcism, if her most commonly cited date of birth is correct (there is some dispute over this). However, this wasn't her first time being exorcised by Father Riesinger. He had tried to do so in 1912 in a ceremony that culminated on June 18. At that time, it was judged that Emma had been possessed for the prior four years. This initial exorcism was only partially successful, in that the symptoms of possession were mollified but would later return with a vengeance.

By 1928, Father Riesinger assessed Emma Schmid as once again showing the signs of being possessed. He asked a long-standing friend (Reverend Steiger) whether the exorcism might be conducted in the relative seclusion of the convent at Earling, rather than the hustle and bustle of Emma's home in Milwaukee, where it would be all but impossible to protect her identity. With permission obtained from both Steiger and the Mother Superior who oversaw the convent, and formal sanction obtained from the presiding bishop for an exorcism to be carried out, Emma Schmid was duly brought to Earling by train. In a tantalizingly opaque reference, Carl Vogl notes that the male employees on the train—men who had been tipped off that one of their passengers might be troublesome—"had their hands full." What this means is impossible to say, but the implication is clear: all did not go smoothly on the journey to Earling.

Taken immediately to the convent, from the outset, Emma reacted violently to anything associated with the church, particularly the presence of holy water, which was surreptitiously mixed in with her food. Despite its being colorless, tasteless, odorless, and theoretically completely undetectable, Emma Schmid flew into a rage when it was placed in front of her, insisting that it burned her. She was, however, able to tell when her food was "uncontaminated" with holy water. Emma also seemed to possess a sixth sense regarding the presence of religious objects in her immediate proximity, even when they were hidden in the clothing of the people who were taking care of her.

Once the rite had begun, Riesinger's working method during an exorcism entailed his forcing the possessing entity to tell him its name, and when it is going to depart the body of its victim. In the case of Emma Schmid, there was no single occupying entity, but rather—to borrow a Biblical phrase—there were legion. Most prominent in terms of the demonic pecking order was Beelzebub, the titular Lord of the Flies, Prince of Hell, and head of all demons according to the New Testament. If Beelzebub truly was in possession of Emma Schmid's body, that would have been akin to an army putting its field marshal on the front line.

Nor was Beelzebub the only infamous entity that was claimed to infest Emma. Upon close and insistent questioning by Father Riesinger, a male voice claimed to be none other than Judas Iscariot, the disciple who betrayed Jesus Christ to the Romans in exchange for thirty pieces of silver. After Jesus was crucified, a remorseful Judas is said to have hanged himself from a tree branch. Theology holds that this would have consigned him to Hell for all eternity, as the prevailing Christian beliefs of the 1920s held that suicide was a mortal sin and an act of blasphemy against God. Speaking through Emma Schmid's mouth, whoever (or whatever) claimed to be Judas told Father Riesinger that the prime objective of the possession was to torment her so badly that she took her own life by hanging, thereby depriving God of one of his children and gaining another soul for Satan.

Jacob Schmid and Emma's Aunt Mina/Minnie were also in the mix, answering the exorcist's questions in separate and distinct voices. Under interrogation, the voice that claimed to belong to Minnie confessed to having murdered her own children. It also admitted to having given Emma the food and drink that acted as a conduit for the possessing entities.

As if a demon, a treasonous apostle, and the spirits of two malicious family members weren't enough for Father Riesinger to contend with, there was an ever-present chorus of damned and tormented souls vying for the use of Emma's mouth. The people of Earling got used to hearing their shrieks and cries coming from behind the closed doors of the convent, often accompanied by a noxious and sulfurous odor. Few who heard or smelled them ever forgot them. Nor were Emma's utterances restricted to human voices. There were also animal noises, such as the baying of hyenas, and the more familiar sounds made by dogs and cats—even cows. To those listening, it must have sounded as if the small woman's increasingly frail body contained an entire zoo.

Equally strange was the nature of Emma's speech. Although she spoke in a multitude of different voices and several distinct languages, her lips did not actually form words in the conventional manner. The sounds *did* come from somewhere within her mouth—the question is, from where? Father Steiger observed that the voices were heard even when Emma's mouth was shut, and her lips were not moving. Were her vocal cords oscillating, or were the sounds of paranormal origin? In Britain's infamous 1977 Enfield Poltergeist case, the scratchy, croaking voice of an old man was heard to emanate from the mouth of one of the young female residents of the house. Paranormal investigators Maurice Grosse and Guy Lyon Playfair documented the voice being clearly audible even when the young girl's mouth was filled with water and her lips taped shut. Could a similar mechanism of speech have been at work in Earling?

Some aspects of possession cases that speaks to their potential legitimacy are the instances in which the possessed person seems to violate the laws of physics. Floating above the bed in apparent defiance of gravity is one of the better-known examples. In Earling, Emma Schmid is said to have been able to alter her mass density at will, becoming so heavy that even a group of priests and nuns working in concert could not heave her up from the floor. The reverse was also true, as those present discovered when Emma bounded into the air, taking up position above them all, looking down on Father Riesinger and his assistants with contempt before they dragged her back down onto the bed.

The exorcism itself was a lengthy process that was equally physically and spiritually exhausting. Afterward, Riesinger would note that many exorcists tended not to live for long once the ritual was concluded, though he would turn out to be an exception. One can only imagine how much brute strength was required to keep Emma Schmid's body down on the bed while the exorcist carried out his work. Her body is said to have contorted itself into an array of painful positions as the spirits possessing her writhed and struggled.

In *Begone, Satan!* Vogl describes Emma's appearance thus:

Her pale, deathlike, and emaciated head, often assuming the size of an inverted water pitcher, became as red as glowing embers. Her eyes protruded out of her sockets, her lips swelled up to proportions equaling the size of hands, and her thin emaciated body was bloated to such enormous size that the pastor and some of the sisters drew back out of fright, thinking that the woman would be torn to pieces and burst asunder.

From the perspective of a medical professional, the protruding eyes and swollen lips conjure up images of anaphylaxis, a severe, systemic allergic reaction that is life-threatening. The "glowing red eyes" might equate to bloodshot sclera caused by the accumulated fatigue and physiologic stress of many days' worth of exorcism. On the other hand, anaphylaxis is usually accompanied by great physical weakness, not strength, along with wheezing and hives across the trunk. Anaphylactic patients do not howl and scream, because their airway is usually swelling shut. Nor would this explain the claims that *her abdominal region and extremities became as hard as iron and stone*. These bizarre physical characteristics were not consistent throughout the entire period of the exorcism; they came and went with no apparent pattern behind them, rather than progressively deteriorating, as might be expected of a worsening disease process.

Directly confronting the evil entities tended to evoke plenty of threats, although that never seemed to deter Father Riesinger from carrying on. Others around him sometimes paid the price, as happened in the serious car crash Father Steiger suffered at the height of the Earling case. Steiger, who was driving at the time, had his view obscured by a dark cloud that suddenly appeared in front of his face, causing him to lose control of the vehicle. He came perilously close to driving the car into a ravine when it collided with the side of a bridge they were driving across. The car was a complete loss. Fortunately, Father Steiger escaped with only minor injuries.

An apparently unruffled Father Riesinger observed that such setbacks were par for the course whenever he was dealing with an exorcism case, and he remained on his guard against such attempts to derail it. In an intriguing sidenote, when Steiger returned to the convent in order to further assist with the exorcism, he found that word of the collision had beaten him there. Emma taunted him about the crash, something she should not have been able to know. Having such a seemingly preternatural knowledge of things is one of the signs of possession.

This cautionary note is still echoed today by those who perform exorcisms: the possibility of the dark powers reaching out into the material realm to inflict harm upon those who confront them. This harm is said to take many forms, ranging from inflicting physical injuries or unexpected illness to psychological trauma and potentially even the possession of the exorcists themselves. At the height of the ritual, Emma Schmid lashed out and punched the convent's Mother Superior in the face, slamming her across the room in the process. This heightened strength is another commonly reported characteristic of possession. Skeptics often attribute this to the surge of adrenaline that can be experienced while under duress. While this is a legitimate observation in certain cases, it should be noted that Emma Schmid barely ate during the course of her own exorcism—she relied on infusions of liquid nutrition. She vomited up fluid "between twenty and thirty times per day," meaning that in all likelihood she was dehydrated, borderline malnourished, and plagued with electrolyte abnormalities. By all rights, Emma Schmid ought to have been as weak as a baby and growing more so with every passing day.

The exorcism culminated in a seventy-two-hour continuous battle of faith between Father Riesinger and the entities infesting Emma Schmid. With neither participant stopping to rest or sleep, it was a final slugfest, Riesinger's last push to drive the devils out of the innocent woman. He wasn't alone in his efforts. In addition to the support of his fellow priests and nuns, the exorcist also enlisted the help of the people of Earling, who gathered in the church and prayed for Emma's release from possession. Two days before Christmas, on December 23, 1928, they were victorious. Emma Schmid was restored to her former self, her tormentors finally departing her body. The only trace of their presence was a disgusting odor, which completely stunk out the convent.

Emma Schmid's torture seemed to be over...

...except, it wasn't.

Enter Therese Neumann, a holy woman born in Germany in 1898 in Konnersreuth, Bavaria, who gained renown for developing the wounds of stigmata and experiencing faith-based visions. Neumann claimed to live without eating and drinking, sustaining herself only spiritually by taking regular communion. She attracted a large following, who gathered to hear about her spiritual visions. One of the most intense visions related to what she described as the battle between the forces of good and evil taking place in Earling, Iowa. Ominously, Therese Neumann declared that Emma Schmid would endure at least one more round of possession. This does indeed appear to have been the case, although it was reported to have been less intense than the earlier possession. Once again, Theophilus Riesinger stepped in, continuing to exorcise Emma while also chronicling the messages she began to channel. Matters had taken a stranger turn when some of the voices speaking through Emma seemed to come from angelic spirits, vying for attention with their dark counterparts—one claimed to be none other than Jesus Christ himself.

Seven years after its supposed conclusion, *The Denver Register*, a weekly Catholic Press Society publication, printed an article about the exorcism on Sunday, January 26, 1936. ("Weird Exorcism Case Related in Pamphlet.") The account was extremely popular and equally controversial, so much so that it caused Theophilus Riesinger to be profiled by *Time Magazine* three weeks later, on February 17. ("Religion: Exorcist and Energumen." An energumen is a person possessed by a demon or evil entity.) This brought the events in Earling to a national audience and resulted in a blizzard of correspondence from readers wanting to know more or weigh in with their own views on the matter.

On March 8, the *Des Moines Register* published an interview with Father Riesinger ("Priest Reveals How He Exorcised Iowan"), which originated in the *Milwaukee Journal* the month before. The article by journalist Francis Stover states that Riesinger prefers the term *casting out devils* to the word *exorcism*, as the former is less dogmatic. In the case of Emma Schmid, who is not named in the article, readers were told he exorcized her "in 1926 and again in 1928." At that time in his career, he claimed to have performed exorcisms on twenty-two different individuals, one of which was Emma.

The interview is illuminating in more ways than one. Father Riesinger notes that few of the hundreds of potential possession cases that were sent his way turned out to be legitimate, in his judgment. Riesinger admits that some of the behavioral abnormalities evidenced by the truly possessed often mimic the signs of hysteria and mental illness, then goes on to list some of the symptoms he considers to be genuinely demonic in nature. One in particular raises an eyebrow: "Strange cats and dogs talk to them in the night." Echoes of the Salem Witch Trials, in which feline familiars were invoked as so-called spectral evidence.

Perhaps most remarkable of all is Riesinger's take on why the possession of Emma Schmid went on for as long as it did. He said that while she was possessed, Emma acted as a kind of prison for "billions and billions of devils" who were "locked up and unable to do harm." She was to remain that way until God declared she could be set free.

Father Theophilus Riesinger died in 1941. His career as an exorcist had taken a toll upon him physically, but he still lived to be seventy-three years old...thereby refuting the claim that exorcists tended to die shortly after performing the ritual.

It is believed by some that Emma Schmid died in 1964, aged eighty-one. If *this* version of events is true, in what seems like a particularly cruel twist of fate, she shares a gravestone not just with her mother, Anna, but with the man whose spirit was her alleged tormentor—her father, Jacob.

Why do I say "it is believed by some" that Emma Schmid died in 1964? Because there is still much confusion concerning her identity, and it is here that we run into a huge problem with the narrative of the Earling exorcism: it took place in the latter half of 1928, divided into three distinct phases. However, the Jacob Schmid some accounts claim to have been Emma's father died in 1936, which means he would have been alive at the time he was supposedly possessing his daughter. So, which is the truth—do we have the wrong Emma Schmid? Was whatever possessed her lying when it claimed to be the spirit of her dead father?

The fact of the matter is that, despite exhaustive research by scholars such as Dr. Joseph Laycock, nobody has ever been able to definitively identify Emma—if that was even her name. Her role in the story ends with a maddening degree of uncertainty.

I walk around the church, sweltering in the early afternoon sun. I'm holding a printed photograph from the early 1900s, taken directly across the street. To the left of the church is the rectory, which still stands today. To the right, the convent, which has since been demolished. All that remains is a rectangular stretch of grass bordered by trees, though when I look more closely, I can still see traces of the convent's foundation.

Standing here for a while, I close my eyes, ignoring the sunlight and trying to appreciate the fact that I'm standing on the very spot where Father Riesinger and his cohort fought for the soul of Emma Schmid/Anna Ecklund. I don't claim to have any sort of psychic sensitivities, but I am nonetheless grateful for this moment of connection with a case and the personalities involved.

Walking toward the front of the church, I climb the steps and hesitate. *I am the door of life. I entreat all "enter"* declares signage on the glass door. Taking that as an invitation from the master of the house, I walk inside, passing from blinding daylight into the shadowy interior. It takes little imagination for me to picture Theophilus Riesinger and Joseph Steiger walking the long path between the rows of pews, deep in conversation concerning the lengthy process of exorcism. The church interior is magnificent, a series of arches leading up to the star-shaped ceiling. Statues of saints and holy figures adorn every wall. Walking slowly up the nave, I spot a large urn of holy water and a cross bearing eight blessed rosaries of varying types. A handwritten sign declares that they are free, so I help myself to one, slipping it over my neck. I might be an agnostic, but I'm an agnostic who's researching a book about demons. I figure I can use all the spiritual protection I can get.

As a mark of respect and gratitude, I slip twenty dollars into the donation box. There's not a living soul around. Part of me is disappointed; I'd been hoping to discuss the exorcism with the current priest or pastor. However, I'm not sure what kind of reception I would have gotten after raising such a contentious subject. I can only imagine that this particular subject has more than outworn its welcome by now.

There are no echoes now of the animalistic grunts and howls or the shrieking cries of lost souls that were documented by Father Vogl. St. Joseph's Catholic Church is as tranquil a place as any I've ever visited. I make my way outside, heading for my final stop of the day. St. Joseph's cemetery is on the outskirts of town. Parking my car outside the gates, I follow a long road uphill. At the top is a large stone cross. To get there, I climb past row after row of gravestones. I feel drawn toward a dark metal urn, in front of which lies a simple flat marker adorned with two crosses.

Rev. Joseph Steiger. Ordained June 4, 1914.

The stone bears the date of Reverend Steiger's birth—December 11, 1881—and of his death on November 8, 1938. He was fifty-six years old at the time of his death from a cerebral hemorrhage.

I suddenly feel guilty for not having thought to bring flowers or some other offering along, some token of remembrance. Hopefully he would think that the donation to the church fund was a sufficient show of respect. I stand there as the sun climbs, lost in thoughts of the dark things the man at whose grave I now stand once struggled with.

The events that took place in Earling in late 1928 strained the friendship of Fathers Riesinger and Steiger. That saddens me. I hope they found rapprochement at some point. Once all has been said and done, there are basically two conclusions we can come to regarding the case. The first is that Emma Schmid was exactly what she appeared to be: a devout woman who was possessed by evil spirits. This is the conclusion Fathers Riesinger and Steiger reached, along with their peers in the church. Of course, this was viewed through the lens of their Catholic worldview and brings to mind the old saying that "when you're a hammer, every problem is a nail."

The second possibility is that the accounts we have are distorted by bias, only marginally accurate, or just plain wrong. This isn't to say that any of the participants were lying, just that they may have lacked objectivity. Wisconsin-based writer Frank Anderson, a keen student of all matters related to Theophilus Riesinger, believes that the whole thing was essentially a storm in a teacup. He attributes many of Emma's symptoms to a potential autoimmune disease, a hypothesis that is impossible to verify or rule out. In Anderson's view, the events described in *Begone, Satan!* were inflated by its author, Carl Vogl, with the superhuman feats ascribed to her being nothing more than exaggeration.

In all likelihood, the truth of the matter will never be known. For those who believe, the anecdotal accounts constitute more than sufficient proof. For the skeptic, no amount of eyewitness testimony will be enough.

The exorcism is still talked about in Earling to this day. It is, as one might expect, something of a divisive and controversial subject. There are those who believe wholeheartedly that it happened. Many of these people were raised on spine-chilling stories of the unearthly screams, which are said to have emanated from the old convent building, coupled with an unexplained foul stench that pervaded the area at the height of the case. Others are more dismissive, believing it to be the stuff of lore and legend. Based upon the limited sampling of people I could get to talk to me about it, I suspect the former group outnumbers the latter significantly.

Dr. Joseph Laycock has done more than any other writer to demystify the events that took place in Earling. An associate professor of religious studies at Texas State University, the good doctor is also a respected author and an expert on this particular case. He was gracious enough to share his insight with me during an interview. The story behind the Earling exorcism is a tangled web indeed, and Dr. Laycock is just the person to help unpick its threads.

In terms of his personal belief system, Dr. Laycock is agnostic, which means he holds a similar lack of belief but willingness to consider the evidence as I do concerning the potential existence of demons.

"I tell my students that the main thing we try to avoid in class is smugness," he chuckles, referring to those who smugly assert that something cannot possibly exist and therefore does not. I'll be the first to admit that not all my fellow agnostics and atheists are that evenhanded. When they're reading studies on cases such as Earling, Dr. Laycock wants his students to avoid blithely dismissing the accounts and eyewitness testimony simply on the basis of their own bias. This also extends to those who belong to certain faiths, who insist that their church, and *only* their church, holds all the answers when it comes to demons. "I don't categorically have an opinion as to whether demons are real."

That, to me, seems like a very reasonable approach.

"If demons *are* real," Dr. Laycock goes on, "if there is such a thing as a sentient with superhuman abilities and no physical body…well, if it doesn't want you to know it exists, then we're not going to find out about it. This falls more into the realm of philosophy than it does that of testable scientific claims."

He takes a moment to give me a brief history lesson. During the 1960s, there was no shortage of priests who were willing to state quite openly that demons were a metaphor. In 1969, a Catholic priest and author named Herbert Haag published *Farewell to the Devil*, which posited that neither the Devil nor demons actually existed. In Haag's view, Satan was a metaphor for sin itself, a personification rather than a literal being. This was a revolutionary thing to say at the time.

Haag argued that the idea of a Devil and demons had no place in modern religion. The actual effect of this was to make *The Exorcist* seem even scarier when it was released a few years later. The ante was upped, with some people thinking that they couldn't even turn to the church for help fighting off a demon, if Haag was to be believed. Running contrary to that was Vogl's book, which painted this big win for the Catholic Church over the forces of darkness.

In the past, I've said that *The Exorcist* had the same effect on bringing new converts to the Catholic faith that *Top Gun* did for US Navy recruiting. In the wake of its release, there was a significant influx of new adherents. Continuing with the movie theme, *Begone, Satan!* is more like *Rocky*, with the big slugfest at the end culminating in a knockout blow by Father Riesinger against his demonic foe.

However, if we take other sources into account, after the last page of Vogl's book is turned, the story goes on. Emma Schmid was not freed from possession, although she did go on to become a figure of some religious prominence.

"That isn't without precedent," points out Dr. Laycock. "Look at the case of *The Devils of Loudun*."

He's referring to a seventeenth-century French case named the Loudon Possessions, later popularized by author Aldous Huxley in his 1952 book of the same name. Taking place within the enclosed confines of a convent, the alleged mass possession of multiple Ursuline nuns had so many lascivious and outrageous features that it seemed tailored for a novelist to use as source material.

Beginning in September 1632, several nuns began to behave in an increasingly bizarre manner. Twitching and spasming, the young women sometimes acted more like animals than human beings. With the benefit of hindsight, some of the reported symptoms bore similarities with seizures and behavioral crises. As the weeks passed, more of the nuns began acting strangely, until the entire convent was affected in one form or another. That classic sign of possession, speaking in tongues, reared its head. The nuns screamed blasphemies and profanities. Some of the behavior bordered on the obscene, particularly for the 1600s. When questioned, some nuns claimed to have had visions of themselves copulating with a man they had never met, someone who was to become the central figure in the story: a priest named Urbain Grandier.

Grandier was a rising star within the church, popular and stylish with a roguish air about him. He also had a wandering eye for the opposite sex, which had already landed him in trouble with the authorities and made him many enemies by the time matters got out of hand in Loudun. With the mass possessions having become the talk of the region, attempts were made by the clergy to exorcise the nuns. Grandier's name cropped up again and again when the nuns were questioned, several of them confessing to having erotic dreams involving him. Foremost among them was Mother Superior Jeanne de Anges.

It is important to note that some of those confessions were extracted as a result of torture. Urbain Grandier, it was alleged, was behind the demonic possessions. The priest had made a pact with the Devil. Indeed, such a document was actually produced, supposedly signed by both the priest and the Lord of Hell. Grandier's reward—as many women as he wanted, a king's ransom in wealth, and immense power. Found guilty of consorting with the infernal powers at the conclusion of his trial in 1634, Urbain Grandier was beaten to within an inch of his life and then burned to death. Despite being subjected to brutal torture, he refused to confess his guilt.

If it had hoped that Grandier's death would quash the disturbances at Loudon, the church was to be disappointed. The nuns continued to display signs of possession, and the exorcisms continued, often performed in front of a crowd rather than behind closed doors. Some semblances of normality finally returned in 1638.

With the benefit of hindsight, some have claimed that the entire episode was a case of mass hysteria. Others maintain that it was a plot by Grandier's enemies, some of whom were powerful and influential—particularly Cardinal Richeliu, who bore Grandier deep malice for both personal and political reasons.

"The Mother Superior of that convent made the transition from being a demoniac to a holy woman," Laycock explains. "She got to tour around France visiting shrines and religious locations. This is why, in the *Rituale Romanum*, it specifically states that nobody engaged in an exorcism should ask questions of the demon. Get its name, and then get rid of it! The intent was to avoid exactly what happened in Iowa, where you have this monk creating a series of prophecies that said the world was going to end in 1955. The exorcism was turned into an exercise in fortune-telling."

Dr. Laycock is referring to Jeanne de Anges, who had seemed to be the "most possessed" of all the nuns. The Mother Superior went on to garner fame and reputation in the aftermath of Loudun, gaining far greater influence than Grandier had ever had. One is forced to wonder whether she incited or actively engineered aspects of the possession for her own purposes. If so, she certainly benefited from it.

I'm by no means claiming that this is also what happened at Earling, but the parallels between the two cases are apparent. One key difference is that Emma Schmid and Theophilus Riesinger were a team. Unlike that of Grandier and de Anges, their relationship as exorcist and alleged demoniac was a mutually beneficial one.

It's fair to say that Father Riesinger had the best interests of his faith at heart, but I'm finding it hard to escape the conclusion that he had something of a hidden agenda. Dr. Laycock notes that the church did not want the Earling exorcism or the events surrounding it to be made public, but Riesinger seemed to enjoy the publicity and fanfare it attracted.

"The story was first published in Germany, and the church figured, *It's all the way across the Atlantic in Iowa, nobody's ever going to really hear about this in the United States...what's the harm?* And of course, word *did* get out in America. It made the pages of *Time Magazine*. Vogl's version is celebratory; Bunse's is not. Because it contained apocalyptic prophecies, it was regarded as having some importance—but it was never meant to be published or disseminated outside the church. Bunse knew it was sensitive material that should only be distributed on a very limited need-to-know basis."

Vogl's account might make the church look good, but it nevertheless still has its detractors. During the course of his research, Dr. Laycock encountered at least one dissenting opinion from a priest who considered its contents to be out of line with good Catholic practice and teaching. The priest maintained that the book should never have been approved by the church for publication.

"William Peter Blatty [author of *The Exorcist*] read *Begone, Satan!*" Dr. Laycock says. "He didn't like how *ra-ra!* it was. Blatty thought that parts of the story were genuine, but it seemed a little too perfect to him."

In a 1988 *St. Louis Post Dispatch* article, Blatty declared, "I in fact did not base my book on *either* of the publicized North American cases." He was of course referring to Earling and St. Louis. However, the similarities between the documented phenomena reported are simply too great to ignore, and while the term *base* may be accurate, it is undeniable that the author was heavily influenced by them.

How convincing does Dr. Laycock find Vogl's take on the case?

"I believe we're *meant* to take it literally, as a reliable account, but I doubt that it really is. Vogl wasn't delivering firsthand information. It's hearsay. The book also has a clear agenda. It isn't even trying to be unbiased documentary reporting; it's meant to celebrate a religious community. It qualifies as propaganda because of the purpose it serves.

"This is something we encounter quite often in religious studies. Consider something like the Gospels. Biblical scholars approach documents like these with the view that they were written with a very specific purpose in mind, and that while the contents therefore aren't completely reliable as a historical text, parts of them are probably true."

Such is the case with *Begone, Satan!* The question then becomes, *which* parts are true, and which are hyperbole?

In Bunse's account, the narrative being pushed is of the "end of the world is nigh" variety. It deserves the same level of scrutiny as Vogl's does.

What manner of man was Theophilus Riesinger? Reading between the lines, in addition to being devoted to his faith, he seems to have been something of a showman. It's my belief that despite the physical and spiritual toll exorcisms are said to exact on those who perform them, he nonetheless thrived on doing so.

"Speaking during an old newspaper interview, Fr. Riesinger said that you lose a little piece of yourself each time you perform an exorcism," Laycock recalls. "He said that God had given him a double dose of strength, which was why he lived as long as he did. I wonder if he really expected to live until 1955, in order to see the prophecy either come true or be disproven."

I have an issue with Riesinger's approach. If he was speaking correctly, and God really *had* given him an extra measure of strength to cope with the hardships of exorcism, why then would God withhold that same strength from all the *other* priests who were out there, performing exorcisms in his name? If it were true, then this would be exceptionally unfair on God's part, to favor one of his servants but not the others.

"The Catholic Church has expressed concerns about this sort of macho syndrome," says Dr. Laycock. "The Church cautions the would-be exorcist on making things all about *themselves*, their own power and willpower, instead of glorifying the power of God. There's also no mention in the Gospels of the disciples having their lives shortened after they cast out demons themselves.

I don't know where this idea about an exorcist losing part of their life force originates. It seems very ego driven."

I'm wondering whether, in Fr. Riesinger's mind, he was the star of the show, and may perhaps have lost sight of what the role of an exorcist was really meant to be about. Risinger became something of a rogue exorcist, performing the ritual more frequently than his bishop was comfortable with—something that earned him a degree of chastisement.

So, where does this leave us? Dr. Laycock sums it up.

"It could be that something truly paranormal was happening at some point, and after that, it was essentially shenanigans. It could also be that Emma Schmid enjoyed being the focus of Riesinger's attention and feared that if she stopped prophesying and appeared to be free of possession, he would simply move on to somebody else. That dynamic happens surprisingly often in possession cases."

Even less is known of Emma, but Dr. Laycock's eye was caught by a reference made in Bunse's manuscript to her symptoms of possession: "Some described this sudden change to an operation she had undergone."

The term *operation* is quite nebulous, but when Dr. Laycock consulted with a colleague in the history department at his university, he was surprised to learn that in the context and parlance of Bunse's document, the operation in question was likely to have been either a clitorectomy or an abortion. During Emma's early lifetime, clitoridectomy, the surgical removal of the clitoris, was usually inflicted on girls and women to prevent masturbation. This barbarity was something for which a female could be committed involuntarily to an insane asylum on the ludicrous grounds that her sexual behavior was a root cause of mental illness.

While Dr. Laycock's colleague said that such a procedure was a definite possibility, given her circumstances and the era in which she lived, it was most likely that the procedure performed was an abortion. This may lend some credence to the claims of her father having been sexually abusive, possibly resulting in a pregnancy through incest. It is entirely possible that part of what Emma Schmid was experiencing involved a degree of PTSD as a consequence of that abuse and emotional trauma, which manifested in the form of some of the bizarre behavior she engaged in.

"For a female Catholic living in that time period, the ability to say *I'm possessed, and therefore not responsible for anything I say or do* may have been the only way she could have spoken out about what had been done to her."

In other words, could the symptoms of possession actually have been Emma's way of telling the world that she had been assaulted by her father? A woman did not simply come forward and publicly claim sexual abuse in those days. If she did, she could become a pariah, ostracized from society.

"I think it's undeniably a possibility," the academic agrees. "Again, let's consider Loudun. Most of those nuns were admitted to a convent at an early age, often against their will, by parents who didn't want them or couldn't afford to take care of them." It would have taken little for the sexual repression inherent in such an environment to boil over into a false form of demonic possession, which allowed them the freedom to behave sexually, in ways that would normally be considered lewd and obscene. It was an early version of "the Devil made me do it," used as a defense for sexualized behavior rather than murder. If they were believed to be possessed, then there was a chance they would not be held accountable for their actions.

What of the claim that Emma Schmid was possessed—were her symptoms and her presentation like those documented in historical documents? Dr. Laycock brings up the story of the Gerasene demoniac, which is recorded in the Gospels of Matthew, Mark, and Luke (albeit with some variances in detail). This is the instance that gave rise to our current conception of what somebody demonically possessed would look like.

"Elsewhere in the Gospels, demons are making people mute, making them lame, or causing some other physical malady. It isn't changing their personality in any way. Not so with the Gerasene demoniac, who is, it's worth noting, found in a cemetery. Jesus asks for the name of the demon and is told, *My name is Legion, for we are many*. The demons entreat Jesus to put them into a massive herd of swine. Jesus obliges. The pigs stampede into the ocean. It's a strange story, and some parts don't make sense. Why are there *thousands* of pigs in this Jewish region? Who owns them, and why? Be that as it may, if we look at other reports of exorcism from the Mediterranean world at about the same time, there are almost always physical indicators to show the spirit has left the demoniac or energumen. Something is knocked over; a statue falls; some kind of objective sign that the possessing entity has gone. In the case of the Gerasene demoniac, the stampeding of the pigs is something many believe spoke to the validity of the possession and its forced resolution by Jesus."

In the Earling case, the physical sign that the demons and/or evil spirits were departing was the sound of their voices departing, and a foul stink pervading the convent.

I ask Dr. Laycock for his perspective on why it is that only those who believe in the demonic seem to become possessed. He refers me to comments made by Father Malachi Martin, an Irish-born Roman Catholic priest who advocated for a concept known as being "perfectly possessed." In such cases, those who are possessed do not resist it and certainly do not want to be freed from it. In fact, the opposite is true. They desire possession and even invite it to happen, becoming willing participants in the propagation of evil.

Martin refers to perfect possession in his 1976 book *Hostage to the Devil: The Possession and Exorcism of Five Contemporary Americans*. It was his contention that the perfectly possessed individual was immune to such religious iconography as crucifixes and holy water, capable of shrugging them off with impunity. Such people are, to all intents and purposes, undercover agents hiding in plain sight and showing few, if any, of the outer signs of demonic possession.

"According to Martin, if somebody is perfectly possessed, there's nothing you can do for them. They can't be exorcised," Dr. Laycock says. "As far as I'm aware, however, there's no precedent for this in Catholic history. Malachi Martin seems to have come up with it himself in 1976. For the Church, it is rhetorically very useful, because it allows the argument *the atheists don't seem to be getting possessed because they are actually perfectly possessed*. Such individuals cannot be saved or freed because they don't want to be. It's a very toxic idea, one that dehumanizes people."

Both Dr. Laycock and I are skeptical of the concept of perfect possession, not least because it hasn't been around for more than a few decades. It's not something that was documented prior to the 1970s, appears to have been the invention of a single individual (or at most a very small number of them), and just seems a little too neat for my liking—something contrived as a loophole to solve the issue of why nonbelievers don't become possessed.

Emma Schmid was a believer and may fit into the category of having been a "victim soul" who underwent a penance possession. The Catholic notion of a victim soul holds that some individuals are specially chosen by God to undergo great suffering and tribulation, which they bear with great fortitude and grace. They willingly accept the burden of suffering far more than most, which makes them purer and holier people due to their being willing victims who are accepting incredible hardship to atone for the sins of the world. The concept is not without controversy, with some Catholics declaring that victim souls do not exist.

A study of exorcism cases shows that "often, those who are possessed are not doing bad things—in fact, they're usually some of the most pious people in the church," Dr. Laycock tells me. This makes such people high-value targets, and it also appeals to the ego...the idea that "if the Devil has little old me on his radar, I must be an incredibly holy and pious person."

It's the ultimate humblebrag.

In that respect, Jeanne de Anges and Emma Schmid have more than possession in common. Both received lots of attention, increased status within the church, and special privileges because of it, both during their respective possessions and afterward. Both cases were immensely dramatic and theatrical in nature. The happenings at Loudon formed the basis for director Ken Russell's highly controversial 1971 film *The Devils*. The Emma Schmid case was dramatized in the 2016 British movie *The Exorcism of Anna Ecklund*, with Swansea, Wales, standing in for Earling. In August 2023, it was announced that a new movie adaptation of the case would begin shooting in October. The film, titled *The Ritual*, would star Al Pacino; Natchez, Mississippi, was to double for Earling, Iowa.

One could easily be forgiven for thinking that the details of the Earling exorcism sound more than a little bit Hollywood in nature. Many of the visceral images contained in *Begone, Satan!* would later be popularized in William Peter Blatty's bestselling 1971 novel *The Exorcist* and its blockbuster movie adaptation directed by William Friedkin. It is difficult to believe that Blatty was not influenced to some degree by the exorcism of Emma Schmid, which he had certainly read about. During his interview with Francis Stover, Father

Riesinger described the subjects of his exorcisms thus: "The body of the possessed person floats in the air. The eyes are always closed. When the eyes are opened finally, they are seen to be covered with a yellow skin."

Moviegoers who saw and were horrified by Friedkin's film will recognize the scene in which the possessed girl, Regan, rises into the air above her bed and opens her eyes to reveal almost exactly what Riesinger describes. Even more infamous is the scene in which she vomits a viscous green liquid that has a similar consistency to pea soup. Riesinger again: "Sometimes there is diabolical material in the body. This must be expelled. As long as it is there, the devil can always come back. This material is given up only through application of holy water and by exorcism."

Although more is known about Theophilus Riesinger's life than that of Emma Schmid, he remains something of an enigma. One man who knows more about him than most is researcher Frank Anderson, who refers to him affectionately as "Father Theo."

Anderson moved to Appleton, Wisconsin, in 1988, which was once home to Riesinger. Although Fr. Theo had died by then, Anderson kept encountering elements of his story as he went about his daily life. For a while, it felt as if he couldn't go anywhere without somebody telling him a story about the Capuchin friar. He was also loaned a scrapbook covering the man's public life and career, which had been lovingly put together and maintained by Riesinger's housekeeper.

After moving into his new office, situated inside a monastery building, Anderson was pleasantly surprised to discover that Fr. Theo's grave was located close by.

Sitting in the library one morning after perusing the contents of the shelves, Frank was momentarily startled when a book dropped down into his lap from above. Nobody was near enough to have pushed it from the shelf. Flipping through its pages, he found that its margins had been annotated in German by none other than Fr. Theo himself. He took it as his cue to learn more about the Capuchin.

"Fr. Theo was something of a superstar around here," Anderson chuckles. "A real celebrity. One of the clippings covered his funeral, on December 9, 1941…picture a horse-drawn carriage, accompanied by two hundred hooded monks, taking him to his final rest."

What Frank Anderson is describing sounds very much like a state funeral, the sort of procession that would be given to a dignitary or public figure of great importance. The Church certainly made efforts to honor its fallen exorcist, which seems somewhat peculiar considering it hadn't really known what to do with him during his lifetime.

"The Church kept sending him out on speaking tours," recalls Anderson. "He drove from one church to another, lecturing on a range of subjects. The man was simultaneously a rock star and a black sheep in their eyes."

Delving into the Earling case, Anderson grew convinced that Emma Schmid had in fact hailed from Marathon, Wisconsin. After immersing himself in the various accounts of the case, Frank Anderson doesn't find it to be a credible case of possession—though it must be pointed out that he doesn't believe there are *any* credible cases of true possession.

"I believe that Fr. Steiger was *very* tightly wound," Anderson explains. "He was dealing with a lot of personal issues at the time and experiencing doubts about his faith when he arrived in Earling. I find his stability to be questionable. The reason the exorcism took place in Iowa rather than Wisconsin was, I suspect, because the

Church authorities in Wisconsin were unhappy with Fr. Theo constantly driving around and performing exorcisms there. It's ironic that it would go on to become the most famous thing he ever did!"

As far as *Begone, Satan!* is concerned, Anderson believes that it was at the very least *highly* embellished and written primarily to push the Catholic agenda.

"As for Fr. Theo, he was described by one of his peers as an amazing entertainer. He was a showman. Whenever that man got behind a lectern to speak in front of a crowd, no matter how big or small, he just lit the place up. Think of him like a Vaudevillian performer."

That's not to say his beliefs weren't genuine. Theophilus Riesinger had a deep and abiding faith. It was the rock on which he built and anchored his entire life. But it's fair to say that there was a whiff of the P. T. Barnum about him as well, the great showman who liked being center stage with the spotlight on him. That's true of a great many orators, particularly in the field of religion.

In 2022, Frank Anderson was invited to give a talk about the life and accomplishments of Fr. Theo. In attendance were several nuns, whose older sister nuns had known the man personally. After the presentation was over, they approached Frank and revealed that they had been told the story of the Earling exorcism from nuns who had actually been present at the time. They each chimed in with their own secondhand accounts, handed down from the previous generation of sisters. Acknowledging that such tales grow tall in the telling, Anderson recalled one nun's testimony: "Speaking through Emma Schmid, the Devil said...*Fr. Theo, you're standing in my way! I would conquer the earth, if it wasn't for you!*"

We both laugh. I have no doubt that this was a close approximation of at least one eyewitness story. It tracks with the dramatic flair imbued in so many stories about Theophilus Riesinger, who would have found the portrayal of himself going mano a mano with Satan himself to be highly appealing. This is evident on every page of Vogl's book.

That's not to say it didn't happen. Or that it did. Most likely, the answer lies somewhere in the middle of the road, as tends to be the case.

The parallels between Earling and William Peter Blatty's novel seem clear, yet Blatty himself denied that what happened in Earling was hugely influential during the writing of *The Exorcist*. He told the *St. Louis Post-Dispatch* in an April 1988 interview, "I, in fact, did not base my book on either of the publicized North American cases."

The first of those cases Blatty referred to was, of course, the exorcism in Earling. The case that served as an inspiration for *The Exorcist* took place in 1949, and while there are similarities with the exorcism of Emma Schmid, there are those who consider the latter case even more remarkable.

Before we analyze the most famous of all exorcism cases, however, I'd like to delve deeper into the psychology of demonic possession. What role, if any, does an individual's state of mind play in all this? For that, I'm going to need a psychologist.

nine
THE DEVIL IN MIND

Dr. Travis Langley holds the post of Distinguished Professor of Psychology at Henderson State University. He is known for having written and edited sixteen books (with more on the way), many of which place elements of popular culture under the lens of psychology.

I first encountered Dr. Langley at a convention devoted to all things relating to comic books, superheroes, and the media of the fantastic. We sat on a panel together and talked about the craft of writing and the publishing process. Arrayed in front of him were a series of books he had written, which covered the psychology of everything from Batman to the TV show *Supernatural*. When the time came for me to explore the question of the demonic and its relationship to the human mind, Dr. Langley was the obvious person to call.

The first thing to note is that the good doctor is not part of the paranormal community, and therefore has no skin in the game. He doesn't spend his free time poking around supposedly haunted houses or popping up on TV shows to give his opinion on the validity of paranormal phenomena. He does have friends who are involved in the field, however, and takes more than a passing interest in some of the strange goings-on that take place.

"I don't believe in ghosts and spirits," he tells me, "But I would love to be proven wrong. I show respect for what paranormal investigators and ghost hunters do and appreciate them and their work. At the same time, I can go through and offer a valid psychological explanation for most of the things they report."

In other words, Dr. Langley takes the position of the open-minded skeptic, adhering to the perspective of legendary science fiction author Robert A. Heinlein: *What are the facts, and to how many decimal places?*

"I look at evidence skeptically, but also try to remain conscious of my own assumptions—a key element of critical thinking, because assumptions can be wrong. With a topic like this [ghosts, demons, and the supernatural], I want to know what the truth *is*, but I don't necessarily want it to be one way or the other. I'm more interested in the nature of the truth itself than in an investment in either outcome."

On this, he and I are of like mind. This mindset encapsulates my entire paranormal journey and seems particularly on point regarding my search for demons.

Like millions of people around the world, Travis' first awareness of demons occurred when William Friedkin's movie *The Exorcist* was released in theaters. He was a child at the time, and while he would not see the film itself for many years afterward, he did witness the cultural explosion that surrounded it. Adults in his family circle were talking about how scary it was, and how terrifying William Peter Blatty's novel had been.

"It had a very strong impact on so many people," he says. "I'm the son of a Methodist minister. That isn't a faith that spends a lot of time addressing the topic of demons, but I remember people in my father's Texas church expressing their fear and concerns regarding the Devil and demonic possession back then. I'd never even *heard* of the concept until then, and now even kids were talking about it—this fear that the film itself had demons within it."

The furor surrounding the film is well documented and was an absolute boon to the marketing department at Warner Bros film studios.

Our conversation turns to what many refer to as the subliminal sounds and imagery embedded within the movie. The most common example is a garish demonic face with pointed teeth and bulging eyes, which appears for just an instant during a dream sequence. In reality, this isn't truly subliminal, it's a quick interspersion of a couple of frames that flash quickly enough to disturb the viewer but can still be consciously perceived. Countless theories, which director Friedkin dismissed as being groundless, have sprung up around this aspect of the film.

"The 1970s were a time when people were terrified by the possibility of subliminal influence," Dr. Langley goes on. "People were lumping CIA mind control and demonic influences being subliminally hidden in songs and movies. Society at large was deeply afraid of Satanism at the same time. A few years later in 1976 we get *The Omen*, which tapped into that same vein."

Director Richard Donner's story of the antichrist being born on Earth and adopted by an unwitting US ambassador to Great Britain was a sibling to *The Exorcist*, playing on the same widespread fears of the demonic.

"Whereas before, people with strange things going on at home thought they were being haunted by ghosts, now an increasing number believed them to be demons."

The popularity of cultural phenomena such as *The Exorcist* and *The Omen* led to a swing away from garden variety hauntings toward darker, nastier demons. Much the same happened in the late 2000s and early 2010s with the prevalence of "demonic cases" on paranormal reality shows...an effect that has yet to dissipate.

I ask Dr. Langley why this belief remains so firmly entrenched in our minds to this day.

"Because it adds mystery to our world and the universe," he says after giving the matter a moment's thought. "We *want* mysteries, perhaps more than we want answers. This may explain the popularity of conspiracy theories, which weren't as widely believed in the 1980s and 1990s. The internet only empowers that, particularly as algorithms steer people closer toward these things they already believe in. That's why we see such polarization of beliefs. In the past, some of these fringe topics would have died out. Now, with everybody being online, you *will* find somebody willing to reinforce a belief of almost any kind, no matter how bizarre or improbable it may be.

"When it comes to ghosts and demons, we desperately want there to be something else...something higher. We are keenly aware of our own mortality, and that awareness influences many of our actions and beliefs. It predisposes us to interpret some things as being signs that there is something greater beyond this terminal, mortal existence—even if that something is both terrifying and dangerous."

That's a very astute observation. None of us wants to die, or at least, wants to die and be erased forever. The possibility that we are all alone in the universe, that we came from nothing and will return to nothing after our deaths, terrifies us on a deeply primal level. We need our ghosts. We need our gods. It may be that we also need our demons.

"Those demons also serve as an excuse for the bad things happening in the world," Travis goes on, echoing the point made by Jeff Belanger. "They provide a reason for why people do bad things to others. There's a reason we *demonize* others, those who aren't like us...people with different beliefs, politics, or races."

What about the portrayal of demons in comic books? They generally didn't appear in that particular form of entertainment until after the 1970s. That was a decade of increased mass communication.

"The nightly news was showing body bags coming back from Vietnam, and the carpet-bombing going on in Southeast Asia. The world was starting to look darker and scarier. People needed something *worse* than Dracula and his universal monsters to bring them the scares they wanted. The Dracula type of creature doesn't explain atrocities committed by humans, but demons can—with the added benefit that they worked as scapegoats too."

In April 1991, the ABC network broadcast an exorcism on its national television show *20/20*. To describe the show's tone as being alarmist would be something of an understatement, not least because it was accompanied by a blistering rendition of "O Fortuna." The subject of the exorcism, a sixteen-year-old girl, said that she saw visions of demons and the spirits of the dead. For years, she had suffered from seizurelike activity. She began speaking in voices other than her own, usually at night in her bedroom. After spending two months in a children's psychiatric facility, the psychiatrist overseeing her case described her behavior as "psychotic." She made little to no progress at the hospital and was discharged home without definitive answers.

Understandably, the girl's mother sought those answers from the Catholic Church. Representatives conducted an investigation into the case. While members of her family claimed to have witnessed the girl levitating and being pulled through the air, it's notable that no photographic or video evidence of this was offered. (On the other hand, not everybody had access to a camera in 1991.) Harder to explain was her knowledge of the attending priest's activities, including specific details pertaining to his movements and activities that she could not have known by conventional means.

After six months of inquiry, authorization was granted by the bishop for an exorcism to be performed. A team was assembled, including priests, assistants, and a doctor. Preliminary proceedings began with the girl drinking a glass of holy water (crucially, we're not told whether she *knew* it was holy water), followed by retching and the appearance of what seemed to be an entirely different personality. The newcomer was belligerent, speaking in a staccato, rough voice. The girl grew combative, requiring her to be forcibly restrained.

Once her normal personality returned, the girl named two of what were claimed to be multiple entities possessing her. Rather than a demon, one is said to be the spirit of "an African." Another, named Minga, she described as being "a short woman."

The final decision was taken to go ahead with the exorcism. The energumen shrieked a series of shrill cries, alternately weeping that "she" did not want to leave and calling for help. A team member commented that this could be a prelude to levitation, in which she would rise to the ceiling...unless she was held down. I suspect that television viewers had never wanted to see a hypothesis tested more than they did in this instance. Had levitation truly been possible and allowed to occur, then having it happen in front of an ABC camera crew would have offered world-changing proof of demonic possession. Unfortunately, this doesn't seem to have crossed the minds of anybody present.

Instead, the possessed girl thrashed and squirmed as the ritual went on, before finally calming down as it reached its conclusion. When all was said and done, there was nothing to differentiate a case of demonic possession from a psychotic episode, of which the unfortunate girl had a documented history. More than thirty years later, watching the show with the benefit of hindsight, there's no proof that what took place was anything more than a performance, the result of a behavioral disorder. Then again, many believers would say that there was no proof this *wasn't* a genuine case of possession either.

Later that night, members of the church team went to the girl's home and carried out "an exorcism on the house," in order to drive the evil spirits out. The girl was readmitted to the psychiatric unit at the children's hospital for a further two weeks.

"She was still distorting reality," observed her psychiatrist, "but not to the degree that she had previously."

The girl was also less agitated than before. This suggests that the exorcism did *some* good. A fundamental question is this: Were demons and evil spirits driven out of her, or was something akin to the placebo effect at work? The psychiatrist concluded that she had "gradually responded to a combination of medications and various psychotherapies." In the eyes of the Church, she was successfully exorcised—and the medical therapies had at best simply helped control her symptoms. It was a clear case of religion and psychiatry, each claiming credit for making her feel better, while pointedly denying that the other had played an important role.

The girl's condition continued to improve in the weeks after the exorcism and being discharged from the hospital. She remained convinced that she was possessed by evil spirits, and that the Church—not the psychiatrists, nor the antipsychotic medications they prescribed—freed her from their clutches.

The *20/20* broadcast was a controversial and polarizing one. What it undeniably achieved was to help keep the subject of demonic possession in the public consciousness during the early 1990s.

"ABC made such a big deal about showing an exorcism for the first time on national TV," Dr. Langley says. This was a year after the movie *Exorcist III* hit was released. Fifteen years after *The Exorcist* first reared its head, people were still fascinated by the demonic. Church attendance was declining globally, and an interest in demons served to bolster it to some degree.

Dr. Langley brings up the topic of dissociative identity disorder, noting that DID is primarily found in North America, particularly the United States—so much so, in fact, that some clinical professionals regard it as being a culture-bound syndrome.

"DID and possession have this in common: the notion that *something else is in the person*," he tells me. "This other part of you, with its own separate existence—whether it's an alter personality or something demonic. In both cases, that extra piece is something you have no control over, and it remains largely unknown to you. It can cause you to do things you and others are afraid of…and can also serve as an excuse for doing them."

Karen A. Dahlman's encounter with an alter named Demon supports his contention. We have to wonder whether the fact that a belief in demons is so persistent in the United States *and* the fact that DID is so US-centric, there may be a common underlying root.

Our capacity to believe in fantastic things is part of what makes us human, and what some find easy to accept, others find impossible. Go to any paranormal convention, and you're going to find those who believe in the existence of ghosts, extraterrestrials, time travel, magic, elementals, faeries, lake monsters, and, of course, demons. Yet not all those people believe in all those things. There are those who don't bat an eyelid when the prospect of Bigfoot is mentioned, but absolutely draw the line at the existence of demonic entities. What seems patently ridiculous to one is accepted truth to another.

"When evaluating the rationality of a person's beliefs, they have to be assessed in context of their life, their biases, and their culture, all of which has shaped their frame of reference," Dr. Langley explains. "It's more challenging to explain the person who believes they are demonically possessed when that concept wasn't part of their upbringing. Psychiatrically speaking, that's of greater concern than the person who was raised with the existence of demons as accepted fact."

He uses the example of a person who lives in a village where part of the everyday fabric of life involves the presence of dark forces. If such an individual starts hearing voices in their head, it is perfectly natural—completely rational—for them to ascribe those voices to demonic influence or possession. The same cannot be said of a stringent atheist.

"It can be less scary to think that demons are talking to you than to consider the possibility that a psychological illness may be the cause…not least because the demonic explanation seems more *fixable*."

A case in point involves notorious gangster Al Capone, who was supposedly tormented by the ghost of one of the many men he was responsible for killing. It's a spine-chilling story, but there's a twist. Capone was riddled with syphilis, which he contracted as a young man. One of the insidious effects of that particular disease once it reaches the brain is a propensity for vivid hallucinations.

Some people find it easy to believe that a vengeful ghost made the crime lord's life miserable. Others blame syphilis. Either (or both) could be right. Whichever side you come down on, however, speaks volumes about the way in which you personally view the world. For Al Capone, the ghost explanation was almost certainly less frightening than the possibility that his brain was slowly being eaten away by an uncontrollable disease.

As strange as it may sound, does a belief in demons offer us a more comfortable alternative to fearing such things as dementia and other illnesses that rob us of our fundamental self?

"Demons, in some ways, can be *less* scary than ghosts," Travis says. "The existence of ghosts means that you or your loved ones could be left behind on Earth in a tormented state, enduring *centuries* of being an incomplete version of yourself. For those who accept the notion that these entities are in fact demons pretending to be ghosts, it can be comforting to believe that we humans are not at risk of suffering in that way."

Our conversation has left me with a great deal to think about, not least in terms of my own personal biases on the subject. Before we part, I ask him what advice he would give me as my search for demons continues.

"Protect yourself."

I frown. Isn't this the guy who just challenged the existence of ghosts and demons?

"The lack of belief in demons is the best protection you could possibly have," he clarifies. "If you don't believe in them, you'll be safe."

Time will tell if he's right or not.

ten
ILLUSION, DELUSION, AND POSSESSION

Aiden Sinclair knows a thing or two about belief.

The former US Recon Marine turned confidence man turned magician makes his living convincing people to believe things that aren't real.

After leaving the Marine Corps, Sinclair became, by his own admission, a grifter. A con man. For a time, living under aliases, he lived the highlife, exploiting others for his own gain. But Sinclair is also that rarest of things: a con man with a conscience. He willingly turned himself in to the authorities, where he served prison time for his crimes. In prison, he learned the art of the illusionist, passing the long hours learning card tricks and sleight of hand.

Upon regaining his freedom, with his debt to society paid in full, Sinclair set about becoming one of the most sought-after stage magicians in the country, a master illusionist who still cons people for a living—but this time with their full consent, and while being paid handsomely for the privilege.

I am also proud to call him a friend.

Sinclair now uses his background as a cautionary tale, encouraging prisoners and wayward youths to stay on the straight and narrow. I first met him in a hotel renowned for its colorful (and many would say haunted) history. I was giving tours, and he was performing stage magic. We have remained good friends, and with his skills in professional deception, he seemed like an excellent resource to speak to about the fraudulent side of the demonic world. Surely, I opened our conversation with this question: How many signs of demonic possession could be faked by a sufficiently well-versed illusionist? Aiden Sinclair is capable of making things disappear and reappear; of causing his fellow performers to levitate, seemingly in defiance of the known laws of physics; of making a planchette fly around a talking board and shoot up into the air in front of the astonished participants.

If anybody could detect deception during a case of alleged possession, it would be him.

Not for a single moment did I consider the possibility that he may have encountered the genuine article. Aiden drops that particular bombshell on me partway through our interview.

Let's start out with that old chestnut of the illusionist's performance: levitation. In the context of demonic possession, this brings to mind the unforgettable image of Linda Blair's Regan levitating above her bed in *The Exorcist* (or alternatively, Sigourney Weaver's Dana Barrett floating above her bed in *Ghostbusters*).

"It's an easy thing to achieve, but only if you control the entire environment," Sinclair explains. "Which means that every single person present has to be in on it. Otherwise, they'd see the illusion for what it is, or find out about the mechanical apparatus that makes the illusion work."

For the stage or street magician, making themselves or their assistant levitate is child's play. There are multiple techniques for doing so, many of which are in the public domain. At the low end of the complexity scale is the Balducci trick, named after the illusionist Ed Balducci. This simple visual trick uses a specific angle of the feet to fool the observer into thinking that both the performer's feet are leaving the ground, when in reality, the ball of one foot remains firmly planted.

Other methods of staging a levitation involve cutting clothes and positioning shoes in a specific way and using metal stands and frames concealed by clothing and the illusionist's body to support the levitating person.

If some of the eyewitness testimony from Earling, St. Louis, and other cases of alleged possession is correct, then theatrical tricks simply cannot account for the reports of levitation or paranormal floating. A case in point: the infamous 2012 Gary, Indiana possession in which a young boy is said to have walked up a hospital wall to the ceiling—*backward*. In addition to members of the boy's family, this gravity-defying behavior was said to have been witnessed by a caseworker from Child Protective Services and other members of hospital staff.[7]

---

7. It seems odd, however, that in 2012, with the prevalence of cell phone cameras and security cameras proliferating throughout emergency departments across the United States, that no footage or photographs were taken of that incident, or any of the other demonic phenomena said to have taken place inside the home—such as the boy's sister being raised into the air in her bedroom. I am not stating the possession was real or not real, just pointing out that in a twenty-first-century case such as this, it should have been relatively easy to obtain proof in the form of photographic evidence. Yet none is known to exist.

"All it would take to debunk a faked levitation would be one legitimate person in the room to see it and call it out," Sinclair goes on. "When a mechanical apparatus is used, they make noise—and how can you conceal that? Looking under the bed or close to it would give the game away very quickly and obviously."

As part of his act, Aiden has a specially constructed chair that contains a hidden mechanism, capable of floating somebody approximately five feet above the surface of the chair. The resulting "levitation" is extremely impressive...until you get to within six feet of the chair and hear the sound of the motorized mechanics that power the illusion.

Which prompts the question: What would a highly insightful observer like Aiden Sinclair have to see in order to be convinced that he was witnessing a genuinely paranormal occurrence?

"I'd want to be within a foot or two of the person in question, and have the ability to place my hands on them, to feel them rising and to rule out mechanical assistance. These machines cause tremors and vibrations, which I'd be able to pick up. I'd have to walk three hundred sixty degrees around them, look under whatever they're sitting on."

The priests, monks, and various assistants in both the Earling and St. Louis cases were all within very close range of their subject on numerous occasions. None of them ever cried foul.

I'm now satisfied that there's nothing even an expert illusionist could do to make the participants in an exorcism believe that their subject truly was levitating due to demonic influences.

I'm also convinced, based on the matter-of-fact tone of his voice, that the very rational Mr. Sinclair doesn't believe in such things as demonic possession. Not for the first time in my search for demons, I'm proven wrong...or at least, partly so.

Aiden regularly performs for sold-out audiences at a historic hotel in northern Colorado, where he is the resident illusionist. One night several years ago, he was performing a theatrical séance of his own design—an act with its own unique supernatural theme. On that night, he would encounter a man who changed the way Aiden looked at the concept of possession forever.

At the end of the show, he likes to stick around and mingle with guests, being a gracious host. One of the attendees was a priest from nearby Wyoming. The elderly gentleman stuck around until the rest of the attendees had left, seeking a quiet moment to talk with the illusionist.

"I've been to your show four times now," the priest said, handing Aiden a business card. "I understand that you live in Wyoming."

Aiden nodded, scanning the card indicating his status as a member of the clergy...and an exorcist. Intrigued, Sinclair agreed to meet the man for a cup of coffee. As they talked, the priest quickly steered the conversation toward the subject of demonic possession, asking the illusionist whether he would be able to tell whether a supposedly possessed individual was faking it or not.

"Yes," Aiden replied, "I believe that I can."

What impressed him most was the priest's approach to the subject. He was also a qualified psychologist and had gone to great lengths to rule out medical and behavioral conditions before tentatively considering the possibility of demonic possession...definitely an appropriate horse before the cart approach.

It's not every day that one is invited to attend an exorcism. Aiden agreed to meet the priest at a residence in Wyoming. After meeting the family of the possession victim, he was given free rein to look around the house and examine anything he wanted. The illusionist searched high and low for signs of a setup, including hidden mechanical devices, speakers, fans, and other gadgets. He found nothing that aroused suspicion.

Aiden was then introduced to the subject, a female who greeted him pleasantly. At first, he found nothing out of the ordinary about her. Out of the blue, she had what Aiden refers to as "an episode." She slumped to the ground and began to convulse, arms and legs twitching and jerking spastically in what looked like a grand mal seizure. As a former paramedic, Sinclair has seen plenty of those, and the similarity was striking. The key difference, however, was that in a grand mal seizure, the person is completely unresponsive. The electrical storm going on in their brain puts them in a state of grossly altered consciousness, in which they have no awareness of their own actions or the world around them. In the case of the young lady, she was not only still conscious, but her behavior quickly turned violent.

She began lashing out at anybody within range, punching and slapping, kicking whenever somebody got close enough. There were four grown men in the house. All four of them were required to restrain the subject in such a way that she could harm neither herself nor others. This is all the more remarkable considering the young lady's relatively slight build: five feet tall and weighing approximately one hundred pounds.

"It was surreal," Sinclair recalls, shaking his head. "I've never seen anything like it."

The priest immediately began saying prayers over her body. After a few moments, he handed Sinclair a St. Benedict medallion and, in a hushed tone, asked the illusionist to try placing it on the woman for her own protection. Each time he brought the medallion within two feet of her, she lunged at Sinclair, trying desperately to smack it out of his hand.

Changing tactics, Aiden took a card printed with a prayer to St. Benedict and palmed it. This time, when he brought the medallion close to the struggling female, he slipped the prayer card into the pillowcase behind her. She fell backward, her head coming into contact with the pillow at exactly the point at which the prayer card sat—and just like that, it was over. The thrashing, flailing young woman closed her eyes and instantly passed out.

Skeptics might suggest that she was simply faking it for her own purposes, yet crucially, she could not have known that the prayer to St. Benedict was inside her pillow. Not only was it behind and beneath her, but it had been put there quick as a flash by a man who makes a living performing sleight of hand. The timing of her sudden change in behavior seems, to this author at least, far more than coincidental.

"I've got nothing," Sinclair says, when asked to explain it. "No explanation whatsoever. It certainly wasn't a seizure."

In all, the episode lasted thirty minutes. Had it been a seizure, not only would she have lost all motor coordination, but she would have been at great risk of brain damage and possibly even death. She had suffered multiple episodes of this nature, and always returned to normal afterward. By the time her head hit the pillow, every other person in the room was drenched in sweat and physically exhausted from the struggle they had just gone through.

"When she woke up," he continues, "she was a totally different human being. Just the sweetest person you could ever meet. She professed to have no memory of what she'd done. This didn't come across as an act—and I *know* con artists."

It's time for me to ask the sixty-four-thousand-dollar question.

"Aiden, do you truly believe that you were in the presence of a demonically possessed individual?"

"I think there was *something* going on," he hedges, "but I don't know exactly what. Some people would say demons. Others might call it an elemental, or a ghost…or is this something that all of us have in our brains somewhere, an unlocked capacity. Maybe sometimes that switch gets flipped, and we call the results possession."

Although many would, Aiden Sinclair is clearly not comfortable labeling this as a demonic possession. That doesn't fit with his worldview. He makes a good point, though: what he experienced that night in Wyoming was some kind of phenomenon. He's keeping a broad mind as to what it was, so I try to narrow things down a little.

"Is it your belief that she was overcome by something, whether intrinsic or extrinsic, that night?"

"I feel like it was a supernatural experience," he admits, which can't be an easy thing for someone who's known for their skepticism to say. "I spent hours analyzing this afterward, questioning what I saw and experienced, looking for another explanation. It's one thing to hear about something like this. It's very different when you're actually present and witness it firsthand."

He points out that there is a degree of religious theater whenever an exorcism is performed, which casts a theological light over the events taking place. I'm curious to know whether the subject of the possession was a Christian or held any sort of religious or spiritual beliefs.

"The whole family was Catholic. That's why they went to the church for help."

Aiden and I debate the possibility that the religious undercurrent that ran through the case might have reinforced the idea that this was a demonic possession. By the same token, if you're Catholic, it's tempting to label this type of occurrence as demonic possession. We have to wonder what else it could have been. After we rule out a medical condition such as a seizure, then we're left with fakery—something that the experienced illusionist is adept at spotting—or mental illness. Efforts were made by the priest to rule out the medical and psychological possibilities prior to even considering the ritual of exorcism. While illness of one form or another cannot completely be negated as an explanation, neither can the possibility that this was exactly what it looked like…

…a case of possession.

"Bottom line," Sinclair concludes, "I just don't know what it is."

That makes two of us.

Has he ever experienced anything else remotely like this?

In fact, yes. While working as a paramedic on a 911 ambulance, Sinclair encountered patients who seemed to be overcome by something…uncanny, for want of a better word. Many first responders recount similar experiences, usually when called to treat somebody who is acting wildly out of character. Often, the explanation is a simple one: intoxication, or acute psychosis, to name just two. At other times, the presentation just doesn't quite fit either category. Consider those patients who somehow have an in-depth knowledge about the personal lives of the responding medics, knowing personal, private things about them that they could not possibly know by conventional means.

I have interviewed a number of responders who report this eerie phenomenon. Others were covered on the TV show I appear on, *Paranormal 911*. When it fit within their personal belief system, some became convinced that their patients were possessed. One paramedic told me about the 911 call she ran after dark, in which she was called to treat a man who had begun acting aggressively for no apparent reason.

"I looked him in the eyes," she told me, all but shivering at the memory. "Whatever was looking back out of them at me, it certainly wasn't human."

Those emergency professionals who came from a more secular background tended to dismiss the encounters as being "just one of those things."

"If you talked to them about this, 90 percent of magicians would tell you confidently that there's no such thing as the supernatural," Aiden goes on. "I'm in the remaining 10 percent. My life experience no longer lends me to that belief."

So, there we have it. After years spent working in haunted historic places, and an inexplicable brush with what may have been a demonic possession, the master illusionist, formerly skeptical of otherworldly experiences, had become a believer.

Not necessarily in demons, he would point out, but after ruling out deception and clinical causes, what else is there?

It's a question that will be foremost in my mind as we approach the most notorious case of them all: the 1949 St. Louis exorcism.

eleven
DEMONS AND DIARIES

The chances are that because you're reading this book or have even the slightest of interest in its subject matter, then you've seen a certain movie at least once. Even for jaded twenty-first-century audiences, *The Exorcist* has lost none of its ability to instill shock and fear. Many consider it to be director William Friedkin's cinematic masterpiece, his *Citizen Kane*. The movie has gone on to be spoofed, lampooned, criticized, lauded, and frequently ripped off in the half a century following its initial theatrical release in December 1973.

It is no exaggeration to say that this movie, more than any other factor (including the novel on which it was based), did more than just about anything else to put demons squarely in the public consciousness.

To understand how cultural juggernaut this came to be, it's necessary to go back to 1949. Much has been written about what is now referred to as the Hunkeler exorcism over the years, including numerous books and articles. For a truly in-depth analysis of the case, I highly recommend Troy Taylor's *The Devil Came to St. Louis*. Perhaps more than any other researcher, Taylor has contributed greatly to our understanding of what happened when a teenage boy was allegedly taken over by the Devil himself, and in my opinion, his book presents the most rounded appreciation of the case yet committed to print. Taylor spent decades on the Hunkeler trail, interviewing witness after witness, painstakingly gathering information, and even speaking in person—albeit briefly—to the subject of the exorcism himself, Ronald Hunkeler, shortly before his death. In writing his book, Taylor made a concerted effort to untangle the many disparate and sometimes contradictory narrative threads surrounding the case.

Born in 1935, Ronald Hunkeler was thirteen years old when the first inklings arose to suggest something odd was taking place: scratching from behind the walls of the family home in Maryland. (It should be noted that a number of those involved in the exorcism of Emma Schmid experienced similar scratching, which kept them awake late into the night.) A ratcatcher was duly brought in but found no vermin to account for the scratching.

This was January of 1949. After the death of Ronald's aunt, Tillie, with whom he had been close, the phenomena increased both in frequency and intensity. The furniture shook; objects moving of their own accord when they were around him. In one particularly notable incident, a dresser moved across the room entirely of its own volition, an incident that was recreated to terrifying effect in Friedkin's movie.

Some of those who knew Ronald Hunkeler during his time in Maryland recalled him as having been a "troubled" boy, whereas others noticed nothing particularly unusual about him at all, even with the benefit of hindsight.

Apart from the obvious, what else might have accounted for these bizarre phenomena? Rather than demonic possession, one potential explanation might be telekinesis: the capacity to move objects with one's mind. This is a hypothetical paranormal ability that has been documented anecdotally but never scientifically proven. Perhaps the best-known example comes in the form of Stephen King's 1974 debut novel *Carrie*, in which the titular protagonist is a teenage girl who undergoes such severe bullying that the stress unlocks latent telekinetic powers in her brain. Brian DePalma's 1976 movie adaptation memorably ends with Carrie, drenched in pig blood after being humiliated at the prom, using her mental powers to set the hall on fire and seek retribution upon her tormentors. Telekinesis is once again a hot commodity in the entertainment world these days, thanks to the success of the Netflix series *Stranger Things*.

Stepping away from the realm of fiction, we have celebrity figure Uri Geller, who rose to prominence in the 1970s with claims that he was able to bend spoons, forks, and other items with the power of his mind (and also by lightly stroking them). A former paratrooper in the Israeli military, Geller made a number of high-profile television appearances in Britain and the United States, seeming to demonstrate talents many audiences found jaw-dropping. Always a controversial figure, one thing is clear: whether one believes his claims or not, neither Uri Geller nor anybody like him was ever able to produce telekinetic effects even remotely on a par with those reported in the Hunkeler case.

Multiple eyewitnesses reported objects seeming to take on a life of their own in Ronald's orbit. This included his parents and other members of his immediate family—none of whom had any vested interest whatsoever in making this stuff up. In fact, the reverse would have been true. The Hunkeler family were Lutheran traditionalists, which framed the way in which they viewed the world. Paranormal activity cropping up around their son could have only one of two possible explanations: the restless spirit of Ronald's dead Aunt Tillie was to blame, or...it was the work of the Devil. The fact that the paranormal activity began days *prior* to the death of Aunt Tillie makes the former possibility extremely unlikely.

Little wonder that Edwin and Odell Hunkeler turned to the church for comfort and a possible solution to their family's troubles.

As matters progressed through early 1949, Ronald's mental health took a turn for the worse. It might be tempting to believe that the teenager was simply experiencing mood swings and the symptoms of depression, something for which he could be treated with counseling and possibly medication in this day and age. However, nothing to be found in the pages of the DSM-5 (*Diagnostic and Statistical Manual of Mental Health Disorders*) can explain the poltergeist activity, which is also said to have taken place around him. This even occurred when Ronald went to stay with the family's minister for the night at his home. The guest bed in which the boy was supposed to sleep rocked and shook, all without any movement on the part of its occupant. A presumably exaggerated form of this made for one of the more memorable scenes of Friedkin's film, when Regan's bed is seen floating up into the air and swaying from side to side, in complete defiance of gravity.

Nor did assessments of Ronald Hunkeler by psychiatrists and physicians find anything psychologically or medically wrong with him—at least, nothing that could account for the remarkable constellation of bizarre symptoms he was exhibiting.

Involving the family's Lutheran minister had not helped matters. To the contrary, after his engagement in the case, things escalated to the next level: physical violence. Scratches and cuts started to appear spontaneously on Ronald's body, apparently inflicted upon him by some invisible tormentor. The wounds happened in full sight of eyewitnesses, who vouched that they were not self-inflicted, and sometimes spelled out letters, words, and names. It's worth noting that this type of phenomenon is not unheard of in some of the more violent poltergeist cases on record.

Shortly afterward, the decision was made to consult with representatives of the Catholic Church. The belief was starting to take hold among members of the Hunkeler family that Ronald Hunkeler was possessed by an evil spirit…or possibly spirits, plural.

What followed was a maelstrom of fantastic claims, strange phenomena, aggressive behavior, and, ultimately, a pop culture phenomenon that shows no signs of slowing down seventy-five years later.

Today, the only building still standing that played a pivotal role in the story of Ronald's exorcism is an unremarkable-looking house in Bel Nor, a suburb of St. Louis, Missouri. At the time of the ritual—March 1949—it was owned by Ronald's uncle, and it was here that the youth was taken in an attempt to rid him of whatever it was that had (quite literally, it was believed) gotten into him.

Standing in the street outside the house on a sunny morning in March of 2021, some seventy-two years after the exorcism took place here, I'm struck by its sheer *ordinariness*. It looks like one of a thousand other houses in the state of Missouri. There's not one single thing to suggest the two-story home has any kind of sinister history. In fact, I even double-check the address in my research file to confirm I have the right place.

This is the house where, if contemporary accounts are to be believed, a small cadre of Jesuit priests went toe to toe with a demonic foe in the struggle for Ronald Hunkeler's soul. A primary source for what happened during the exorcism is a diary kept by a priest named Father Raymond Bishop, who kept detailed notes throughout the duration of the case. The diary was never meant to reach the public domain, but events nonetheless contrived to place its contents there. When the wing of the Alexian Brothers Hospital in which the exorcism took place was being torn down, construction workers found a copy of the diary in a drawer inside a room that had been kept permanently sealed. This was not the original handwritten document penned by Fr. Bishop, but rather, a duplicate. Although the idea of the room being kept shut off after the exorcism may seem far-fetched, author and researcher Troy Taylor was able to verify this from multiple independent sources.

Raymond Bishop, in turn, involved Father William Bowdern, a friend and colleague—not to mention a World War II combat veteran. That experience must have been helpful, because unbeknownst to him, Father Bowdern was about to engage in a bout of spiritual warfare that would take a heavy toll on him, both physically and spiritually.

After hearing about the phenomena that surrounded Ronald Hunkeler, Fathers Bishop and Bowdern visited Ronald and his family at the house in Bel Nor, intending to assess the youth's condition and suitability for treatment.

The priests left the house convinced of the need for an exorcism. On that night, and those that followed, they witnessed phenomena that seemed to defy any rational explanation—and pointed toward demonic possession as the only answer. Permission for an exorcism to be carried out was granted on March 16, and the ritual began posthaste.

Father Bowdern would be the lead exorcist. Frs. Bishop and Bowdern also enlisted the aid of fellow Jesuit Walter Halloran, a student who helped with some of the more physical aspects of the ritual...such as restraining Roland when it became necessary to do so. This would prove to be a real boon to future students of the case, as Halloran would go on to provide extensive information to author Thomas B. Allen as he worked on his manuscript for *Possessed*, a written account of the Hunkeler case that would be turned into a Showtime movie released in 2000.

Ronald Hunkeler seemed like a fairly ordinary youth during daylight hours—albeit one who was behaving in ways that were inconsistent with his established personality. The formerly well-behaved Ronald had become something of a problem child, having grown uncharacteristically aggressive and unruly. Once night fell, it was as if an entirely different persona emerged…one who was much darker, seeming to hold complete dominance over Ronald's body. Screaming, crying, and combative behavior became the norm at night. Histrionics tended to continue until the early hours of the morning, at which point the exhausted youth would fall asleep, usually waking up around noon that same day.

Much like the exorcism that took place in Earling, the phenomena that were reported in St. Louis seemed to defy the laws of science and nature as we currently understand them. Ronald is said to have suffered vicious bruises, scratches, welts, and other injuries, many of which spontaneously appeared on his body…sometimes within full sight of the priests, his family, and other observers. On occasion, raised weals formed words on Ronald's skin. The word *Louis* preceded the family's journey to St. Louis, as did *No*, *Hell*, and other words, as did an image of what Father Bishop described as a *devil*. It did not matter whether he was wearing clothes or not. During one of his lucid intervals, Ronald said he was fighting "a huge red devil" who wanted to prevent him from escaping. This boss creature was not alone; it was accompanied by a host of smaller demonic minions.

Pieces of fruit and books flew across the room at great speed. Furniture moved, some of it heavy and solid. Whenever Ronald lay in bed, or above the covers, the mattress tended to shake violently, even when he was perfectly still. He developed a strong aversion to holy water, religious icons, and relics. When he was in the grip of possession, Ronald cursed the priests and monks attending him, lashing out with punches and kicks that were extremely painful whenever they landed. These blows were more powerful than those an average thirteen-year-old should be capable of delivering. One particularly accurate punch broke Walter Halloran's nose.

The possessed Ronald was a spitter, hawking gobbets of phlegm at targets of opportunity whenever they presented themselves. He preferentially targeted the faces of his victims, and achieved an unerring degree of accuracy, even when his own eyes were screwed tightly shut. He was also a biter. The priests soon learned to beware of Ronald's teeth and made every effort to keep their arms and hands out of range.

On March 23, Ronald claimed to have seen a "dark cloud of black vapor" in his room, within which was a black-robed figure. This brings to mind the dark cloud that suddenly appeared in front of Father Steiger in the Earling case, causing him to crash his car and almost topple into a ravine. The literature of demonology is replete with instances of these dark, shadowy forms, which crop up again and again in accounts of possession.

As the days went on, Ronald's behavior continued to worsen. As with the Earling case, his angry shouts were punctuated by animal sounds, most notably a doglike barking. He began to use profanity, swearing like a sailor at the exorcists and making crude sexual references that were clearly intended to shock and horrify. This was counterbalanced by periods in which he sang in a clear, melodic voice that lacked any apparent trace of the demonic.

With the symptoms of possession growing worse, it was decided to transition the exorcism to the rectory located in the

campus church at St. Louis University and also to the nearby Alexian Brothers Hospital. Both offered a degree of security and privacy that the house in Bel Nor lacked.

Although the tenets of exorcism maintain that the exorcist
should never make casual conversation with the possessing entity,
there was nothing to prevent Ronald from making statements in
writing. Through this medium, he claimed to be "the Devil himself" and stated his purpose as being "I will, that is the Devil will
try to get his mother and dad to hate the Catholic Church."

It is a common trait of the exorcism ritual that, when com-
manded to do so, the possessing entity will usually give its reason
for possession. Of course, exorcists are also cautioned to anticipate
deceit. In the Hunkeler case, this comment was made at a time
when Ronald was being immersed in the teachings of the Catholic
faith. Was this a true statement made by "the Devil" that possessed
him, or the pushback of an angry boy who was bombarded with
Catholic doctrine morning, noon, and night?

At the rectory, with the permission of his parents, Ronald was
baptized a Catholic. During the process, he fought the priests tooth
and nail and had to be carried kicking and screaming to its conclusion. It was a titanic struggle but was completed successfully. It did
not lessen the severity of his symptoms, however. The newly Catholic Ronald Hunkeler was still afflicted with fits, outbursts, and spontaneous physical trauma. Scratches tore open his skin until it bled.

Matters came to a head on April 18. The day started out with
a violent outburst, Ronald throwing a bottle of holy water at the
priests attending him. The exorcism continued throughout that
day and into the evening. Later that same night, there came a seis-
mic shift in events when a new voice began speaking through. It
claimed to be St. Michael and boomed, "I command you, Satan,

and the other evil spirits to leave the body in the name of Dominus, immediately…Now! Now! NOW!"

And leave, they apparently did. After a brief period of intense thrashing and contortion, Ronald declared in his normal speaking voice, "He's gone!" Ronald described seeing a man in white robes surrounded by a brilliant light and carrying a "fiery sword" and a set of scales. This is, of course, a nearly textbook description of St. Michael, who was said in Biblical scripture to have used the sword in combat against Satan and his demons. He is also the saint charged with assessing the souls of the departed, determining their suitability to either enter the kingdom of Heaven or be consigned to the fires of Hell.

Ronald Hunkeler told the priests he watched as St. Michael banished Satan and his acolytes into a fiery cave, presumably representing the entrance to Hell, and described a "tugging" sensation in his stomach as the demons left his body.

The clock struck eleven. It was an hour before midnight, and the Hunkeler family's ordeal was finally over.

The bigger story, however, was only just beginning.

After Ronald's return to normality, Father Bowdern and Father Bishop continued to serve the church. The "Roland Doe" exorcism, as it came to be known when aspects of the case entered the public eye, would cast a long shadow, but it still remained a single, albeit exceptional, incident in their respective careers.

Walter Halloran went on to serve as a chaplain in the Vietnam War, as part of an airborne unit. He was a tough man whose story concerning the exorcism of 1949 did not waver. He died in 2005, at the age of eighty-three. Until his death, he steadfastly maintained his belief that Ronald Hunkeler truly had been possessed.

Although the similarities between the St. Louis and Earling exorcisms are manyfold and very apparent, one key difference is that Emma Schmid was said to have become possessed again in the aftermath of the 1928 ritual. This was not true of Ronald Hunkeler. He went on to have a family of his own, becoming an engineer for the National Aeronautics and Space Administration (NASA). Employed by the agency's spacecraft technology division, he worked on the ceramic tiles that form a key part of atmospheric reentry systems on the space shuttle. He died on May 10, 2020, aged eighty-five. Understandably, Ronald guarded his privacy, not wanting to be known as the boy who inspired *The Exorcist*. To the very few who became aware of his past, he refused to talk about the exorcism or the events surrounding it, stating that he did not remember a thing about the ordeal he underwent in 1949.

Ronald Hunkeler did everything in his power to keep a low profile where his alleged possession was concerned. The church helped protect his identity, and for decades, his true name and much of his backstory remained hidden from public sight. Due to inaccurate newspaper reporting, it was erroneously believed that he was a resident of Mt. Rainier, Maryland. A specific address was even circulated in the media: 3210 Bunker Hill Road, an empty, burned-out lot, which attracted late-night thrill seekers, partiers, and those who wanted a personal encounter with the Devil. This information appeared in a 1985 *Washington Post* article in which several murders and a fatal arson fire on Bunker Hill Road were tacitly linked with the possession.[8] There was just one problem: the Hunkelers never lived there. It was a derelict house the local fire department acquired in order to burn to the ground for training purposes.

It is true that Ronald and his family *had* lived in Maryland, both before and after the exorcism. Their home was in Cottage City, and

---

8. Brisbane, "Violent Deaths Plague Old 'Exorcist' Haunts."

it was there that the first signs of possession had reared their head. In the late 1990s, author Mark Opsasnick played the role of sleuth.[9] Any author writing about the Hunkeler case is standing on Opsasnick's literary shoulders and owes him a debt of gratitude. After a great deal of investigative work, he managed to put the pieces of the puzzle together, identifying both the correct residence in Cottage City and the Hunkeler family by name, effectively debunking the Bunker Hill Road rumors in the process. While researching this book, I could find no claims at all that the Hunkelers' Cottage City house was or is haunted, in contrast to what has been said about the house in Bel Nor.

Robert Murch, chairman of the Talking Board Historical Society (TBHS), also managed to track Ronald down and obtain his phone number. The mission of the TBHS centers upon the scholarship of talking boards in their many varied forms. Fascinated with the case for years, Murch gathered his courage and cold-called Ronald, who promptly hung up the phone without saying a single word. Murch couldn't blame him in the slightest.

Fast-forward several years. Once again, Robert Murch decided to phone Ronald Hunkeler, who surprisingly had not changed his number.

"I realize you're probably just going to hang up on me again," Murch blurted, trying to get the words out before the inevitable click of the line going dead, "but I just *have* to know…sir, is it true that before all the unpleasantness happened in 1949, you and your aunt were playing with a talking board?"

Murch waited with bated breath. Surprisingly, the line stayed active. There was even an amused chuckle at the other end. After

---

9. Learn more at http://www.strangemag.com/exorcistpage5.html.

a pause, Ronald Hunkeler said, "Well, I guess you're just going to have to ask the board."

Then he hung up again.

Robert Murch never got up the nerve to ask a third time.

The author of over one hundred and fifty books, author and researcher Troy Taylor spent years piecing together the facts in an effort to shed light on the murkiest depths of the Ronald Hunkeler case. In the process, arguably the biggest service Taylor performed was to debunk some of the wilder myths, exaggerations, and outright falsehoods that surrounded the alleged possession and exorcism. He also consulted as an on-camera expert for the TV documentary *The Exorcism of Roland Doe*.

Taylor is kind enough to take time out of his busy writing schedule to share his thoughts and expertise. There's a great deal on which I want to pick his brains. After we've exchanged pleasantries, the first thing I want to know is the author's stance on the subject of demons. Does a man who has written multiple books on the subject believe in their actual existence?

It turns out that he does, after a fashion, although he cautiously defines it as "the possibility of something we might *call* a demon." Taylor believes the word itself currently has a rather narrow Judeo-Christian connotation, when in reality, he points out that every culture has some sort of evil spirit or entity that is roughly analogous to a demon. This evil presence, he emphasizes, has been around much longer, and is far older, than that one particular belief system.

In other words, Taylor accepts the potential existence of demons, but rejects the label as the Western world tends to use it.

What about possession—and therefore, exorcism?

"Often, possessed people are being influenced by *something*, and an exorcism serves as a placebo to push whatever that influence is, out of them," he opines.

While researching his book on the Hunkeler case, Taylor interviewed a prominent Catholic exorcist, who revealed that the majority of the services he was called upon to provide were not in fact exorcisms at all; he referred to them as *infestations*, lower-level paranormal phenomena in their homes that could be addressed with lesser rituals such as blessings or with a form of what he termed *spiritual counseling*.

"I've come to believe that if someone believes they are possessed, then it's worth just giving them an exorcism," he goes on. "It might just clear the whole thing up."

There are many cases of fatal exorcisms on record, so while Taylor does have a point, great caution should always be taken. If somebody truly believes themselves to be possessed, what harm is there in having them *safely* exorcized—assuming that they have already been evaluated by qualified medical and mental health professionals, and that the ritual is conducted under controlled conditions and is closely monitored?

All of which brings us back to the case of Ronald Hunkeler. Was he really possessed—or at least, did he truly believe himself to be? The writer pauses to gather his thoughts.

"The people I spoke with who were actually in attendance at the exorcism of Ronnie Hunkeler were all convinced it was real. *All of them.* Even Father Halloran, who was more skeptical than anyone else...he just kept telling me that he didn't feel qualified to answer that question, but that was his way. I interviewed one of the monks who was present there for several days, and he told me over and over again what he had seen, and how compelling he still found it to be, even seventy years later."

On the other hand, Taylor cautions that every single one of the forty-eight people who signed the equivalent of an affidavit detailing the seemingly paranormal events that had taken place during the exorcism were all related to the church in one way or another. One of the individuals involved was a Lutheran minister, not part of the Catholic Church as the others were; he nonetheless wrote a letter to the parapsychologist J. B. Rhine, describing the uncanny phenomena he witnessed during the Hunkeler exorcism. Taylor has a copy of the letter in his possession, if you'll pardon the pun, and has used it as a primary source for his work.

"When I look at the totality of evidence," Taylor muses, "if this was not an instance of possession, then the only other thing it might equate to is a poltergeist case. Yet that explanation just doesn't encompass all of the phenomena. The priests involved all thought it was genuine. The people who were there were convinced, and I have to give that some weight."

Why didn't Ronald Hunkeler ever try to cash in on his status as "the Exorcist boy?" For one thing, he valued his career at NASA too highly, and was afraid at what effect his being associated with the infamous case might bring. Additionally, Taylor adds, "Nobody would have believed him. There was no evidence of it in the public realm at that time. I don't know if the church would have backed up his story if he had come forward—Father Bowdern refused to even give William Peter Blatty his name."

One of the primary reasons Troy Taylor sat down to write *The Devil Came to St. Louis* was the avalanche of rumors, ill-founded speculation, and outright misinformation that emerged in the wake of Friedkin's movie. He set out to correct as many of those misconceptions as he could.

"The idea that the possession arose from the use of a Ouija board was something I wanted to address," Taylor says. "That came straight out of Blatty's book. He needed a way to kick this whole thing off in his story. If you look at the time period of the real case, the late 40s, talking boards weren't even all that popular. By the time the 1970s came around and the novel was written, the occult was back in vogue, which made it easy for Blatty to use the board as a catalyst for his plotline. The Hunkeler family members I talked to all said that they were unaware of Ronald or his relatives ever using a board."

It's worth noting that the term *Ouija board* appears only twice in Father Bishop's journal. One reference involves Ronald's desk at school moving about on the floor *similar to the plate [planchette] on a Ouija board*, and the other referring to the time Ronald drew a sketch map and said, "Yeah, this is what I got on the Ouija board," implying that he had tried the board at least once. (After drawing the map, the teenager drew a face and added the words *Dead Bishop*. Whether this referred to an actual bishop or one of Ronald's two own personal exorcists, Father Raymond Bishop, is unclear.)

"Then there was the rumor of an earlier exorcism making the rounds, one in which Ronald had supposedly been taken to the hospital and had acted up so violently that he slashed the attending priest's arm open, seriously injuring him. That claim doesn't stand up to any real scrutiny. It was all just a made-up story."

As part of his research, Taylor happened upon a letter written by Father Bowdern to William Peter Blatty in 1967. The letter mentioned several Jesuit priests at St. Louis University telling stories regarding the exorcism that were completely inaccurate, their gossip simply adding fuel to an already growing fire. Father Bowdern himself did not speak openly about the exorcism because he was under strict instructions from his superiors not to do so.

Taylor still runs into this same problem decades later, including false claims that various different buildings were used as part of the exorcism. One of them is an apartment building in St. Louis that was formerly a hospital. Supposedly haunted, legend now has it that Ronald Hunkeler was held there and exorcised for a time. In reality, Taylor says, there's no record of the boy ever setting foot in the building. It is a myth Taylor has to dispel repeatedly. The problem rears its head every time a sequel (or TV version) of *The Exorcist* hits our screens. With three more movies scheduled from Blumhouse Productions, I get the feeling the author is going to have his hands full for quite some time to come.

A key primary source for Taylor's book was Father Halloran, who was able to fill in some of the blanks in the exorcism diary, casting light on some of the incidents that Father Bishop had documented rather sparsely. "I was lucky to have the access that I did, because Father Halloran died in 2005." Without his recollections and Taylor's research, we would know far less about the Hunkeler possession case than we do.

The burning question remains: Was Ronald Hunkeler genuinely demonically possessed? Taylor exhales as he lays out his complicated thoughts on the matter.

"Was it a mental illness? I've got psychiatrists telling me that there's no single condition that encompasses all the boy's symptoms. If it was mental illness, how exactly was it so miraculously *cured*? It apparently just went away, and never happened again. I find that hard to believe.

"In this day and age, when everybody has a high-definition camera, there's absolutely no excuse for exorcisms not to be recorded, and to have those recordings shared with the world," Taylor insists. "The Catholic Church says it's training more exorcists than ever before, because the calls for their services are coming in in record numbers. If that's the case, then surely one of the best ways to attract new members to the Church and convince them of not only the existence of evil, but also the superiority of God over Satan, would be to show them a successful exorcism?"

It's a compelling point. Director William Friedkin was one of only a handful of individuals permitted to commit an exorcism to film for his documentary *The Devil and Father Amorth*. The resulting footage, while interesting, offered far from definitive proof of demonic possession. Although the allegedly possessed party was aggressive, there's no levitation or any other hint of preternatural ability on display...nothing sufficiently compelling to convince the skeptical that she was possessed by a diabolical force. Assuming possession victims still levitate in the digital age, Taylor points out, wouldn't 4K ultra high-definition video footage go a long way toward convincing millions of people that demonic possession is real?

I can't pass up the opportunity to ask the author what it was like for him to personally step foot in the house himself.

"There was nothing really odd about the house, for me," Taylor recalls. "I could feel a change in the atmosphere when I went into the room where Ronnie was exorcised, but I'm positive that was because I was just so excited to be there, in a place I'd researched and written about for so many years. I don't claim to have any psychic abilities, and I don't sense anything in that house."

He goes on to add that while standing outside that particular room, he and his companions did hear strange noises coming from inside the empty bedroom, but he doesn't assume they were necessarily paranormal. Taylor feels that any residue of the 1949 exorcism is probably long gone.

It was impossible for me to write this chapter in good conscience without at least visiting the house in Bel Nor myself. The house in question seems to encapsulate the Hunkeler case in a way that no other building can. For many years, the house had a dark (or at least very colorful) reputation, having been seen as a sort of "best-kept open secret" among those who live in the St. Louis area. It was not always easy to find, particularly before the advent of the internet.

Although the lion's share of the exorcism took place in buildings that have since been demolished (Alexian Brothers Hospital was demolished in 1978), it was inside this two-story house, so much alike others in the neighborhood, that visiting Catholic priests first encountered the dark side of Ronald Hunkeler in March of 1949. I like to think of myself as a reasonable and rational man, yet standing here in the street late one afternoon, looking up at the window of what was once Ronald's bedroom, my heart begins to race as my mind conjures up images of a violently rattling bed; of furniture moving across the room of its own accord; and of scratches spontaneously forming on the bare skin of a traumatized youth...a youth who, many believe to this day, was possessed by a demonic entity.

I still don't know what to believe where the case of Ronald Hunkeler is concerned. The chill that runs along my spine has its origins in many places. First and foremost, it can be attributed to the work of the two Williams, Blatty and Friedkin, who burned stark images and equally disturbing sounds into my impressionable brain when I was about the same age as Ronald at the time of his possession. *The Exorcist* was and remains one of my favorite films, not least because of the visceral shock it hit me with the first time I saw it on a grainy bootleg VHS tape—the movie was banned in my native Great Britain until 1999, which didn't prevent every schoolkid I knew from passing the tape around with gleeful abandon, eagerly anticipating the sleepless nights it would cause.

Hollywood horrors aside, there is a more fundamental reason for the slight unease I feel standing in front of the house in Bel Nor.

My quest in search of demons is far from over, and I remain to be convinced one way or the other as to their existence, but…

What if? a voice whispers in the back of my mind. *What if it's true?* It's a valid question. What if the tens of millions of people who believe in the literal existence of demons are right? Let's sit with that idea for a moment. The idea that the modest home I'm looking at right now was once a battleground between the forces of light and darkness, a sort of celestial tug-of-war for the soul of an innocent youth Satan wanted for his very own.

Looked at in that light, it's a terrifying possibility.

Or maybe…just maybe…what happened there was something different. An outbreak of intense and violent poltergeist activity. A prolonged episode of mental or emotional disturbance. Or, as some have claimed, a hormonal young man who was entering the most difficult phase of his life, coping with it as best as he could in the most unconventional of ways.

If only those walls could speak to us, what stories would they tell?

Ever since Ronald Hunkeler's last day at the house in Bel Nor, most of the subsequent residents have lived there quite happily… but not everybody who steps across the threshold agrees. In 2005, Chad Garrison of the *Riverfront Times* interviewed a prospective buyer of the house, whose wife became suddenly and inexplicably unwell while climbing the staircase.[10] Understandably, that put her off buying the place. Garrison also spoke to a neighbor, who relayed claims that the bedroom in which Ronald's exorcism took place was perpetually cold no matter the season.

That same year, on October 30 (Devil's Night, appropriately enough), a TV show titled *Exorcism Live* aired. It centered upon an

---

10. Learn more at https://www.riverfronttimes.com/news/hell-of-a-house -2491650.

attempt to cleanse the house of whatever evil energies remained. The show was controversial from the outset, drawing fire from the St. Louis Catholic diocese, which objected to airing the ceremony of exorcism on television "for entertainment purposes."[11]

The exorcism was conducted by a representative of the Old Catholic Church. Was it successful? An equally valid question would be this: Was there anything there to exorcize in the first place? Ronald Hunkeler had not been inside the house in fifty-six years, and by all accounts, his exorcism had been a complete success. However, there are those who believe the presence of whatever demon or entity may have possessed him could possibly have left behind some sort of psychic taint or residue. This might account for what had so unnerved certain visitors to the house.

The TV production took over the section of street for several days prior to the broadcast. Ouija historian Robert Murch was part of the cast, brought on to speak about talking boards and their connection with the case. Although there's little evidence that such a board was ever used at this particular house, a Ouija session was going to be part of the show. Things took a turn for the surreal when Murch spotted what was either a drone or a remote-controlled model aircraft flying over the house. It was being operated by a small cadre of Satanists, who were standing in a nearby street and using the drone as part of a ritual to spoil the impending exorcism—a truly creative merging of technology and the occult!

Although nothing happened inside the house that Murch considered to be paranormal or demonic in nature, he does admit to

11. Learn more at https://www.catholicnewsagency.com/news/32908/exorcisms-for-entertainment-terrible-idea-st-louis-archdiocese-tells-cable-network.

having felt distinctly strange while spending time in Ronald Hunkeler's old bedroom. Picturing the boy lying there on the bed while attempts were made to cast out the Devil sent a chill down even the seasoned researcher's spine.

Reflecting on that night some eighteen years later, Murch admits that he might just have been apprehensive because of what he knew had taken place in that small upstairs bedroom— the power of suggestion. On the other hand, perhaps something entirely more sinister was to blame. He remains unsure.

In 2013, cast members of the TV show *Ghost Adventures* filmed their hundredth episode at the house. Lead performer Zak Bagans also posed the question: After leaving Ronald Hunkeler, did the possessing entity return to the house? Bagans and his team met on camera with the niece of Father Bowdern, who flatly refused to go anywhere near the house for her interview. Her rationale: "I know that whatever my uncle dealt with, was very powerful and very evil."

It's difficult to fault her for her concerns. She laid the blame for Ronald's possession squarely on what she says was his nearly obsessive use of a Ouija board, adding that such boards "open doors." It's an avenue I'm determined to explore further during my own search for demons.

She firmly believes that a remnant of the demonic infestation is still embedded within the house in Bel Nor. Based upon interviews I conducted for this book, she is most definitely not alone in this belief. Also wary of the house is Gregory Myers, a local paranormal investigator who claims to have been attacked inside the house in 2009. He recalls being skeptical of the property being paranormally active at first, making the very valid point that it ought to be "the most blessed house in the St. Louis area." To his dismay, Greg would learn differently while spending some time in the upstairs bedroom where Ronald's exorcism took place.

When seen on this episode of *Ghost Adventures*, Ronald's old room is small and cozy, painted in mute pastel colors and adorned with several mirrors and several pieces of colorful artwork. It looks like the kind of place you could peacefully curl up and take a nap… if you were unaware of its history, that is.

Standing at the scene of the attack, Greg recalled feeling a strong sense of heat on the side of his face, coupled with a sudden sense of fear and disorientation. It quickly intensified, Greg claimed, until his skin actually turned red and blistered.

Equally interesting was the interview that host Bagans conducted with a next-door neighbor, who proceeded to tell him that many of the owners of the house experienced runs of bad luck in their lives after becoming associated with the house. This resonates with the warnings I have been given by numerous members of the religious and paranormal communities regarding my involvement with this book project: the concern that expressing an interest in the demonic may cause it to take an interest in you right back. It's an ever-present thought lurking in the back of my mind as I work on this project.

This seems to be borne out when the exorcist brought in to work with *Ghost Adventures* fails to arrive at the house, after suffering a "freak medical emergency" while driving to St. Louis.

"People move in here…" the neighbor muses, refusing to enter the house at Bagans' invitation. "It just never seems to have a happy ending."

Greg Myers' account is remarkable, and I want to hear about it firsthand, so I reach out to him and ask if we can set up an interview. Fortunately, he's willing to talk about his experience at the house in Bel Nor, and I can't wait to hear what he has to say. He's a seasoned paranormal investigator with many years of experience and time spent living in St. Louis. He first went to the house to work with filmmakers Christopher and Philip Saint Booth, who were making a documentary titled *The Haunted Boy: The Secret Diary of the Exorcist*.

The first thing I want to know is just how paranormally active the house was. I'm intrigued to hear that, with the exception of the intense events he experienced in Ronald's old bedroom, he didn't find the house to be particularly haunted when compared with other cases on which he's worked. Then again, considering the sheer amount of spiritual firepower brought to bear on the residence by Frs. Bowdern and Bishop during the 1949 exorcism, that makes sense.

Greg and his colleagues had the opportunity to walk around the house before shooting started, getting acquainted with the layout and taking baseline readings. This is a key part of any reputable paranormal researcher's investigative process. Things began quietly enough. "During a production shoot, it's hard to get things to manifest sometimes," Greg recalls. "I went in with the mindset that very little was going to happen, because the house had been blessed several times by the priests."

There were a few EMF (electromagnetic field) anomalies, which may sometimes be paranormal in nature, but are just as likely to have a rational explanation. Harder to explain was the disembodied voice Greg and his companions began to hear talking to them from thin air as their investigation progressed. This was a male voice that did not belong to any of the production crew, although the words themselves were unintelligible. It was most often heard on the second floor of the house, and nobody was able to identify the source or figure out what it was saying.

I ask Greg whether, in his opinion, the main paranormal hot spot in the house is the bedroom. His answer is surprising: in Greg's view, the basement of the home is far more active than the rest of the house. On one occasion, as a colleague went downstairs, they were followed down the stairs by disembodied footsteps—truly an unnerving experience. The steps followed them around the basement before stopping abruptly.

"You'd get the feeling someone was right there behind you, that you couldn't see," Greg recalls. "It's been theorized by other investigators that the basement may contain a portal."

Portals are believed by some to be a sort of interdimensional doorway through which entities can come and go. Their existence has never been proven by science, but belief in them has been widespread throughout the paranormal community for years.

As previously mentioned, by far the most alarming encounter, as Greg related on television, happened in the upstairs bedroom. It's this I want to delve into a little deeper. He and a colleague, Sandy Oates, were standing still, asking questions and hoping to generate a response. It's fair to say that Greg got more than he bargained for. The side of his face began to feel warm, then hot. A fellow investigator who was monitoring a thermal imaging camera observed this rise in heat show up on the screen, offering tangible proof to back up what Greg was feeling. He broke out in a sweat as the intense burning sensation grew. The skin itself grew red, and as Sandy looked more closely, she saw the imprint of what looked to her like a white cross had risen up in the center. Greg adds that there were also a handful of small blisters on the periphery.

Although he wasn't given to flee the scene of a paranormal investigation, Greg only stuck around for a short while after this incident, before finally becoming discomfited enough to get up and leave. This was the first time in his career that Greg ever felt compelled to make an early exit from a haunted location. Leaving is something that no seasoned investigator does lightly—the equivalent of the fire department pulling out of a burning building because the conditions appear to be too unsafe to remain inside.

"I didn't want to sit there and take the chance I'd get roasted," he says drily.

"Did you ever return to the house?"

"I did...because I'm stupid." One of those events was to shoot *Exorcism Live*. Never again did he experience anything even remotely like the burning in the bedroom. The house was quiet on each subsequent occasion, with the exception of the phantom footsteps, which once again followed investigators down into the basement.

Does he believe in demons?

"Yes," Greg tells me without equivocation. "Whether or not they're from Hell, I can't exactly say that, but demonic entities *are* out there."

And is there a demon inside the so-called Exorcist House? Greg's answer catches me completely off guard.

"I don't believe I was burned by a demon. I think it was the spirit of Father Bowdern."

"Father Bowdern?" I'm having a hard time keeping the surprise out of my tone.

"I think he left the cross on my neck to send me a message. During our case research, we talked to many family members of those who were involved in the exorcism. We asked a lot of questions. This may have been a warning from Father Bowdern, telling Sandy and me to back off...to stop digging into the case and poking around—or else."

I have to admit, the concept of the spirit of a deceased exorcist deliberately injuring a paranormal investigator in an attempt to shut them up was something I hadn't ever considered.

"If it really was a demon, it could have burned me a lot worse," Greg adds. "That's my theory, anyway."

The house in Bel Nor is still occupied at the time of writing. It is privately owned, a family home, and one suspects that the tenants have had their fill of the curious onlookers who stream through the neighborhood each fall, particularly when October comes around. Should you ever decide to pass by the house for yourself, I entreat you to please not bother the residents, and to refrain from trespassing on what remains private property. Although an essential piece of history, it is, first and foremost, somebody's home.

The alleged possession of Ronald Hunkeler is as complex as it is fascinating. Broadly speaking, there are two schools of thought on the matter. The first holds that he was simply "troubled," "disturbed," or even just a "bad kid," in the parlance of the time. A number of friends and acquaintances, usually speaking off the record, voiced the opinion that Ronald was just making the whole thing up for his own purposes—possibly to get attention, or purely for his own amusement. One childhood friend of his, interviewed by author Mark Opsasnick, recalled young Ronald as being "a real mean little bastard" who took delight in setting his aggressive dog on other kids for kicks. There is also the possibility that Ronald was suffering a period of mental illness, which seemed to subside after the exorcism.

The second explanation is that Ronald Hunkeler was indeed the victim of demonic powers.

Was this truly a genuine case of possession? Father Halloran was noncommittal on the matter when interviewed by Mark Opsasnick—who ultimately concluded that there was likely no possession at all. Troy Taylor maintains that "something happened" to Ronald Hunkeler but, despite extensive study, is not sure precisely what that something was.

William Peter Blatty certainly believed so, as did Father Bowdern, the exorcist himself. The novelist's original intention was never to fictionalize the Hunkeler case. He had wanted to document the events at Bel Nor and the Alexian Brothers Hospital in a factual book, a work of historical accuracy rather than a novel. A lack of permission from the church and the Hunkeler family prevented him from doing so, leading Blatty to instead write a creative piece that drew heavily from what information he was able to glean.

Few people seem to consider a third possibility: that in a possible case of "one from column A and one from column B," *both* explanations might be true. Could the truth have been that Ronald Hunkeler was dealing with emotional issues that in turn made him vulnerable to a demonic possession?

In the years afterward, the Hunkeler family understandably shunned the spotlight, particularly Ronald, who sought to actively disassociate himself from the exorcism until his dying day. This speaks in favor of not just his own credibility, but also that of his parents. Nobody can accuse the Hunkelers of having concocted the whole thing as a cash grab or an attempt to become famous. When the tidal wave of publicity poured out after *The Exorcist* premiered, Ronald could very easily have taken center stage and cashed in on his status as "the Exorcist Boy." Instead, he did the opposite, choosing a quiet and productive family life over one of fame and notoriety. For all that we do not know about the life of this very private man, with all things being equal, I suspect he made a wise choice.

I have completed work on this chapter of the book you're now reading by mid-August of 2023…or so I think. Unbeknownst to me, I'm about to be blindsided in the most spectacular way, by a man whose chosen profession is to take ordinary members of the public and convince them that black is white and up is down. This is a man we've met before, stage illusionist Aiden Sinclair.

Time is a subject very much on my mind as the end of August approaches, bringing as it does my fiftieth birthday. Fifty is one of those landmark numbers that has the capacity to make someone look back over the course of their life, take stock, and critically analyze every single life choice that has ever been made. Ten years ago, turning forty had made me realize that celebrating my next major decade of life held the potential to make for a melancholy experience. In order to head that off at the pass, I accept an invitation from Aiden Sinclair and his partner Becca Knight to attend a public performance of their magical illusion show at Sinclair's Underground Theater in the Rocky Mountains. Accompanying me is psychic medium and paranormal investigator MJ Dickson. MJ is joining me not in a professional capacity, but rather just as good company to help me celebrate. We plan to enjoy a good meal, a couple of drinks, and be wowed by Aiden's stage magic.

All of that happens, and so much more.

As we file into the auditorium alongside—appropriately enough—fifty other members of the audience, expectations are high. There's a sense of anticipation building in the room, born out of Sinclair's reputation for excellence (he got his big break on the popular TV show *America's Got Talent*).

The room is laid out with rows of tables, around each of which are several chairs. Part of Sinclair's extensive collection of historic—and, he points out, sometimes haunted—objects can be seen in the many small display alcoves set into the walls.

Chapter Eleven

Although I don't know it yet, the contents of one of those alcoves is the equivalent of the Holy Grail for the book I'm currently working on…the book you now hold in your hands.

Sinclair's show is packed with illusion, misdirection, and spectacle, a series of impressive set pieces that go far beyond mere parlor tricks. No rabbits are pulled from hats on this Saturday evening, but there is at least one card trick that leaves a lasting impression. A collector of obscure and mystical arcana, Sinclair has in his possession a set of historic tarot cards more than two hundred years old. They once belonged to the celebrated magician and mystic Anna Eva Fay (1851–1927), who made her living as a stage medium, among other things, at the height of Victorian spiritualism. This particular set of cards was printed in 1713 and belongs to the *Tarot de Marseilles (Marseilles Deck)*.

I won't give the game away—not least because I have absolutely no idea how he does it—but part of Sinclair's act this night involves bringing five members of the audience up onto the stage. The tarot deck is shuffled, cut into five piles, and shuffled again. Then each of the five selected volunteers examines their unique pile, which only they can see, and at the illusionist's urging, chooses the card they feel speaks to them the most.

With it being my birthday and the illusionist one of my best friends, it's inevitable that I'll get picked. I'm given a set of pristine white museum gloves with which to handle the historic cards. Keeping them close to my chest, I go through my possible choices, almost settling on *Le Fol* (the Fool) as the card that best suits my personality and life path—after all, this is an adventurous idiot who is pictured with a playful dog tearing out the seat of his pants. It's safe to say I can relate.

Then I get to the final card, and the choice is made for me. It's *Le Diable*—the Devil.

Not for the first time on my journey in search of demons, a chill rushes through my body, that unsettling feeling that some people like to describe as somebody walking over their grave. I handle the thick card stock carefully, staring back at the leering face of a winged demon...the lord of *all* demons, Satan himself.

How could I possibly pick any other card?

I set the remaining cards facedown on the table when directed to do so by Sinclair, shielding *Le Diable* from sight. There's no way either he or the audience can possibly see which card I've picked, and there's no way on Earth he's going to have marked such a valuable and historically important set of tarot cards in order to pull off a stage illusion.

One by one, Sinclair turns his attention to each of my fellow volunteers on the stage and correctly tells them which tarot card they've selected. He's right every time, as the incredulous *oohs* and *aahs* from the audience attest. My brain is trying to figure out how he's able to pull this off. Even if it's by calculated guesswork, there should only be a one-in-five chance of him getting it right—which he has pulled off every time so far.

Then he looks at me and makes a show of "reading" me, admitting to the audience that we're friends, and that as a paramedic and writer, I have by necessity a fairly dark sense of humor.

"Your card," he concludes in the same matter-of-fact tone of voice one might use to announce the weather, "is *Le Diable*. You chose the Devil."

To say I'm impressed is to put it mildly. I turn the card around to show the audience, which quite rightly erupts in thunderous applause. I go back to my seat, shaking my head in bemusement, and enjoy the remaining thirty minutes of the show. I'm trying very hard not to dwell on the fact that another demonic image has just popped up in my life again, this time on stage in front of fifty people.

Surely, it's just another coincidence...right?

The show ends at ten o'clock sharp. The audience files out, shaking hands with Aiden and exchanging a few complimentary words. While he's greeting his public and signing autographs, MJ and I are poring over the artifacts encased in the wall displays. Many of them have been purchased at auction. The first to catch my eye is a straight razor that once belonged to Aaron Kosminski, one of the prime suspects in the Jack the Ripper murders. As a barber, Kosminski was well versed in the use of such a blade. Many believe he used it to deadly effect on the streets of Whitechapel, London, in the late 1800s.

There are also artifacts that belonged to passengers of the 1912 *RMS Titanic*, items that were taken aboard the ship and left on lifeboats with some of the fortunate survivors prior to the liner sinking.

Then, I happen upon a strange book. Its black cover bears signs of both flame and water damage. Emblazoned front and center is a silver cross with a crucified Christ. The book sits vertically on an ornate stand. Laid on the shelf in front of it are six St. Michael medallions, presumably for protection.

I don't hear the magician approach, but suddenly he's right behind me, looking over my shoulder.

"Is this...?" I begin, knowing the answer already thanks to a small title card next to the display. He nods.

"This is the diary of Father Raymond Bishop," he confirms.

"The *actual one*?"

"Yes, the actual one."

I'm immediately beset with so many questions. How did it come into Sinclair's possession, if you'll excuse the pun again. How long has he had it?

Most importantly of all…can I open it up and look inside?

I'm fully expecting him to say no. Instead, Aiden reaches past me, opens the case, and reverently takes out the book. Setting it down on a nearby table, he tells me how he came to be the custodian of the book. After Father Bishop's death in 1978, the diary and other personal items became the property of his next of kin. To say that they were not thrilled by this is an understatement, according to Aiden; this is evidenced by the many scorch marks that mar each page. At least one attempt was made to burn the book. When he was given the opportunity to take it off their hands, Sinclair jumped at the chance, recognizing that such a culturally important artifact needed to be preserved for posterity.

I look inside the cover. Somebody—presumably Father Bishop—has glued a St. Michael medallion on the very first page. Written above it is Fr. Bishop's name, and the address of Jesuit Hall on the campus of St. Louis University. The magician slowly turns the pages with great care, wary of the risk that the damaged paper might simply come apart if too much force is applied. I photograph some of the pages, watching as the story of Ronald Hunkeler's exorcism unfolds before my eyes. Each entry is written in neat, capitalized handwriting, dated, and contains the location for the day, and the names of those present. All end with Bishop's flourishing signature, preventing any false additions from being added below the last line.

The April 23, 1949, entry discusses Ronald's move to the St. Louis College church rectory because of the family's "desire to no longer host the boy." His dad spent the night sleeping in the same room as Ronald. When the bedtime of 9:30 p.m. came around, prayers were said, after which Ronald flew into "a tantrum" and began spitting at and physically attacking those present. Father Halloran's nose was broken in what proved to be a remarkably accurate punch, given the fact that Ronald's eyes were closed. He "urinated copiously" and "complained of burning sensations." Another priest, Father Roos, also developed a nosebleed after taking another hit from the thrashing boy.

Swearing loudly, Ronald declared that Father Bowdern would go to Hell in 1957, a prediction that proved to be untrue. (He died in 1983.) The day's entry ends with Bowdern standing vigil over Roland while he slept.

Aiden carefully advances a few more pages to the entry for April 30. By this time, Ronald was back in the Bel Nor house belonging to his family. They called the priests for help at midnight, at which point Frs. Bowdern and Bishop went over to perform the exorcism. According to Father Bishop's notes, Roland had written on his bedsheets the words *Dead Bishop* and *Believe in me or Ronald will suffer*.

After Ronald fell asleep in the small hours of the morning, the priest remained to watch over him. Father Bishop's entry for the day ends on a downbeat note: "The family was much disturbed by these happenings and found little comfort in the presence of the clergy."

And so it goes on. Aiden turns the pages while I soak it all in, picturing the scenes in Ronald's Bel Nor bedroom, the rectory, and the Alexian Brothers Hospital. Finally, we come to the entry for April 25, where it is noted that Ronald awoke on April 19 with no memory of what he had suffered. He continued to say Hail Marys and stayed there for just under a week, without any resurgence of the demonic phenomena. Finally, on April 25 (the Feast of St. Mark), he was returned to his family, where he "remained normal."

The journal ends with a list of ten Jesuits who saw Ronald "under possession" and one final flourishing signature from Father Bishop.

It's only when the last page is turned that I realize I've been holding my breath. Although I've read digital transcriptions of this material, to actually see the primary source document itself, to touch it with my own hands, is jarring. I feel a sense of connection with the Hunkeler case that nothing to this point has been able to create, not even standing outside the house in Bel Nor looking up at the bedroom window where much of Ronald's ordeal took place.

This book, with its scorched patches marking every single page, was at the heart of it all...*if* it's the real deal, that is. While it's unclear whether Father Bishop physically took the journal into the room when Ronald was being exorcised, it is certainly possible this was the case on at least one occasion—if not more. Now that the human beings who participated in the exorcism are dead, the Alexian Brothers Hospital and the rectory are torn down, the only tangible links to the case that remain are the house in Bel Nor... and this handwritten journal.

And that's assuming, of course, that it really is what it purports to be. There's no way I can tell for sure whether it really is Fr. Bishop's diary or whether my friend has been the subject of an elaborate prank. All I can do is take it at face value and, acting like the paranormal investigator I am, treat it as I would any other allegedly haunted object.

I can hardly take my eyes off it. Now, another thought pops into my brain. I don't know what to make of the stories surrounding that house, but could it be the case that something...some attachment, some residual form of energy...may have been soaked up by the journal somehow?

It's time for us to find out.

I set out two digital voice recorders, one on either side of the book, and start them running. The intent is to capture what paranormal investigators refer to as electronic voice phenomena, or EVPs—believed by some to be the voices of the dead, or disembodied intelligences of some kind. If there is any kind of psychic energy associated with the journal that has the ability to communicate, now would be its chance.

"C'mon, Houdini," I say, gesturing at the illusionist to take a seat next to MJ, Becca, and myself.

"Here's the reason I don't think we'll get anything," he says, pulling up a chair and sitting down. He proceeds to tell us about the many ghost hunts he has conducted on the haunted cruise liner the *Queen Mary*. The events were usually paranormally active, with one glaring exception: the night a lady who did not want to be there spent the entire session saying prayers of protection to Saint Michael. Somewhat afraid of all things paranormal, she had only gone to the ghost hunt in order to please her daughter, whose birthday it was. The prayers seemed to have a dampening effect, as virtually nothing strange happened during the event.

Sinclair opens the diary to the first page, onto which a silver St. Michael medallion has been affixed. My eyes shift to the cubbyhole in the wall, where the diary's usual but now empty resting place is surrounded by six more of them. I'm reminded of the Secret Service details flanking the presidential limo as it rolls through the streets.

"Faith is immensely powerful," the illusionist opines. "This was owned by a Jesuit priest who had an immense amount of faith. It's filled with religious iconography, and although I personally don't have faith in those things, the person who owned it and wrote in it, absolutely did."

I'm beginning to get a sinking feeling in the pit of my stomach.

Looking at my watch, I see that it's ten minutes to midnight. How very apropos. We're going to investigate the book over the witching hour. Let's do this.

MJ closes her eyes and attempts to tune in psychically to the book. After a pause, she opens them again and says, "Nothing."

"Nothing at all?" I ask hopefully. She shakes her head sadly.

"There's not a shred of psychic residue emanating from this thing."

Nothing strange has ever happened around the book while it has been in Sinclair's possession, but there might be a reason for that. He might be a skeptic, but he does believe in binding, the idea that paranormal energies can be intentionally attached to an object. This is why, on those rare occasions when the Exorcist Diary is moved or transported, he places a ring of protection around it in the form of religious icons such as the St. Michaels, essentially creating a mobile jail cell for it. This is the first time ever he's taken the book out of that protective circle, removing it from lockdown.

I invite any communicators present to speak, welcoming them to tell us their name. After leaving a suitable pause for a response, we each begin asking questions in turn. What can they tell us about this book? Is anybody staying with it? Are there any energies imbued within the book?

We allow the two recorders to run, recording not just the formal EVP session but also some casual chat afterward. The rationale is a simple one. Some of the best EVPs I've ever gotten have occurred when my team and I were just shooting the breeze, chitchatting about nothing of particular importance. It's almost as if an invisible somebody wanted to get in on the conversation.

Playing the recordings back, we hear our own voices accompanied by the occasional crackle of static. No ghosts, spirits, and, most importantly, no trace of a demon. If anything demonic was ever attached to this book, it would seem that the many blessings and protections the diary has undergone have broken that connection somewhere along the way, cleansed it of any dark traces.

There's just one nagging doubt in my mind. Although the diary looks authentic, there's no cast-iron guarantee that it isn't just a clever fake. I trust Aiden's word implicitly. However, the identity of the person who delivered it to Father Bishop's family in unclear, and I can't discount the possibility that somebody created this artifact and passed it off to them for reasons known only to themselves.

The mystery deepens.

I won't deny experiencing a twinge of disappointment when MJ's psychic abilities and our EVP session both turn up nothing… yet as we say our goodbyes, and Aiden carefully returns the Exorcist Diary to its rightful place, I am reminded that sometimes it is a privilege just to have a personal connection with such a remarkable piece of history. From the events it chronicled in its pages sprang a global phenomenon that continues to terrify and enthrall readers and viewers today.

It's time to take a closer look at the role played by demons on the silver screen, and their place in popular culture.

twelve
DEMONS ON THE SCREEN

In 1949, when Ronald Hunkeler was undergoing the rite of exorcism in St. Louis, future screenwriter William Peter Blatty was a student at Georgetown University in Washington DC. An acclaimed educational institution, Georgetown was Jesuit in nature, which made it a perfect fit for Blatty. It was here that he heard for the first time about the Hunkeler case. The idea sat in the back of his brain, bubbling away, percolating for more than twenty years.

Blatty was not known for writing horror movies, having written primarily comedy screenplays for such movies as Blake Edwards' *A Shot in the Dark*. Yet it was his novel about a teenage girl possessed by the devil that forever altered the course of his career, ultimately putting him in the director's chair for 1990's *The Exorcist III*.

The Hunkeler case provided a solid foundation for a plot. In writing his novel, Blatty kept the age of his teenage protagonist about the same, but gender-swapped Regan MacNeil and relocated the scene from St. Louis to his beloved Georgetown. Given the connection between Georgetown and the Jesuits, the shift made eminent sense, and the backdrop would give Friedkin's future film adaptation a suitably brooding, overcast look.

The route of possession in Blatty's novel involves Regan messing around with a Ouija board, conjuring up an "imaginary friend" named Captain Howdy. Although there were rumors of a similar board being used by Ronald Hunkeler prior to his possession, author Troy Taylor was unable to find concrete evidence to validate these stories. (However, when interviewed by Zak Bagans of TV's *Ghost Adventures*, the niece of Ronald's exorcist, Father Bowdern, claimed that Ronald and his aunt used the Ouija board "all the time.") Nor was the Ouija board blamed for the possession of Emma Schmid, who was supposedly made vulnerable after consuming a cursed meal. I make a mental note to interview a leading expert on such boards and explore their reported connection with the demonic in greater depth.

Once Friedkin's movie really gets going, the various manifestations of Regan's possession seem to have been borrowed liberally from both the Hunkeler case and that of Emma Schmid—with the dial turned all the way up to ten. Regan becomes increasingly demonic in appearance as the second half of the film progresses, brought to disturbing life by the prosthetic skills of makeup artist Dick Smith. She vomits a green pea souplike substance into the faces of Fathers Karras and Merrin, which may have its genesis in the frequent vomiting attributed to Emma Schmid in *Begone, Satan!* In the later stages of her exorcism, Regan is fed via a nasogastric tube; this mirrors Carl Vogl's statement that "during all this time, she could not eat solid foods, but nourishment in liquid form was injected into her."

Regan's bed levitates and shakes, just as Ronald Hunkeler's was said to have done. In some scenes, the teenager is tied to the bed in four-point restraints, as happened to Emma Schmid; in others, she floats above the mattress, levitating without any apparent effort.

During our interview, Dr. Joseph Laycock observed that an exorcist only knows the ritual has been successful in terminating the possession when a specific sign takes place, a kind of capstone to the entire grueling process. In the Earling case, Emma Schmid is said to have flown up to the ceiling, then gone completely limp and dropped back down onto the bed. Accompanied by what Vogl calls "a piercing sound," the names of the four principal entities possessing Emma were repeated over and over, progressively diminishing in volume as though the unseen speakers were receding into the distance. The final word spoken was *Hell*. The final capstone came in the form of a dreadful stink, indicating that the possessing spirits had been ejected.

They say that art imitates life, but Friedkin's version of *The Exorcist* ups the ante considerably, as befits a major motion picture. With Father Merrin dead at his feet, Father Karras allows the demon Pazuzu, expelled from Regan MacNeil, to enter his own body, as evidenced by his eyes turning an evil shade of yellow. Karras then hurls himself from the bedroom window, falling head over heels down what are still widely known today as "the Exorcist steps" before taking his final breath on the street below, after being given the last rites by his friend, Father Dyer. (As it turns out, Karras and Pazuzu are not really gone, but that's a story for another day—and a sequel.)

The Exorcist exploded onto movie screens in a storm of controversy, which made it onto TV news shows, newspaper headlines, and the covers of popular magazines such as *Newsweek*. Proving that there's rarely such a thing as bad publicity, the brouhaha surrounding the film only served to sell more tickets, helped by claims of viewers vomiting, having seizures, or fainting in the aisles during screenings.

For the Catholic Church, the success of *The Exorcist* was very much a double-edged sword. On the one hand, some of its more shocking imagery, such as the possessed Regan masturbating with a crucifix before thrusting her mother's face into her bloodstained crotch, led to widespread revulsion and condemnation. The evangelist Billy Graham took every opportunity to decry the film, both from the pulpit and during interviews, declaring that the Devil was "in every frame" of the movie. It's worth noting that Graham was not a Catholic.

On the other hand, the theme of faith—explicitly the Christian, *Catholic* faith—winning out over evil worked very much in favor of the Church. The movie delivered a recruiting coup for Catholicism, showing an idealized version of the organization performing heroically and saving the day. The movie generated a fresh wave of interest, not only among churchgoers, but also among those who aspired to make the Church their calling. As was the case with *Begone, Satan!*, *The Exorcist* has been accused by some as being nothing more than Catholic propaganda.

In the wake of the film, exorcists and exorcism became a hot topic. In the United States, the church experienced a sharp uptick in cases of reported possession, and subsequent requests for exorcism—the vast majority of which were rejected out of hand. At the time of writing, the demand for exorcism is at an all-time high.

Both at the time of its release and for decades afterward, much was made of the so-called curse of *The Exorcist*—the claim that a string of deaths and unfortunate incidents were attached to the movie, either directly or indirectly. Cited foremost is the death of actor Jack MacGowran, who portrays Burke Dennings, the director of the film within the film. Production had already wrapped on

The Exorcist when the fifty-four-year-old actor, who was not in the best of health to begin with, contracted influenza and died. The flu kills thousands of US citizens each year (particularly in years when the disease reaches epidemic status).

"The cast and crew of the film were so freaked out that they had the set blessed," says author Troy Taylor, referring to blessings performed by two priests who served as advisors on the film.

Still, reports of misfortune continued to surface during and after production on the film. Close family members of two of its stars also died. While the film was still in production, the grandfather of star Linda Blair passed away. Axel von Sydow, Max von Sydow's brother, was sixty-five at the time of his death in 1972. (By comparison, the titular exorcist himself, Max, lived to be ninety.) As time went on, an increasing number of deaths among the cast and crew, plus their families, were attributed to a demonic curse. This included illness, injury, and even a fire that damaged the set. During its shoot, *The Exorcist* gained a reputation for being a troubled production. Aided by director Friedkin, Warner Brothers' publicity department fanned the flames, hinting at a diabolic attachment being a possible cause of the film's woes. Whether or not it was cursed remains up to the individual to decide, but it was undeniably great PR.

It also prompts the question: If *The Exorcist* was truly cursed by diabolic influences because of its fictionalized depiction of demonic activity on celluloid, why wasn't Friedkin's subsequent documentary *The Devil and Father Amorth* also cursed? That film purported to show a case of actual possession and exorcism, instead of a dramatized version. Surely that would anger the dark powers even more. Yet there are no such accounts surrounding the lesser-known film.

To discuss the influence of the demonic in television and film upon our mass perception of the phenomenon, I sit down to chat with Aaron Sagers, a mainstream journalist with expertise in paranormal pop culture. He has also worked extensively in paranormal television, both in front of and behind the camera.

"Friedkin's movie came out at a time when people were losing faith in national institutions," he begins. *"Rosemary's Baby* had already had a massive impact. Both movies talked about faith in opposition to nefarious forces, and explored the possibility that the power in which you place all your faith—God—is perhaps not as powerful as you might think. A lot of people saw *The Exorcist* and thought *I too might want to become an exorcist, or maybe need the services of one."*

We both agree that a similar effect is seen today in the realm of paranormal television, with an increasing number of individuals watching shows about hauntings (both demonic and traditional) and believing that something similar is happening to them in their own lives. Some human beings are wired to see something told dramatically on the screen and to apply those same events to themselves, in much the same way that after reading an article on WebMD or any other healthcare-related website, it's possible to convince oneself that we're having a heart attack or some other malady.

"You watch a movie like *The Exorcist,*" Sagers muses, "and you reflect on it. A mental pattern starts to form, incorporating potentially strange things taking place in your own life. It's a very powerful movie, one that still holds up well today. You walk out of that film *shaken,* and while some viewers can find a catharsis in that, others find that it preys on their preexisting spiritual fears. When it came out, the movie also aligned with the *Satanic Panic* movement of the time."

Burning its way across the United States during the 1980s, the Satanic Panic was a widely held false belief in Satanistic ritual abuse and cult activity that was said to permeate all levels of society. Everything from restaurant chains to rock music and roleplaying games such as Dungeons & Dragons were said to be playthings of the Devil, tools that dark forces could use to make entry into the lives of the unwary in order to corrupt them. In addition to the aforementioned *Rosemary's Baby* and *The Exorcist*, the popularity of Hollywood's version of the Antichrist story, *The Omen*, also stoked the fires of public fear and outrage. Claims of animal and human sacrifice arose, some of which were linked with false memories brought out while the claimant was under hypnosis. In an eerie and disturbing echo of the Salem Witch Trials, accusations and counteraccusations were hurled back and forth. Despite a lack of any solid evidence, innocent people were convicted and sent to jail. Lives were ruined on the basis of sheer paranoia and ignorance.

"Christian fundamentalists were warning the public of dark forces lurking around every corner, cults carrying out heinous ritualistic acts that were threatening to corrupt America's youth," Sagers goes on. "The timing was, for want of a better term, nefariously perfect. Those demonically themed movies came in at exactly the right time to stoke the fires even further."

Much has been made about the supposed curse of *The Exorcist*, and with his extensive knowledge of the movie history and its production, I put the question to Aaron: Was the production really cursed? Did dark forces truly intervene in an attempt to stop the movie being made?

"A lot of the time when people talk about cursed films, they're referring to a series of accidents, mishaps, and trauma that take place around a movie production, where *after the fact*, we try to discern a pattern that connects them. Once you dig deeper, however, it becomes clear that some of them can be ascribed to negligence and a lack of attention to safety. Linda Blair was thrashed around on set, subjected to some very harsh conditions, and on the movie's release, this poor child became the focal point for a mob that wanted to point fingers at the movie in a negative way. The movie was incredibly successful, yet she bore the brunt of much of the fallout from it. We don't need the occult to explain things like that."

Sagers makes an excellent point. However, he isn't ruling out the possibility of diabolic interference entirely.

"I theorize that when a movie's intent is to create and film certain subjects and rituals, such as a séance or black magic, including the summoning of dark forces into our world, I can't say for certain that those forces will just sit back and say, *Oh, we won't bother them, because they're just filming a movie.* I think that even if you are *pretending* to conjure things and stir up entities, you might actually be doing that!"

The idea isn't all that far-fetched, but it prompts the question why each and every movie and TV show that has a conjuration and summoning scene doesn't bring in those forces to curse their production. Why don't we hear similar reports every time a movie set in the Conjuring universe wraps shooting?

"Sometimes the stories are just put out by the marketing department," Sagers allows, "but I have spoken to numerous people who worked on paranormally themed productions who insisted some very weird stuff took place on set. I sometimes wonder whether the subject matter is putting out a kind of psychic beacon, which starts attracting some kind of supernatural attention. On the other hand, you have to consider the possibility that because these people are so steeped in the material, they begin to interpret every creaky floorboard and bump in the night as being something ghostly or demonic. That's not going to happen if you're working on a Marvel superhero movie, because you're going to have a completely different mindset."

As has happened so often in this journey in search of demons, the subject matter has come back to the power of belief and the human mind. Indeed, in the days before our interview, reports have surfaced from the United Kingdom of ghostly goings-on during the filming of the new *Ghostbusters* sequel *Frozen Empire*. In an April 14, 2023 article in Britain's *Daily Mail* newspaper, reporter Gemma Parry wrote that the film crew was spooked by weird noises while they shot scenes in central London.[12] One source was quoted: "They have been hearing really weird noises, and it's freaking people out. It's spooky enough being in a dark tunnel deep underground, let alone there being ghouls too."

This exemplifies Aaron's point about the crew being steeped in ghost lore during the course of production, yet at the same time, London's underground subway system is renowned for being extremely haunted—something I can confirm, having investigated parts of it myself. Perhaps *both* explanations could be true in cases such as this.

Our conversation turns to the popularity of demons on the big screen. "Paranormal movies have been around for a long time," Sagers points out, "but only a few find a spot in the top ten moneymakers each year...films like *The Sixth Sense* come to mind. What demons do is allow the filmmaker to have a strong twist and finale to a ghost movie, which is why so many start out as a vanilla haunted house movie and then—*surprise!*—there's some bigger, more nefarious dark force revealed partway through the

---

12. Learn more at https://www.dailymail.co.uk/news/article-11974997/Ghost busters-crew-spooked-weird-noises-believe-haunted-tube-tunnel-set.html.

film. Demons raise the stakes…and this is also true of paranormal reality TV."

Hunting ghosts is one thing. Hunting demons—or being hunted *by* demons—takes things to an entirely new level of scary. Demons take things far beyond the realm of ghosts, heading into the murky domain of nonhuman creatures that can't be negotiated or reasoned with. They can only be expelled by an exorcist, sometimes at great cost. No wonder viewing audiences respond so positively to them.

Year 2009 brought the blockbuster movie *Paranormal Activity*. Shot on a shoestring budget inside a house, it tells the story of a couple who is stalked each night by a demonic entity. Replete with night vision shots that wouldn't look out of place in a paranormal reality show, part of the plot involves the couple in question using a Ouija board—with predictably dire consequences. The runaway success of *Paranormal Activity*—the movie made almost two hundred million dollars and kickstarted a franchise—also provided a huge shot in the arm to ghost hunting shows on TV, a number of which then began to encounter demons on a weekly basis.

It's possible to make a direct connection between the success of *Paranormal Activity* and the proliferation of demons throughout popular culture, in both reality and drama. Aaron experienced this personally when pitching TV shows to executives, when the question was frequently asked: "How can we make this *scarier*? Is there any demonic activity taking place?"

Shows featuring demons became more popular. In turn, paranormal enthusiasts visiting haunted locations began to claim they were encountering demons at more and more haunted locations. Some would say that demonic activity was increasing across the globe—certainly, the Catholic Church would take that line—

whereas others would say that the slew of shows and movies featuring demons was introducing a bias.

"Sometimes, we find exactly what we go looking for," Aaron tells me, speaking of this very same bias, "but we also can't discount the possibility that we are *attracting* that very thing to us. We could hypothetically be manifesting this very activity ourselves when we intentionally seek it out."

As we conclude our discussion, Aaron Sagers has left me wondering how much of what is termed *demonic activity* may simply be misinterpreted by individuals with a strong predisposition toward believing in it...and whether some could possibly be genuine, attracted by the paranormal enthusiast's interest in and fascination with the darker side of things.

As the old saying goes...be careful what you wish for.

thirteen
A TWENTY-FIRST CENTURY DEMON

Thus far, we have looked at cases of demonic activity and possession throughout different stages of history. But what about today? To what demons does the twenty-first century lay claim?

Since the days of antiquity, demons have been described as beings of immense power that live for thousands of years. Many of their names are listed in books such as M. Belanger's *A Dictionary of Demons*.[13] One name that does not appear in that book is a relative newcomer to the scene: a demon named Zozo.

With the benefit of hindsight, unearthing an old talking board in 1982 came perilously close to ruining the life of a young man named Darren Evans. The board was hidden beneath the house of Darren's girlfriend at the time, located in Oklahoma. Who put the board there, and why, was a mystery, as was the name carved

---

13. Belanger, *The Dictionary of Demons*.

into it: *Zozo*. It was found by a plumber, and ultimately ended up in Darren's hands.

I'm fortunate to have the opportunity to discuss Darren's Zozo experiences with him directly. He's a little wary of being interviewed, feeling that his views have been misrepresented in the past. I'm aware that some have criticized his story and either mocked or even attacked him personally, and what I really want is to hear his side of things directly. Darren speaks clearly and earnestly, giving thought to each of my questions before answering each one.

It's hard to think of a *good* reason for somebody to bury a talking board in the dirt beneath their house. There are several different techniques for destroying one, such as cutting or tearing it up and burying it in salted earth; however, there are those who believe this might release any dark energies that are attached to the board. In the case of what Darren would soon come to call the Zozo board, whoever placed it beneath the house had also positioned four jars around it, one at each corner. Inside the jars were the remains of four blackbirds.

"I was fifteen, and I'd never seen a Ouija board before," Darren remembers.

As soon as it was unearthed, Darren felt somehow drawn to it, an odd attraction that he could not explain. His interest in the board quickly developed into a full-blown obsession. He never missed an opportunity to break out the board, to show friends and acquaintances what it could do. His involvement with the board seemed to coincide—if coincidence it truly was—with a series of increasingly troublesome events. A stranger caught looking through the window turned out to have escaped from a mental health facility. He was apprehended and returned to the care facility only after scaring Darren and his friends halfway out of their wits. His response, when asked why he was looking in windows, was chilling. He said that the Devil had made him do it.

"I became convinced that I was some sort of chosen one," Darren shakes his head ruefully. "I believed the board—and Zozo—had bestowed special powers upon me. After suffering a nervous breakdown, and undergoing a couple of unsuccessful exorcisms, I became convinced that I was being manipulated by an actual, literal demon."

Attempting to destroy the Zozo board, Darren doused it in gasoline. Incredibly, the board survived the intense flames without a mark on it. His best friend, Michael, was not so lucky; his arm caught on fire, causing sufficiently serious burns to merit a hospital visit. Matters turned even nastier a few years later when Darren and his friend used the board together again. Although they blew it off when the planchette spelled out the word *murder*, Darren looked on with horror when Michael was found dead. The diagnosis: poisoning.

With his life sliding deeper into negativity, Darren realized he had to get rid of the board. He abandoned it at an old campsite in the woods. Walking away, he experienced what can only be described as withdrawal symptoms. The Zozo board preyed on his mind day and night. Darren began to fear for his mental health.

Finally, when he just couldn't help himself anymore, Darren went back to retrieve it—only to find that it had been chewed apart by rats. The board was damaged beyond all repair, but Zozo apparently was not. Darren moved on to other boards, and it wasn't long before Zozo cropped up again, the planchette moving rapidly between the Z and the O to announce its presence.

It's fair to say that, despite his best efforts to stay away from them, Darren had developed a talking board obsession. No matter which board he used, Zozo was a constant presence on it. Darren almost died when his wife attacked him with a kitchen knife one night, stabbing him repeatedly. Fortunately, he survived, though he could easily have been killed during the assault. He attributed the surprise attack to the influence of the Zozo demon.

Evans and Guiley point out that the name Zozo is mentioned as being a devilkin—also known as an imp, or inferior demonic minion—in the 1818 *Dictionnaire Infernal* by Collin de Plancy...so there is precedent for its appearance in the literature of demonology. Darren has spent years attempting to track down other instances of Zozo throughout literature, in both fact and fiction.

In the September-December 1876 edition of *The Month and Catholic Review* can be found a reference to "the Mass of Zozo," known as the *Commune Omnium Daemonum*. It clearly links the word *Zozo* to *daemonum*, the Latin phrase for "of demons."

"This thing would tell me that there was a power in its name," he recalls, "and I've uncovered evidence during my own research that suggests it may be correct—such as references in an eighth-century Buddhist manuscript to Zozo being the Lord of Demons. The word *Zo* appears elsewhere in connection with evil and demons. It even appears in popular culture, such as the 2000 movie *Cecil B. Demented* in which a character named Raven, played by actress Maggie Gyllenhaal, declares "my father is Zozo, the three-headed guard dog at the gates of Hell."

One has to wonder what the likelihood was of writer/director John Waters pulling the name Zozo out of thin air, especially when it's placed into an infernal context.

"That's not all," Darren continues. "During the 1950s and 1960s, UFO contactee George Hunt Williamson used a Ouija board in an attempt to summon UFOs. He communicated with an entity calling itself Zo."

Zo claimed to live on Neptune and issued various ostensibly helpful predictions about humanity's future via its board sessions with Williamson. Darren wonders whether "Zo of Neptune" was actually Zozo, trying to pass itself off as a benefactor of mankind, while in reality its intentions were quite the opposite.

"I even found a child-eating monster called Zozo in a vintage book for children!" Darren tells me, consulting his notes. "The list goes on and on."

It came as something of a shock to Darren to learn he was not alone in being tormented by these deeply unpleasant happenings. The arrival of easy internet access in the early 2000s allowed him to connect with others who had their own Zozo experiences. Virtually none of them were positive in nature. Although he did not lack for detractors, talking board users from multiple countries related their own run-ins with the entity. Hundreds of stories came in, all revolving around what claimed to be the Zozo demon.

"It was only when I found out that other people were having similar experiences that I really began to accept that I wasn't just crazy. I began documenting as many Zozo encounters as I could. That's why I started my website: to document the reality of this phenomenon, not just for myself, but also for the public benefit. I had to warn people what this thing was capable of."

In 2014, Darren participated in an episode of *Ghost Adventures* at the house in which many of his Zozo experiences had taken place. With the Zozo board long since gone, a new board was needed for the show. Cue talking board expert Robert Murch, who loaned the show a board that had been sent to him by someone who reportedly had a horrific encounter with Zozo. Darren had tried to put using talking boards behind him but agreed to join cast member Nick Groff this one time. Almost immediately, the planchette announced the arrival of Zozo. The episode proved to be extremely popular with viewers, and equally controversial. Darren and his wife took a lot of heat when the episode aired, with some claiming that they were influenced by drugs during the shoot. It is an accusation that he strenuously denies.

Although the paranormal community only learned of the Zozo phenomenon en masse with the advent of Darren's blog post in 2009, followed by a huge boost of awareness when the *Ghost Adventures* episode aired in 2015, it is believed that accounts of board users encountering Zozo date back to the 1980s. Since he began writing publicly about his encounters with Zozo, Darren has been the recipient of hundreds of accounts from those who have experienced something similar.

"Do you think the internet just brought greater awareness of Zozo," I ask Darren, "or did it serve as an actual means of transmission—a medium exploited by the entity in order to spread, in the same way that infectious diseases have vectors?"

"Both of those possibilities could be true. Some of those experiencers who contacted me had already heard of Zozo prior to using the Ouija board. That could have led to confirmation bias. What interests me more are those cases in which the participants had no knowledge of Zozo whatsoever until they first encountered it. Some skeptics have claimed that there were no reports of Zozo surfacing prior to 2009, when I first went public with my story. That simply isn't true. For example, Zozo (or Zo) was mentioned on a Nigerian message board in connection with a Ouija board in 2004. There are numerous others—*and some of those mentions predate the invention of the board!* They're almost always associated with evil, unclean spirits…or demons."

There is a wide range of phenomena reported by those who claim to have fallen afoul of Zozo. A fairly common example is the sensation of being watched by an unseen observer. Taking that up a notch, others claim to be physically touched, pushed, or pulled by some sort of invisible force. Sometimes there are minor injuries, scratches on the skin with no apparent cause. Disembodied voices, usually male, can be accompanied by shrieks and cries that chill the blood.

Zozo apparently loves to dish out predictions of death to those using the board. Conventional wisdom in talking board circles holds that one should never ask questions regarding one's own mortality. Asking how or when you're going to die is considered to be both bad form and ill-advised, and every experienced user has their own stories of encountering trickster spirits, who seem to like nothing better than to spread fear and anxiety among the sitters. Zozo will sometimes offer such information without being asked, and if Darren Evans' fears are correct, it has been accurate about the method of an individual's death on more than one occasion. Just as often, Zozo engages in scare tactics, often telling participants that it intends to take them to Hell.

Nobody likes a party crasher. Many of those who claim to encounter Zozo while using a talking board do so when it breaks into the middle of a conversation with another communicator. It's the equivalent of being at a party, where a boorish individual jumps right in the middle of a polite chat and hijacks it. Initially, Zozo can be charming and playful. Often, it will assume the guise of someone known to one or more of the sitters, a dead friend, or family members. However, matters quickly devolve into vulgarity, profanity…and threats. Whatever Zozo might be, whether it is an independent discarnate intelligence or entity, or part of the board users' own subconscious, it seems to delight in causing fear.

Seasoned board users know that there is a definite process to opening a board up, and another for shutting it down again. If you believe, as many do, that using a talking board opens up a door to some other realm, then it only makes sense to close that door once you've finished using it. Otherwise, the reasoning goes, who knows what might come through, uninvited? It doesn't take much in order to close down a board, a statement of intent that takes less than a minute to deliver. One common characteristic of the Zozo stories, however, is that Zozo—whoever or whatever it may be—tends to linger around the participants long after the session has ended.

Those aftereffects usually come in forms that paranormal investigators would recognize as those attributed to a haunting. Disembodied voices and footsteps. Objects moving from one place to another without human intervention. Doors and cabinets opening and closing of their own volition. Icy cold spots and drafts. Pets and other animals acting strangely, appearing to react to something humans cannot see. Shadowy figures appearing and disappearing, either in plain sight or from the corner of the eye. Perhaps most common of all, the unshakeable feeling of an unseen presence lurking in close proximity to the person who used the talking board. This is often accompanied by terrifying nightmares in which the dreamer feels trapped, desperately trying to escape from something that either stalks them or holds them captive.

More ominously still, Zozo sometimes appears to exhibit the behavior of an incubus or succubus, with interactions of a sexualized nature being reported. These do not tend to be pleasant.

Sometimes, these preternatural effects last for a relatively short time; in other cases, weeks, months…even years. While I'm admittedly biased by my background as a medical professional, the Zozo stories put me in mind of an infection—albeit a psychic, rather than a biological one. Sifting through the online accounts of Zozo encounters, one doesn't have to look too far to find reports of emotional symptoms, such as feeling suddenly overcome with feelings of intense anger or deep depression. While these fit the criteria often cited for demonic oppression, it should also be borne in mind that a psychiatrist would consider them to be potential clinical symptoms.

"The more I learn, the deeper this demonic rabbit hole goes," he tells me. "*Demonic* is simply a term we use to label something we truly do not understand. Just using that word in conversation generates a response that is regulated by not only a person's belief system, but also whichever horror movies they've seen, and a variety of other factors."

He points to the explosion of interest in talking boards over the past few decades, with tens of millions now in circulation, and more being sold each year. In a particularly canny marketing move, Hasbro, which owns the Ouija brand, put their support behind Hollywood movies such as *Ouija* and *Ouija: Origin of Evil*, feeding into the scare factor that has been associated with the boards since the 1970s. The movies came out several years after Zozo first began popping up on boards around the world.

Although Zozo is commonly believed to be a demonic entity, there are other potential explanations. The idea that a talking board is simply being manipulated by the participants themselves (usually without their knowledge) is commonly proposed by skeptics as an explanation for why the planchette moves, seemingly of its own volition. It is a reasonable explanation, as far as it goes.

In my experience, some people simply aren't aware that they are working the board themselves. However, this is by no means true in all cases. It is possible to incorporate control measures into talking board sessions in order to help verify the authenticity of the answers. For example, having somebody who is not participating in the session write a number between one and one thousand on a piece of paper and leaving it faceup in an adjoining room, then asking the board to repeat the number, is a valid test of its abilities. There's a one in one thousand chance that this number could be guessed by one of the sitters…not great odds if you're a gambler by nature. I have used this technique personally and can verify that there are instances in which, even against those great odds, the board is capable of delivering accurate answers. This doesn't happen *all* the time, or even the majority of the time, but it does happen often enough to make the talking board a valid tool—if a proper set of controls is put in place.

"The origins of the Zozo board I unearthed are still a mystery," Darren says, "Somebody took the time to combine a classic William Fuld Ouija board with a homemade talking board, with Zozo's name inscribed on it. I don't know what the purpose of that was. I stashed it inside an abandoned Austin-Healey car in a clearing outside Jennings, Oklahoma. The way it was devoured by a nest of rats was just so bizarre."

In the interests of fairness, I should point out that although cardboard, wood, and paper have no caloric value, rats will chew on them habitually not for food, but as a means of keeping their constantly growing incisors under control. I personally find the destruction of the Zozo board to be far less curious than its origin story, something that will never fully be known.

Taken as a whole, it's easy for some to dismiss the Zozo phenomenon as being nothing more than the product of the sitters' imagination. Such a dismissal is, I feel, overly simplistic. The sheer volume of encounters that are reported from around the world bears further scrutiny. Undoubtedly, there are many instances in which a supposed Zozo encounter was the product of nothing more than an overly active imagination. There was a tidal wave of such cases after the *Ghost Adventures* episode aired, giving Zozo its big media break. Yet there were reports of Zozo interactions prior to Darren publishing his own experience on the internet, and even if we dismiss the vast majority of Zozo stories as being little more than that—just stories—that still leaves a core of bizarre experiences that demand further investigation. I for one am not comfortable with simply sweeping the whole thing under the rug and dismissing it.

In their book *The Zozo Phenomenon*, Darren and his coauthor Rosemary Ellen Guiley posit that Zozo might be a thought form or *egregore*. Simply put, this is the idea that if enough people tell a story sufficiently often, imbuing it with a kind of energy we do not understand, then that story somehow takes on a life of its own. There's reason to believe this may happen more often than we think.

The more publicity Zozo got, the more it was talked about, and the more fear became associated with its name, the likelier it became that these thoughts would coalesce into something almost tangible, capable of interacting with talking board users across the planet. In other words, the hypothesis holds that, if Zozo didn't objectively exist before it went viral, it does now, empowered by a massive bolus of energy that stemmed from its television appearances and viral internet posts.

Throughout my years as an investigator and author in the field of paranormal nonfiction, I have encountered this hypothesis numerous times. It has been advanced as a possible explanation for the haunting of Malvern Manor in Iowa, where the spirit of a hanged little girl is still said to walk; and of the Villisca Axe Murder House, and the other house in the Midwest, both of which are discussed elsewhere in this book. The idea that collectivized thought can give rise to an independent, intelligent entity is becoming more widespread. Then the question arises: Would such an intelligence, created by human thought, truly qualify as a demon? Most, I suspect, would say not by the traditional definition, but it certainly seems to *act* like one…so is there really a difference, or are we just splitting hairs?

Zozo has the distinction of being the foremost demon of the internet age—the first demon to have truly gone viral, its name trending on Twitter and spreading with lightning rapidity across the comments section of websites. In a time when fictional memetic entities such as Slender Man have taken on lives of their own (and in Slender Man's case, been the cause of attempted murder), questions should rightfully be asked about the origin and reality of the Zozo phenomenon. To Darren Evans, and those who have suffered terrifying experiences, the reality of Zozo has already been proven beyond question. To the rest of us, the jury is still out. After my interview with Darren, I ponder this for a few days, thinking about my next best step.

Steve Higgins, author of *The Rational Demonologist's Handbook* and analyst of paranormal trends, confirmed for me that he still hears of Zozo encounters happening frequently to this day. At least some of these cases can be explained by the planchette listlessly drifting between the Z and the O, he tells me, and while they may be so in some cases, I'm not personally convinced this would account for them *all*.

It's not that I disbelieve Darren, or side with those who question his integrity. He's been accused of making the whole thing up. If that's so, then I can only say he hasn't exactly made big bucks cashing in on Zozo. He coauthored one book and appeared on a couple of TV shows. Raking in the millions, he is not.

No, it's more accurate to say that I remain willing to be convinced, one way or the other. What might convince me, I ask myself? There's really only one answer to that question.

I need to go and meet Zozo, so I can ask it myself.

Before going any further, there's a point I need to emphasize. The whole point of embarking on this journey was for me to find answers, and share them with you, the reader. It is *not* an attempt at thrill-seeking or showmanship. During my time as a writer and field investigator, I have endeavored to be as hands-on and experiential as possible. When I write about a specific battle, I walk the battlefield, rather than simply poring over maps. In haunted locations such as Fox Hollow Farm, former home of the serial killer Herb Baumeister, I did not simply turn up, interview the owners, and leave. I spent days and nights there, swimming in the same (allegedly haunted) pool in which a number of the murders took place, walking the same woods in which the bodies of the victims were disposed of. My hands-on approach is intended to uncover as much new information as possible, and to provide a fuller account of whichever subject I'm writing about.

One does not have to go far in the field of demonology to encounter warnings about the dangers involved with getting in over your head. There are countless stories out there concerning those who have used a talking board in a cavalier manner and gotten more than they bargained for. Although I have used the board frequently over the past thirty years and have suffered no apparent ill effects (possibly because I am diligent about opening and closing it at the beginning and end of each session), I still proceed with the utmost caution each time.

I advise you, Dear Reader, to do the same.

Please do not take the talking board lightly. If you're going to use one, specify at the very outset that only truthful communicators with good intentions and strong ethics are permitted to come through. Make it clear that no deceitful or negative communicators will be tolerated, period. Sometimes, this stipulation means the board will not work at all. In such cases, so be it. It is far better to be safe than sorry. Please don't throw down a board and try talking to Zozo or any other dark or demonic entity…whether you believe in them or not.

In this one case, I ask you to please forgive me my hypocrisy and do as I say, not as I do.

Over the space of three months, I visited multiple haunted locations in the United States, Canada, and the United Kingdom. Each time, I took along a talking board and enlisted some trusted friends and colleagues to help me out. I outlined my search for demons, and after making sure everybody was comfortable, we opened up the board and tried to make contact with Zozo.

Nine different sessions, on six different talking boards, with a mix of seventeen separate participants later, we had communicated with what claimed to be the spirit of a soiled dove from the Wild West; a monk who had died hundreds of years previously; and a disgruntled doctor who said they'd dropped dead in the very same hospital they now claimed to haunt. These are just three of the many communicators who came through on the board.

Of Zozo, there was no sign.

It wasn't for lack of trying. In each case, once the board was open, we made sure to invite Zozo to the session. After interviewing Darren and hearing his story, I half expected Zozo to barge onto the board midstream, rudely shoving aside the current communicator and hijacking the proceedings…but it never happened. I've been using talking boards for more than a quarter of a century and have never encountered it before.

Does this mean Zozo does not exist? Not at all, in the sense that one cannot prove a negative. If I post a Facebook status every day inviting John Smith to drop by my house for a cup of tea, and they never turn up, it does not disprove the existence of John Smith. Likewise, the lack of Zozo at any of my talking board sessions does not refute the experiences of those who claim to have encountered it during their own.

Despite my failure to connect with Zozo, I'm left with a deep fascination for the connection between demons and talking boards. Despite all the bad press they get, I've always felt that boards have been unfairly maligned. To explore this connection further, I need to visit an expert. A man whose business card bears the title Chairman of the Board.

fourteen
BOARD MEETING

The notion that talking boards can open gateways through which demons can come and go is extremely widespread, and it has been that way ever since the release of *The Exorcist*. Although negative encounters were reported before the 1970s, they were not nearly as frequent. This is one of the key aspects of the demonic phenomenon I want to explore. Just how valid is it? To find out, I visit the home of Robert Murch, Ouija aficionado and chairman of the Talking Board Historical Society. Murch, as he prefers to be known, owns thousands of boards, ranging from the cheapest mass-produced commercial models to intricately handmade one-of-a-kind custom jobs. He's also the guy Hollywood movie producers consult on all things Ouija, which has led to him having an extensive collection of screen-used prop boards from productions such as *Ouija: Origin of Evil* and *Stranger Things*.

Although the TBHS has an official museum (located, appropriately enough, in Salem, Massachusetts), Murch's home in a Colorado suburb is the next best thing to going there. The walls are covered with rare, framed boards, each one with its own unique backstory. Bookshelves overflow with talking board–related titles, including DVDs of virtually any movie you can think of that might contain a Ouija scene. Everywhere the eye looks, there is either a talking board or some piece of associated memorabilia.

If anybody is qualified to talk about a potential link between demons and talking boards, it is Robert Murch. After petting his three adorable dogs and greeting his husband, I'm led downstairs to a quiet spot where I spend the next two hours getting schooled on the finer points of Ouija history.

We start in 1886, when Spiritualists are using talking boards in an attempt to communicate with the dead as part of a post–Civil War mass fascination with the afterlife. As popular as Spiritualism was, however, enterprising individuals saw an opportunity for marketing the boards to a wider audience. Some people wanted to ask the mysterious boards about their future, how they might go about getting rich or finding the love of their life.

"The board wasn't necessarily just a spirit communication tool," Murch explains, "it was an oracle, a place you could go to for answers when you couldn't find them anywhere else. When Ouija was patented in 1890 by a businessman named Elijah Bond, it was *not* marketed as being a tool to talk to the dead, because he doubted that alone would be sellable. It becomes a parlor game, and the manufacturers explicitly say they don't know how or why it works."

The late-nineteenth-century originators of Ouija were all fascinated with the occult, but they were also interested in making money. Their focus was on commercialism, not talking to ghosts or demons, which meant playing up the *fun* aspect of the board. Millionaires were made during the Ouija boom of the 1890s.

To emphasize his point about the benign nature of the board, he shows me a piece of original marketing material from those days. It shows a family happily gathered around a Ouija board, including a young child holding a teddy bear. Not a whiff of sulfur and brimstone is anywhere to be seen. They look like they're having an absolute blast.

This positive perception of the board continued well into the twentieth century.

Then along came *The Exorcist*.

"*The Exorcist* is a huge turning point in the history of the Ouija board," Murch explains, relaxing back into the couch. "After 1973, movies and TV shows depict the board in a *significantly* darker way than they ever did before."

Murch was fortunate enough to interview William Peter Blatty in person. The author told him that the use of a board and the introduction of Captain Howdy was a convenient plot device for having Regan become possessed.

"Blatty told me that the novel was not expressly intended to be a possession book, so much as it's meant to be a love story between a mother and her daughter. It's about being disconnected from the things that truly matter, while very bad stuff is happening right in front of your eyes."

I must admit that I've never seen the book in that way, perhaps because the movie adaptation overshadows much of the relationship nuance with a prolonged, graphic assault on the senses as the possession and subsequent exorcism really take off. Murch's comment is making me reevaluate my overall perception of the film.

"It's never implicitly stated in the movie that Regan became possessed because she played with a Ouija board," Murch observes. "It *is* implied very strongly, however. The connection between the two is made in the mind of the viewer, and the message that comes across concerning the board is *if you use this thing, you could get into deep, deep trouble.*"

That's not to say that the history of the board is all sweetness and light. Murch outlines cases in which people took their own lives because of things the board said, and others who said they felt compelled to commit murder for the same reason. By and large, however, the watershed change in mass perception was Friedkin's film and the book on which it was based.

Darren Evans takes the opposite view to that held by Murch. "During my research, I have uncovered *dozens* of period newspaper articles highlighting the dangers of Ouija boards, describing blasphemous exchanges with unseen entities…some describing the negative effects they had on college campuses across the country. As far as its sinister reputation goes, the Ouija board need only look in the mirror to find its source. There's more behind its bad rap than simply blaming *The Exorcist.*"

Evans also points out that, during the exorcism of Ronald Hunkeler, the word *NO* is said to have appeared spontaneously on the boy's skin. "Turn *NO* on its side," he says, "and you get…*ZO.*"

When he was given the opportunity to visit the house in Bel Nor where Ronald Hunkeler was exorcised, Murch jumped at the chance. He was there to film *Exorcism Live*, bringing his expertise in Ouija history to the show. Walking around the house, he was struck by how mundane everything felt to him—apart from the upstairs bedroom.

"What was once Ronald's room felt unusually claustrophobic to me, even though it was the same size as the other bedrooms," he remembers. The psychic medium who accompanied him felt the same way. "During the shoot, a number of people found the atmosphere so off-putting that they didn't even want to step foot in the house if they could avoid it."

As we start to broach the subject, I notice that Murch seems skeptical of the existence of demons and the possibility of possession, so I ask politely about his beliefs.

"It's all a possibility, as far as I'm concerned. It has to be taken on a case-by-case basis."

"What do you make of the Hunkeler case?" I want to know.

"The most striking aspect is how worried the Vatican was about the case. It *scared* them, and they did everything they could to protect this kid. What was reported in St. Louis genuinely disturbed them. The Church made it their mission to help Ronald Hunkeler disappear, as best as they possibly could."

Although Murch isn't saying the possession was or was not genuine, it's evident that he finds elements of it fascinating. I'm curious as to how many individuals approach him after using the Ouija board, claiming they have interacted with dark or demonic entities.

"Tons," he replies instantly. "It seems that *every* negative experience is blamed on demons, instead of dead people or something else."

Murch notes that this tendency to blame demons for every bad Ouija session was all but nonexistent until paranormal reality TV began featuring them so heavily. A case of unconscious bias, perhaps? I'm curious as to Murch's opinion on Zozo. He and Darren are friends, and Murch insists that Darren is "extremely honest."

With that being said, Murch adds that Darren's honesty does not necessarily mean that Zozo is a real phenomenon.

"Zozo blew up when the internet was relatively new to all of us," he tells me. "It went from there being no awareness of Zozo, to Zozo seemingly being *everywhere*. It's impossible to tell whether this was a meme *[in the sense that it was a concept that spread widely and rapidly from one person to another]* or a genuine phenomenon that was transmitted digitally. We just can't pick the two ideas apart. Did this go viral because of Darren's post, or did it spread spontaneously across the world?"

Murch shrugs as if to say *beats me*.

"This thing all but wrecked Darren's life," he goes on. "It did some major damage. Talking to Zozo was a lesson in abject fear for him…one that he'll never forget."

Having spoken to Darren at length, I have absolutely no doubt about that.

There's a strange coda to this chapter. When I sent it to my test readers for comments and input, one of them wrote back and said this:

In the summer of 1987, my Ouija board was consistently showing the letters ZOZO, over and over in a figure 8 pattern. Then I began to hear voices…Was this the Zozo demon? None of us were educated about it at that point in time. So, am I another victim of Zozo, or was it all just in my mind?

What's intriguing about her story is that Darren Evans didn't publish his own experiences with Zozo until more than a decade later…but they were happening to him at that same time, in a completely different part of the country…

Taking an antique Ouija board down for me to look at, Robert Murch begins to wrap up our conversation.

"Human beings love searching for answers," he opines. "In our twenty-first-century world of click-tap-swipe, the Ouija board is more popular than ever. Our attention span is at a record low, yet people will sit with the planchette and spend *hours* with it. We're fascinated by the board and the things it tells us."

As to whether those things are being communicated via the sitters' own subconscious, disembodied spirits, or even demons... that's the key question. If the Chairman of the Board can't answer it, then I need to look elsewhere for enlightenment. Perhaps an experienced, qualified parapsychologist will offer some insight.

fifteen
PARAPSYCHOLOGICALLY SPEAKING

A parapsychologist and his partner walk into a bar...

It sounds like the setup for a joke, but as I'm about to learn, it's absolutely true. Evincing a dry sense of humor, Dr. Ciaran O'Keeffe, an academic based in the United Kingdom, has titled our Zoom meeting *Out, Foul Demon!* I like his style already.

Many know Ciaran from his media work, appearing on television shows such as *Most Haunted* and both the TV and podcast incarnations of the wildly popular paranormally themed show *Uncanny*.

After exchanging a few pleasantries, we get down to discussing the subject at hand: demons.

"In the contexts of hauntings, demons are very much a North American finding," Ciaran begins. Raised as an Irish Roman Catholic, demons were very much part of his youthful world view. "I've always been interested in them, but I became fascinated even more in 2010 or so because I started to notice them proliferating across American TV shows."

Beginning with *Paranormal State* and *Ghost Adventures*, demons quickly spread like wildfire across the "reality" and dramatic genres of television. They also did solid business at the box office and on DVD.

"In the United Kingdom, one or two people popped up and called themselves demonologists, but there was nothing like the wave of such cases that engulfed the United States."

With a small handful of exceptions, British ghost hunting shows eschewed the American taste for the demonic. Considering the somewhat more secular nature of the United Kingdom, that's entirely understandable.

"On the whole, the British-produced shows tend to be less dark, and don't integrate that darkness into their branding, as some US shows have done," the parapsychologist observes. "It seems that American audiences respond better to the darker side, and that the producers of US-based programming have simply catered to that."

The field of paranormal research has changed a great deal since I first became involved in 1995. Back then, "ghost hunters" were men like the late, great Peter Underwood, who wandered around historic stately homes in tweed jackets, seemingly lost in thought. They performed simple, low-tech experiments and used basic techniques such as pouring flour on the ground in order to figure out whether living human beings might be responsible for the sound of supposedly phantom suspects. There was no screaming, hysteria, or swearing, let alone becoming possessed in front of the camera. Twenty years later, modern-day ghost hunting (including the search for demons) is almost unrecognizable by comparison.

There has also been a vast increase in the number of online agencies that are willing to offer diplomas, degrees, and even "doctorates" to aspiring demonologists. Most such courses are not accredited by any legitimate academic institutions such as universities, and many are not taught by legitimate PhDs. The titles and certificates bestowed after a few hours of learning are rarely worth the paper they're printed on. Contrast this with Dr. O'Keeffe's undergraduate degree in psychology and music from Washington College, his advanced degree in investigative psychology, leading to a doctorate that involved studying and testing alleged psychic mediums and astrologers, and the difference is very easy to see. Ciaran is currently head of the School of Human and Social Sciences at the UK's Buckinghamshire New University, and he brings a wealth of expertise and experience to the study of ghosts, hauntings, and other aspects of the paranormal. His academic credentials are based on years of rigorous research, study, and testing, affording him unimpeachable legitimacy.

Several years ago, Ciaran took the bait and enrolled in an online demonology course, simply for the experience. After paying a hundred-dollar fee, he was instructed to read Gerald Brittle's book *The Demonologist: The Extraordinary Career of Ed and Lorraine Warren*. After finishing the book, Ciaran was then assigned an essay to write, which he dutifully completed and returned to the course administrator. In return, he was sent a certificate stating that he was now a fully qualified demonologist.

"I was horrified," Ciaran recalls, shaking his head ruefully. "There are so many people out there claiming to be demonologists, holding sketchy online qualifications without having any real understanding of the history of demonology, or the controversies surrounding claims of possession."

Of the many career paths along which Ciaran's qualifications could have led him, why did he choose the paranormal—and ultimately, develop a fascination with demons and possession?

Chapter Fifteen

"It begins with what's called *Christian Parapsychology*," he explains, "although I've advocated for a change for the term to *Religious Parapsychology*. It's the study of any parapsychological phenomena taking place within a religious context. Of course, that's primarily centered upon demonic possession, though it does also include stigmata [those who spontaneously develop wounds akin to those suffered by Jesus Christ], levitation, and other claims.

"I'm enthralled with the subject of possession, not least because of the impact that the movie *The Exorcist* had on me when I first watched it at far too young an age. I was also fortunate enough to witness a real exorcism…in Rome, of all places."

That stops me dead in my tracks. This is a story I have *got* to hear.

This wasn't a planned activity, something arranged by Ciaran as part of his lengthy education. It happened purely by chance. In 2012, Ciaran was on holiday in Italy with his then-girlfriend, who is now his wife. After visiting the Colosseum, the couple enjoyed a coffee and meandered through the streets of Rome with no specific destination in mind. Just two tourists, soaking up the atmosphere and seeing the sights of the capital.

Walking along a backstreet, the pair chanced upon a beautiful historic church. On a whim, they went inside. From somewhere at the back, they could hear the muffled sound of somebody moaning. At first, they mistook the noise for being sexual in nature—hardly the sort of thing one expects or wants to encounter in a house of God. It soon became apparent that the intensifying cries came from somebody in distress. A little freaked out, Ciaran's girlfriend went back outside. The parapsychologist, however, allowed his curiosity to get the better of him. He walked slowly down the center of the church, passing rows of pews on either side of him, until he came to a closed wooden door.

Before he could knock or open it, Ciaran encountered the curator. Ciaran could speak no Italian, and neither could the curator speak English, but the two men managed to converse in limited Spanish and French. Haltingly, the curator explained that an exorcism was taking place in the room beyond the door.

Not thinking for a moment that he would actually be granted permission, Ciaran nonetheless took a chance and asked whether he might be allowed to view the proceedings. Remarkably, after the curator made inquiries, Ciaran was allowed to step through and observe things for himself.

"It's so bizarre that they not only allowed me in, but did so *in the middle of the ritual*," the parapsychologist remembers. "Inside the room was a man lying on his back on top of a table. A priest was standing next to him, carrying out the *Ritual Romanum*. It felt like walking onto a Hollywood movie set, to be frank."

Two other participants stood alongside the priest and the subject of the exorcism, praying loudly for the expulsion of whatever demon was thought to possess him. Ciaran watched as the energumen writhed on the table, moaning and crying out in distress. For the next half hour, he continued to struggle. The priest stuck to his guns, loudly and confidently proclaiming the words of the ritual over him. He became sufficiently aggressive that one of the attendants was forced to hold him down, for the safety of everyone in the room.

Finally, before the conclusion of the exorcism, Ciaran was politely but firmly asked to leave. He had done nothing wrong. There was simply a sense that it was time for his very limited participation in events to come to an end. He left the church with a sense of gratitude at having been allowed to witness what is usually a private, sacred practice.

"It seemed odd to me that the demoniac was lying on a table," Ciaran notes. "In footage of other exorcisms that I have seen, they're placed on gym mats or other more comfortable surfaces, to help protect them from injury. I can still hardly believe they allowed me to witness this."

My one burning question comes next. "Ciaran, as a trained scientific observer, based on what you saw inside that church in Rome… did you get a sense that anything otherworldly was taking place?"

He pauses to consider for a moment.

"I wasn't convinced that something otherworldly was going on…but I have to consider my own biases and my frame of reference. Walking into that room was a psychological event for me. I wasn't expecting to see an exorcism that day, and I didn't have time to prepare for it mentally beforehand. I felt a sense of apprehension and could feel my own adrenaline flowing at the prospect of what I might encounter in that room. That same physiological reaction might convince another person, one with different views on the world, that they were in the presence of something demonic because of the way their body was reacting to it."

Ciaran is well versed in the psychology and physiology of fear and is fully aware that none of us are truly objective observers of *anything*—particularly when our hearts are pounding in our chests, blood pressure is rising, and chemical mediators begin flooding through the cardiovascular system. Even for an academic observer such as Dr. O'Keeffe, the power of suggestion played a role in what he experienced while watching the exorcism unfold.

Determined to improve the quality of online classes, Ciaran devised and regularly teaches courses in the study of demonology and possession. These courses attract both skeptics and believers alike. With an almost mischievous smile, he tells me that one of the big take-home points for students is that it's possible to be every bit as skeptical of the skeptical explanations for demonic possession as one can be about the phenomenon itself.

"There are basically three classifications of argument against demonic possession being real: psychology, psychiatry, and neurology…or a combination thereof. You'll often hear ignorant skeptics advance Tourette Syndrome or schizophrenia as being solid explanations."

Usually manifesting during childhood, Tourette Syndrome is a disorder of the nervous system that causes muscular tics and twitches. Equally embarrassing for those who have Tourette's are the uncontrolled outbursts of words, which can include major profanities, that tend to be blurted at the most inopportune moments. There are also grunts and barks that can be mistaken for animalistic sounds (shades of the Loudun Incident) and sometimes nonsensical use of words and phrases.

A relatively rare but exceptionally debilitating brain disorder, schizophrenia causes the sufferer to hallucinate, undergo episodes of psychosis, and experience delusions that can be both powerful and terrifying, not only to the person experiencing them, but also to their loved ones and those around them.

"Both conditions are widely misunderstood," Dr. O'Keeffe explains. "Skeptics often blame Tourette Syndrome in those instances where the demoniac begins swearing at the priest who is exorcising them. Such people often don't manifest the tics that are so common with Tourette's. Similarly, when they begin speaking in tongues, it's easy for some to dismiss that as being schizophrenia, without actually conducting a behavioral assessment to determine whether it is or not."

It is for these reasons, and others like them, that most Church authorities require a psychological evaluation be performed by a qualified clinical professional prior to giving permission for an exorcism to take place.

"It makes sense to be skeptical of the Tourette's and schizophrenia explanations in many cases. DID is also on the list of potential causes, though it's a hugely controversial area of the psychiatric realm. Some psychiatrists say that it does indeed exist, whereas others insist that it does not."

"What are some other possible explanations for apparent possession?" I ask.

"Role-playing is one. This isn't the same as acting or playing something like Dungeons & Dragons. In this context, we're talking about someone who becomes so immersed in their belief system and pattern of behavior that they 100 percent believe they have become possessed."

"They've basically convinced themselves that they have a demon inside them, and now they're acting like they have?"

"Exactly. You start playing the role of what *you* think a possessed person should be…but it's not done consciously. There's no deliberate fraud at work. It's a sort of psychological version of the ideomotor effect."

It's a compelling and believable explanation for some, though by no means all cases of apparent possession, and still requires the person to have a belief system that incorporates the existence of demons.

This leads us to the role played by neurology.

"Another explanation that is frequently put forward is epilepsy," Ciaran states. "Now, in some cases of alleged possession, we are dealing with misdiagnosed epilepsy as the cause, or the condition is taking place in a culture that does not have a strong understanding of it."

It is estimated that epilepsy affects over fifty million people worldwide. The majority of those people do not live in the Western world, and many lack the medications and other therapies that are used to treat or mitigate the condition. It is a disorder that leads to seizures, the equivalent of a "lightning storm in the brain." Rapid, uncontrolled firing of neurons that lead to effects ranging from minor twitching and eye-rolling all the way up to full-body spasms, cessation of breathing, and, ultimately, death.

"Often, when skeptics blame epilepsy for demonic possession, it seems as though they're reaching. This was one answer that was proposed for the Loudun Incident. Yet genuine epilepsy doesn't spread. It isn't infectious. Now, *psychological* conditions can be contagious—we do indeed refer to contagion in a psychological sense, as illustrated by mass hysteria. Much depends on your relationship to the person who is acting in a certain way, and whether they're behaving like that in close proximity to you."

Ciaran and I are in agreement that mass hysteria is a far more convincing answer to what happened at Loudun than epilepsy, Tourette's Syndrome, or schizophrenia, none of which would have struck so many individuals in such a relatively small area.

"Neurologically speaking, there's another explanation that isn't widely considered: anti-NMDA receptor encephalitis."

I blink. As a medical professional by training, a clinical educator, I'm well versed in many pathologies and disease conditions. This is one I've never heard of. As Ciaran talks, I rapidly begin to take notes.

A relatively recent discovery to medical science (circa 2007), anti-NMDAR encephalitis is a disorder of the autoimmune system in which the body turns upon itself, more specifically targeting the NMDA receptors within the brain. As the brain comes under attack from its own antibodies, it can respond by swelling—the aforementioned encephalitis. Anything that impacts the brain in such a way can cause hallucinations, seizures, and sudden mood swings, some of which may be aggressive and make the sufferer combative. They may also thrash and move their arms and legs in jerky, spasmodic ways similar to those seen in the common conception of demonic possession. Speech patterns are also affected, in ways that might be misinterpreted as speaking in tongues.

"Imagine a scenario set prior to the discovery of this disease, in which somebody believes that they might be demonically possessed," Ciaran posits. "Their family take them to a hospital, which tests for epileptiform activity within the brain and finds none. They're essentially given a clean bill of health, in so far as the doctors cannot find an obvious medical explanation for their symptoms. At this point, the patient and their family buy fully into the demonic possession hypothesis."

Friedkin and Blatty use this to great effect in *The Exorcist*, particularly the scene in which Regan is subjected to a battery of extensive (for the time) and frightening medical tests, all of which come back clean. It's from this point on that her mother is sent along the path to seeking an exorcism.

"It's a classic case of confirmation bias. You're hearing something that confirms your personal beliefs once the doctors admit that what they thought could have been epilepsy was in fact not that." Ciaran pauses, before going on. "Skeptics frequently put forward a limited number of explanations for alleged possession, and in many of those cases, that comes from a misunderstanding or ignorance regarding those medical, psychological, or psychiatric conditions. Although an ethical exorcist will first send their potential energumen to a doctor in order to be medically cleared, not every general practitioner is educated on or considers alternative diagnoses such as serotonin syndrome (a reaction to medications which causes the neurotransmitter serotonin to accumulate to dangerous levels within the body) or rabies, to name just two of many possibilities."

What other valid explanation for what seems like possession is science still unaware of? In 2005, anti-NMDAR encephalitis wasn't even on the table. What other conditions are out there, currently flying under the radar, that we will learn about in the next ten, fifty, or one hundred years? It's one of the best arguments to be made for keeping an open mind.

So, what, in Ciaran's view, is the best way to approach an apparent case of possession?

"In an ideal world, an exorcist would consult a psychologist, a psychiatrist, and a neurologist, in order to discount those possibilities first, before ever even considering an exorcism."

What Ciaran describes here is nothing new to the practice of medicine, where it's known as the multidisciplinary care team. These are groups of specialists in different medical subspecialties who consult with one another and pool their expertise in order to better meet the needs of a complex patient. For example, it isn't unusual that a type I diabetic who suffers a stroke to require the skills of a cardiologist, neurologist, endocrinologist, and a multitude of nurses, technicians, dietitians, and others in order to take care of them effectively. Why should instances of supposed demonic possession be any different?

"Some exorcists seem to just pay lip service to the idea," Ciaran goes on, "saying that they have consulted a general practitioner, and while they may have done so, they aren't really bringing in the appropriate level of expertise that is required to rule out more mundane explanations. Far too often, the criteria they use in order to initiate an exorcism is one of their own choosing: a belligerent response to prayer or the presence of a holy object. The late Father Gabriel Amorth (now portrayed by Russell Crowe in the movie *The Pope's Exorcist*) placed great stock in seeing a patient's eyes roll back until only the whites were showing. He believed that was an unmistakable sign of possession."

Any doctor, nurse, or paramedic can list multiple reasons why this might happen to a patient. The list includes alcohol and drug intoxication, closed head injury, seizure, and stroke, to name just a few. These are all potentially serious life-threatening causes that must be ruled out by a qualified medical professional before anybody ever even mentions the word *exorcism*.

Ciaran acknowledges that his passion for the subject of demonic possession is on par with the level of skepticism that he feels toward it. I ask him whether, over the course of his lengthy career as a parapsychologist, he has ever encountered a case of possession that defied easy explanation—one that might possibly, in his view, have been the real deal.

"The only way we could distinguish a genuine demonic possession from everything else would be the presence of truly parapsychological phenomena. Setting aside eyewitness testimony—because time and time again, the record shows that we often see what we want or expect to see—that leaves us with something like levitation and clairvoyance. Those are both paranormal characteristics, far above and beyond merely speaking in a gruff voice or moving the body and limbs in a jerky way."

He's absolutely right, of course. The problem is, there is no credible video footage of levitation out there in the public domain. Clairvoyance, the obtaining of information via paranormal means, is commonly claimed, but its existence has never been definitively proven under laboratory conditions. (That's not to say that it isn't possible—just that it doesn't meet the bar for evidence set by the scientific community.)

There aren't any cases that reach that standard, to Ciaran's knowledge. If we discount cases that depend on the accounts of nuns and priests, all of whom bring a preconceived faith-based bias to the table, then he's still waiting for that smoking gun to rear its head.

We've covered a lot of ground during our conversation, and Ciaran has listed a wide range of medical explanations that may explain some of the possible cases of possession that arise each year. I'm curious as to how a physician approaches the concept of demons and possession, and so my next stop is to switch scenes from the university to the hospital and ask a medical doctor that very question.

sixteen
HERE BE DRAGONS

We live in a world in which doctors are often placed on a pedestal by society. When we or our loved ones fall ill, we look to them for not just a cure, but also for answers. The white coat worn by physicians has an almost Godlike cachet for many people. We trust the men and women who wear it with our lives and sometimes with our deaths.

It is easy to forget that beneath that coat, a physician is every bit as human as the rest of us. Each has their own set of ideals and beliefs. Each has their own spiritual faith, or lack thereof.

Dr. Donald Molnar is no stranger to the paranormal, having experienced a number of strange circumstances throughout his life—some of which intruded into his medical career. A fascination with ghosts and hauntings has led him along an intriguing road… one that makes him the perfect doctor to weigh in on the subject of demons and possession.

"I do believe in spirits and the afterlife," he tells me when I ask about his personal belief system, "but I also retain a healthy degree of skepticism. I have to really be convinced before accepting that something might be paranormal. There are some very compelling studies being done on reincarnation and survival after death."

Considering the scientific training and education required of physicians—a process that spans their entire career—Donald's approach makes a good deal of sense.

After completing his undergraduate education at the University of Akron, Ohio, he completed medical school and residency before relocating to Virginia. He specializes in internal medicine (the care of adult patients) and practices at a sizable hospital.

After speaking at length with Dr. O'Keeffe, I'm curious to learn more about the way in which allegedly possessed individuals are handled by the medical system.

"About six months ago, I encountered a patient who was, at baseline, a really nice guy," Dr. Molnar begins. "Then suddenly, for no apparent reason, he'd be completely out of control. He weighed about two hundred pounds and wasn't all that big, but it took four security guards to restrain him. I'm wondering: *Why is this guy so out of control?* In the blink of an eye, he went from being an every-day pleasant personality to this angry, combative individual who seemed entirely different. I couldn't help but wonder if he might have been possessed."

Once he was in the grip of whatever this new influence was, the man's eyes bulged in their sockets. He began to growl aggressively at the security team and medical staff who were trying to render care.

Elements of what Dr. Molnar is describing will be familiar to EMTs, paramedics, and any other emergency response profession-als. The combative patient type is something we all regard with caution and wariness. Most prehospital care providers have been punched or kicked by somebody like that while attempting to treat their complaint. Usually there is some kind of pathology at work, be it a head injury, stimulant overdose—drugs such as meth, cocaine, hallucinogens—or alcohol intoxication. Others may be having a psychotic break, through absolutely no fault of their own, and suddenly become a menace to themselves and to everyone around them.

Experienced physicians such as Dr. Molnar tend to become very adept at recognizing these specific syndromes and have a number of medications and techniques with which to treat them. The fact that Donald considered that his patient *may* have been possessed implies that in this particular case, the presentation didn't fit with any of the classic patterns.

"Acute encephalopathy was high on my list of differential diagnoses," the doctor goes on. After my discussion with Ciaran, I'm instantly put in mind of anti-NMDAR encephalitis; however, there are multiple causes of brain irritation and inflammation, such as poison and toxicology, medication or drug overdose, infection, and diabetic complications, to name just a few. The fact that the patient had a history of stroke, and subsequent brain damage, may also have played a role in his sudden onset of rage and combativeness. Dr. Molnar considers an organic brain issue such as this to be more probable than something along the lines of possession.

I want to explore the role our personal beliefs play when it comes to making a clinical diagnosis.

"In your opinion, Dr. Molnar, are medical providers who have a deeply religious background sometimes more likely to misperceive a patient like this as being possessed?"

"Yes, I think so," he responds after considering it for a moment. In his view, a clinician who believes in the existence of demons may think, *This patient's behavior has become so radically different than his norm, that he was temporarily possessed.*

Such behavior would be human nature. However, what is left in the doctor's playbook once they have ruled out such explanations as drugs, illness, and psychiatric or psychological causes for a patient's highly uncharacteristic behavior?

"Interesting, isn't it?" he smiles. "We have to ask ourselves: *Exactly where does that superhuman strength come from?* From a physiological standpoint, the explanation tends to be put forward that bursts of adrenaline are responsible for it...particularly when the patient is under great emotional or physical stress."

We've all heard stories of ordinary people temporarily gaining extraordinary strength in the midst of a crisis. There's even a medical name for it: *hysterical strength.* The astute care provider should weigh up the circumstances surrounding the patient before leaping to any nontraditional explanation such as possession. Still, Dr. Molnar agrees that there are a handful of such cases where it is difficult, if not impossible, to ascribe the patient's behavior to a medical or behavioral cause. I'm thinking specifically of the case attended by illusionist Aiden Sinclair, in which the energumen reacted violently to the presence of a prayer, *which she had no idea was even there.*

"There has been some discussion as to whether some people are simply more prone to having paranormal experiences due to their psychological background," he muses. In other words, are some of those individuals who are diagnosed with behavioral conditions actually more prone to having genuine paranormal experiences, only to have them dismissed out of hand by the medical and psychiatric community?

It's now time for me to ask Dr. Molnar the same question I've been posing to many of the experts that have been interviewed as part of my journey. Has he ever witnessed a supposedly possessed individual behave in such a way that defies the laws of science, as we currently understand them?

"No," he replies. "No levitation, no speaking in different languages that should be unknown to the patient. The closest I've gotten is the hyperaggressive yelling, screaming individual who starts fighting for no apparent reason."

The doc and I are in complete agreement that the vast majority of these patients are experiencing a completely explainable behavioral or medical crisis, something that is seen in emergency departments and the back of ambulances around the world every day. With that being said, I have spoken personally with several paramedics and nurses who underwent the terrifying experience of treating a patient who appeared to be, for want of a better word, *soulless*. A phrase that's often used to describe such individuals is that when the medical provider looks them in the eye, whatever it is that's staring back at them doesn't feel as if it's human. While I acknowledge that this is a completely subjective claim, it arises often enough to give one pause to ponder.

"We also have to consider undiagnosed brain tumors, which can induce a significant enough personality change to make somebody *think* they are possessed," says Dr. Molnar. "Frontal lobe disorders can achieve the same effect, as can focal seizures. A lot can be revealed with a head CT scan."

The big take-home point from my discussion with Dr. Molnar seems to be that, while the field of medicine offers sound and credible answers to many perceived cases of demonic possession, by no means does it offer *all* the answers. There are still thousands of medical mysteries to be solved, new conditions to be uncovered, and aspects of the human mind that should still be labeled *Here Be Dragons*.

Chapter Sixteen

Bearing that in mind, I'm getting the urge to hit the road again, to locate one of those dragons for myself. My destination: the state of Indiana, and a house that has caused numerous visitors to flee in terror from what some say is a dark and demonic force.

seventeen
THE DEMON HOUSE

There's something about the American Midwest that seems to attract demonic cases, based on the sheer number of reports that arise there. On my journey in search of demons, I've visited locations in Iowa and Kansas that are said to be demonically infested. Now it's the turn of Indiana, where I'm joined by a small team of trusted paranormal investigators in an attempt to uncover the mysteries at the heart of the infamous Monroe House—known far and wide as the Demon House.

Despite its name, Hartford City has more in common with small-town America than it does with large urban metropolises. Around six thousand people live there, give or take, and when my team and I roll into town, we're a little dismayed to see how many storefronts are permanently closed down. The people in Hartford are friendly, and there's a colorful history going back almost two hundred years.

Considering its age, it's no surprise to learn that several deaths have taken place inside the house. There's also been a fire, though nothing too serious. Far more unusual are the unidentified bones that were discovered in a crawl space beneath the Monroe House. Examination of the remains has demonstrated little about them… other than the fact that they're human.

There has been much speculation as to how the bones ended up there, in the dirt beneath the house. Some believe that the property was built on top of an old cemetery, and that the ground around it may contain more human remains, still waiting to be found.

That's the nicest theory. There are other, darker speculations, including whispers that the bones may belong to a murder victim whose remains were stashed in the crawl space to prevent their discovery by law enforcement.

The Monroe House has had the reputation of being "that haunted house" for decades. Ghost stories have been associated with the house since the 1940s. To my knowledge, none of those accounts were particularly dark or frightening, however, involving such relatively common phenomena as the apparition of a woman in period clothing, and the sound of kids playing when no living children were actually inside the house. Things took a turn for the nasty after an occult ritual took place inside the house years ago. This version of events is bolstered by the fact that a necklace was found in the same crawlspace, laced with human hair, wrapped up in cloth, and then bound with twine. One individual who claimed to have participated in the ritual said that "we made a mistake" and they "didn't know it would really call something in."

"Call something in" is *exactly* what the ritual appears to have done, and that something is believed by some to have been a demon. The list of visitors to the Monroe House who have gotten slapped, punched, shoved, and scratched is extensive, and continues to grow by the week. Paranormal enthusiasts and investigators flock to the house. Some don't make it through the night, fleeing when things turn malicious. While interviewing witnesses and reading accounts of those who tried their luck inside the house, I was struck by the numerous reports of people growing inexplicably angry, sometimes to the point where they would throw down and fight one another—overcome with rage for no apparent reason. The anger would dissipate as quickly as it came on, once the parties were out of the house.

Some chose never to return.

I'm determined that my team and I aren't going to be deterred by whatever happens to us inside the Monroe House. That's an easy thing to say from the comfort of your own brightly lit living room at home, but a different proposition entirely when you're actually standing on the doorstep of the house with human remains in its basement. Still, we've driven more than a thousand miles to get here, and the idea of possibly encountering a demonic entity is in equal parts alarming and intriguing.

The house is large, far bigger than any of the other residences I've investigated as part of this project. Although its owner has renovated the property, nobody has actually lived here for years. It is solely the province of the curious now, primarily ghost hunters and the occasional thrill-seeker. Walking through the house, my team and I find an abundance of talking boards and children's toys, particularly dolls, of which there are at least fifty. Although the living room is brightly lit and almost welcoming, the rest of the house is shrouded in gloom and shadow. It looks like the sort of place in which horror movies are set, and I remind myself that this can have subtle psychological effects that we must guard against as long as we're here.

After touring the ground floor and upstairs, we're eager to see the basement. It's dank and chilly, exactly as expected. The owner has covered the entrance to the crawl space with a large sheet of wood, screwed firmly into place to keep visitors out. I have permission to remove it and venture inside, should I feel the need.

Paranormal investigators spend a lot of time talking to thin air. This often makes us feel slightly ridiculous—until, that is, thin air answers back.

Our stay proves to be an eventful one. Over the span of several days, one of my colleagues, the veteran of countless paranormal investigations, spontaneously develops chest pain, which he's never had before and will not experience again after leaving the Monroe House. He's not the first person to feel this way inside the house, and he won't be the last. Another colleague develops nausea apropos of nothing, while a third is stricken with abdominal pain. I seem to be the only one unaffected by physical symptoms.

After we remove the wooden board, two of my colleagues, Erin and Jason, take it in turns to venture into the crawlspace. They're chosen because each of them is considerably smaller in stature than I am, more than capable of negotiating such a small space. Each is a willing volunteer. Having watched a TV investigator claim to be grabbed and clawed by an invisible force in the close confines of the crawl space, I'm more than a little nervous as I watch Erin slither forward on her belly like a snake, her feet disappearing into the inky blackness beneath the Monroe House.

We can hear the sound of her clothes scraping on mud and dirt. It isn't long before she reaches the far end of the crawl space and encounters what looks to be part of a rib sticking out of the ground. She pauses to take photographs and run some audio recordings, neither of which turn up anything anomalous. Once she's back out, it's Jason's turn. He does the same thing, with the same results.

It's commonly said that ground zero for the Monroe House haunting involves this basement, but so far, nothing out of the ordinary has happened to us down here. Erin and Jason have taken great care not to actually touch the bones, a mark of respect on their part. If they were part of an occult ritual, did it take place down here in the bowels of the house, or somewhere up above us, with the bones being disposed of in the crawl space afterward?

Neither of them is attacked, which comes as a relief. While we're down in the basement, unbeknownst to all of us, the bathroom door on the second floor has opened of its own accord.

Spirit box sessions held in the house yield sinister results. *Don't sleep*, one message tells us, followed by *death*. A second voice follows up with *sleep. Sleep.*

Skeptics believe that the words emitted by these devices are little more than random noise being misinterpreted by the human ear. On the other hand, many of those who find spirit box output credible believe that the words may come from spirits and disincarnate entities. If that is the case, then this message is an ominous one.

Further spirit box sessions herald a conversation between an aggressive, dominant male voice and a submissive, seemingly intimidated female: one who plaintively begs for help. The male voice is angry and combative, swearing vehemently and hissing that we are to leave the house at once. It's as if we're listening in to confrontation between a vicious male bully and his victim, with occasional abusive asides tossed our way for good measure.

Of course, assuming that what we're hearing truly is paranormal communication, then the ranting of an aggressive male entity doesn't have to be demonic in nature. It could simply be the spirit of an awful human being, one who hasn't made any spiritual progress since he passed on. A common paranormal axiom holds that a horrible person in life tends to be an equally horrible person after their death.

Some visitors have heard the sound of children giggling and playing. Not all of them are convinced that these are residual sounds, or the spirits of actual dead children. One of them told me that "I don't think there are any children in that house. Not one. It's pretending to be a child in order to sucker people in."

There have been several deaths in the house, not all of them known to the public, so I'm aware of the possibility that this haunting could be nothing more than an aggressive and belligerent human spirit—or spirits. They can be responsible for scratches, slaps, and other violent activity. Yet the ritualistic aspects of the case imply that there might be an even darker origin to the Monroe House haunting. There is certainly no shortage of investigators who believe it to be demonic in nature.

As the days go by and we spend more time in the house, a narrative begins to unfold. We make contact with what claims to be the spirit of a male who abducted women many years ago and brought them back to the house against their will.

Worst of all, he claims to have murdered one of those victims and placed her remains in the crawl space under the house. His misogynistic and bullying approach cuts no ice with my hardened female colleagues, each of whom is more than capable of standing up to this sort of thug…whether he's dead or not.

Our Estes Method spirit box sessions are chilling. We hear repeatedly from female voices that are in distress, clearly intimidated by this overbearing male entity. There are repeated cries for help, each one tugging at our heartstrings. These are usually met with aggressive shushing and a male voice insisting that the female shuts up. The guy has a liking for profane language and hurls insults at each of us in turn.

Clearly, someone—or something—inside this house has something to hide.

Skeptics tend to dismiss devices such as spirit boxes out of hand, claiming the voices that come through them are nothing more than audio pareidolia—the desire of the human brain to make meaningful patterns out of random chatter. Sometimes, they're right...but there are some phenomena that are much harder to explain away. We encounter one of them ourselves in the living room, which we've been using as our operations center.

Fellow investigator Linda and I are sitting on the couch, each at opposite ends. We're taking a break, doing nothing more meaningful than doomscrolling through our respective social media feeds.

Suddenly, we hear a female voice sobbing her heart out. It's coming from directly between us, from the empty space in the center of the couch.

All three of us present in the room feel our jaws drop at the same moment. At first, we wonder if we're hearing things, but quickly comparing notes, we all agree that we just heard a woman crying in thin air. Could it have been some sort of mass hallucination? That's possible, but when I play back the file on my digital voice recorder, it has been captured loud and clear.

I can't help but wonder if this isn't what it seems to be at all. If there *is* a demonic entity at the heart of the Monroe House, then it may well be capable of imitating others—particularly innocent victims—in order to get what it wants.

Although I have twenty-five years' experience investigating claims of ghosts and hauntings, some of them dark in nature, my journey into the realm of the demonic is relatively new. In such cases, I find it wise to consult with someone who has greater expertise. I reach out to someone who not only has spent decades researching the occult, but who also has spent time right here at the Monroe House—Michelle Belanger.

During her psychic reading of the house, Michelle picked up on the presence of two Caucasian males who were involved in occult practices. These men were most likely those responsible for trying to conjure up a demonic entity in order to serve their own purposes. Michelle did this without any foreknowledge of the property or its history. Although Michelle is hesitant to employ the word *demon* lightly—not least because they think it is greatly over-used—the term seems to fit the dark malevolence that Michelle detected in the basement of the Monroe House.

Michelle developed the strong impression of a woman being choked, accompanied by the distinct sense that she was somehow connected to the males who were dabbling in the occult. Neither of these men were serious practitioners—they were arrogant and cavalier, meddling with something they did not fully understand. Thrill-seekers, and devoid of morals, if Michelle's sensory impressions were correct, and once they began to get in over their heads and realized that matters had gotten out of their control, they turned on the woman, who wanted nothing more than to just get out before the darkness swallowed them all up.

One of the rooms has been painted entirely blue. We're sitting in there, conducting an Estes Method spirit box session. After a burst of profanity, we're told that "he's coming." When we ask who, we're told "evil" and then "devil." I'm not convinced we are literally dealing with a demon here; my mind goes back to Patti Negri's experience of an angry male spirit pretending to be one in order to scare a bunch of interlopers back in Los Angeles. On the other hand, I'm awfully glad that Michelle is on speed dial, ready to jump in and confront whatever it is that currently shares the Monroe House with us.

Michelle is at home in Ohio but remotely sensing events here in Hartford City by projecting themselves in psychically. We're not greatly reassured when Michelle tells us that they aren't sure whether we're dealing with a human spirit, or something that is "just wearing a person suit."

Speaking in a slow, calm tone, Michelle tries to coax whatever it is to come out and engage with us. It appears to be hiding, lurking in the background. This thing responds by calling Michelle a bitch. Rather than lose their temper. Michelle instead tells the entity to bring it on, letting it know that they are more than willing to fight if that's necessary.

"We won!" the entity tells us through the spirit box. It's fascinating to note that the communicator is now referring to itself as *we* rather than *I*. Seconds later, it switches back, stating, "I have it!"

The more calmly Michelle speaks, the more intimidated the responses become. No matter how much Michelle tries to extract the entity's name and its nature—human or something else—it refuses to give up its secrets, finally skulking away after declaring in a rather sulky tone of voice: "I'm a man."

Maybe it was telling us the truth. Maybe it wasn't. I can't be sure either way whether this particular entity, which seems to be top dog of the many that are said to haunt the Monroe House, was human or demonic. Michelle's perspective is that the entity is dark in nature, not necessarily human, and may indeed be what many would classify as demonic. I certainly respect their opinion and experience on the matter, although the time I've spent at Indiana's Demon House has left me with as many questions as it has answers.

Chapter Seventeen

I have a lot to think about as I start back on the long drive west. The Monroe House was reputedly haunted before the occult ritual summoned something dark within its walls. I still feel the need for greater clarity on what exactly that something might have been, which is why my next step is to consult someone who claims to have gone up against demons in the field.

eighteen
PRACTICAL MAGIC

More than three hundred years after the ignominious conclusion of the Salem Witch Trials, the practice of witchcraft is widespread throughout the United States and across the world. What do modern-day witches make of demons? To find out, I sought counsel from the marvelous Patti Negri, known as the Good Witch.

From a very young age, Patti realized that her "imaginary friends" weren't actually imaginary at all. In her own words, she was obsessed with the dead ever since she was little, though not in a dark or morbid way. It was simply where her natural curiosities lay. Patti conducted her very first séance at the age of eight in the living room of her suburban Los Angeles home. When the shadows began to move, young Patti was exhilarated, believing that her attempt to lift the veil had been genuinely successful, and also fully convinced that she was able to control the process.

Relaxing comfortably in her home office, located in the heart of Hollywood, California, Patti is flanked by a bookcase containing a number of magical artifacts, along with a rather tongue-in-cheek sign declaring its owner to be *Witch and Famous*. It's also completely accurate.

Also a practicing psychic medium, Patti's talents are in great demand. She appears regularly on television, offering her insights into all things mystical and spiritual. Although not all witches are mediums, just as not all mediums are witches, she finds that the two aspects of her life act synergistically.

She has graciously set aside time from her busy schedule to enlighten me on the witches' perspective regarding demons.

The first thing I want to know involves conjuring up dark entities. My thoughts instantly go back to the Monroe House and the amateur conjuration that took place there. Patti tells me that it's not really a big deal; she's capable of conjuring up or inviting in light or dark spirits at her own behest. Her preference is to invite rather than to compel, which is aligned with her values as a self-proclaimed "good witch."

"You have to be respectful, especially if you're dealing with the darker side," Patti emphasizes. "This is where inexperienced people can get themselves into trouble. Bad things can happen whenever you drop the ball, ethically speaking, or allow your protections to lapse—if you don't set up your warding correctly, for example. Then you never know what's going to come in. Don't jump in the deep end if you don't know how to swim."

That seems like sound advice to me.

Which brings us to the nature of demons. Are they real, and if so—what are they?

"They are real," Patti tells me confidently. "It's a vibrational thing, high versus low…there's a dark side and a light side to everything, a natural balance, and demons represent the dark side."

She goes on to add that, in her opinion, we tend to give demons way too much credit.

"Ninety percent of what some people think of as demons is actually just a cranky ghost," she chuckles, speaking from years of experience spent in and around haunted places. "Cranky in life, cranky in death, all these entities tend to be of a lower vibration."

Aggressive human spirits are often mislabeled as being demonic, in her view. Everything dark isn't necessarily a demon, Patti points out, and we have to be aware of what she calls "demon wannabes"—malevolent and mean-spirited, perhaps even evil deceased human spirits, who assume the mantle of a demon in order to create fear and further their own nefarious agenda. To borrow a Sherlock Holmes reference, it's a bit like a small-time pickpocket representing themselves as Professor Moriarty. They might be nasty and even dangerous, but they're hardly a world-class criminal. The truly "big bads" are few and far between, in Patti's view, but that's not to say they aren't out there at all.

This prompts the question: How can they be told apart? Patti assures me that she and other mediums are able to sense the difference in energies between a negative human and a legitimately demonic being. Sometimes even nonsensitives know, but often make the mistake of ignoring our intuition.

A case in point involved the time when Patti was filming at a 1920s-era house up in the Hollywood Hills. The property had been built by none other than Charlie Chaplin for one of his paramours. At one point during the 1960s, the Rolling Stones had rented the place, throwing legendary parties; even Marilyn Manson spent some time there.

"It was a party house for many years," Patti recalls, "and while I'm not judging anybody who parties, it's true that drinking, drugs, and that kind of thing can often let in darkness. It lowers your inhibitions and can erode your defenses."

Patti had been asked to participate in a documentary about the house itself, running a séance for the cameras. Her fellow sitters were mostly in their twenties and, in Patti's own words, "very full of the life force we all have at that age." One of the participants disobeyed Patti's golden rule of the séance table: be respectful. In direct disobedience of her instructions, this particular individual started throwing his weight around, challenging the spirits of the home and calling them out in the most disrespectful ways.

"I knew there were three spirits in this house, and they all had a very theatrical flair," she recalls. "After all, this was Hollywood! It wasn't long before some amazing things began to happen. The French doors flew open without anybody touching them. The entire table screamed! All this time, the cameras are rolling, four of them covering the room from different angles. I started to feel a real sense of tension from one of the three spirits, a male entity that wasn't happy with this young man who was provoking so aggressively."

As the drama grew in the séance room, things quickly began to spiral out of control.

"Spirits like funny, and this young man thought he was being funny," Patti goes on. "In fact, what he was saying was *stupid* and it was about to come back and bite him—well, not him, but the cameraman who was directly facing him."

"What happened?" I ask, on the edge of my seat now.

"He caught fire. Literally. A pair of what looked like angel wings burst into flames on his back."

Patti isn't exaggerating; she insists that this case of apparent spontaneous combustion was captured by two of the cameras.

The entire table screamed.

A former EMT, Patti switched from witch to medically trained professional in the blink of an eye, ordering the now burning cameraman to drop and roll in order to put the flames out.

"I don't care about the filming—we are DONE!" the witch insisted, putting her booted foot down literally and metaphorically. "Nobody bursts into flames on my watch."

Once everybody's physical safety was assured, Patti shut down the séance and set about communicating with the spirit responsible for the fiery termination of the night's events. It was, she remembers with a laugh, the theatrically inclined ghost of a dead Hollywood actor who wanted to portray himself as a demon in order to scare off "meddling kids"—to borrow a phrase from *Scooby-Doo*.

The spirit had fed off the energy of those young people present around the table, Patti explains, whose energies were heightened because of the ill-advised, increasingly provocative behavior of one of their number. "I think there's a demon in here with us," one of the speakers had whispered nervously once the atmosphere in the room had begun to darken.

Once the combustion incident was over, the provocateur, suddenly chastened, never said another word. Patti was able to talk the angry spirit down and thereby quash any rumors of the historic old house being demonically infested…which it wasn't.

Has Patti ever encountered an entity she considers to be genuinely demonic?

Yes, she has.

The Good Witch cites two examples. The first is LA's notorious Cecil Hotel, which dates back to the 1920s. In its heyday, the Cecil was regarded as an affordable, if far from swanky, place to lay one's head. Outfitted with seven hundred rooms spread over fourteen floors, by rights the hotel ought to have been a great success story. Instead, the onset of the Great Depression in 1929 started the Cecil on a downturn from which it was never able to escape. Its once swanky neighborhood was dubbed with a name that is instantly recognizable to this day: Skid Row.

Over the years, the Cecil developed a reputation for being cursed, and its primary customers became transients, criminals, and the occasional uninformed out-of-towner. All hotels have their deaths, but some of those that took place at the Cecil were sufficiently gruesome to feed its macabre aura. This included a resident who cut his own throat from ear to ear; a postpartum mother who hurled her baby to its death from an upper floor; and numerous guests who checked in and committed suicide by jumping from one of its many windows. At least two serial killers are known to have stayed there: Richard Ramirez, the so-called Night Stalker, held Los Angeles in a year-long grip of terror spanning 1984 to 1985 before finally being caught. Ramirez rented a room at the very top of the hotel, where he liked to play loud music throughout the night.

Lesser known but no less heinous was Austrian serial killer Jack Unterweger, who stayed at the hotel in the early 1990s while supposedly researching a magazine article on crime in Los Angeles. In reality, Unterweger was adding to the city's crime stats by strangling sex workers to death.

The Cecil was one of LA's worst-kept macabre secrets until 2013, when a Canadian tourist named Elisa Lam disappeared while she was a guest at the hotel. Security camera footage showed her apparently talking to thin air while inside one of the hotel elevators. Her body was subsequently found floating inside a rooftop water tank. Investigators became suspicious when guests complained that the Cecil's tap water had begun to look and taste strange.

Patti visited the hotel in 2020 while shooting an episode of *Ghost Adventures*.

"So much bad has happened at the Cecil over the years, that I'm convinced there's a demonic influence at work there," she says. "It has affected living people for many years, preying on their minds. That place makes you want to kill yourself."

"How did it make you feel?" I ask.

"I came very close to jumping out a window myself! I was speaking in some weird, backward language. I felt myself being physically attacked in Pigeon Goldie's room."

Of the many tragic stories associated with the Hotel Cecil, that of "Pigeon" Goldie Osgood, is one of the most heartbreaking. Goldie was an animal-loving homeless lady who liked to feed the pigeons on Skid Row and bought bags of birdseed with which to do it. She checked into the Cecil on June 3, 1964, and never checked out. An unknown assailant raped Goldie Osgood, stabbed her repeatedly, and strangled her to death. The crime was never solved.

"Every room in that hotel feels different," continues Patti. "I was getting more and more depressed. All seven hundred of those rooms were unlocked and available to us. I was in a trance state, and led the film crew to a window that, unbeknownst to me, somebody had jumped out of and killed themselves. [Host] Zak had to yell at me to snap me out of it—I had this urge to just get out of there by jumping out of that window myself."

The darkness within the walls of the hotel targets and exploits a person's weakest, most vulnerable place. If a visitor is emotionally compromised, the attack will be an emotional one; if they're unwell, they will become even more ill, she explains. In Patti's view, this force, while not having cloven hooves and carrying a pitchfork, is nothing less than demonic in nature.

The second location in which she has encountered such dark energies is every bit as infamous: the so-called Black Dahlia House. In 1947, twenty-two-year-old Elizabeth Short was like hundreds of thousands of other Los Angelenos—simply trying to make enough money to get by in the City of Angels. Her dreams of building a better life and perhaps making it big as a movie star were cut tragically short when she was brutally murdered, her naked body sliced in half and dumped in a public place, to be discovered by a horrified woman who was out taking a walk with her child.

Elizabeth Short's brutal killing vexed LAPD detectives and FBI agents. It shocked the city of Los Angeles and remains officially unsolved to this day. Investigators were able to determine that she had died elsewhere, rather than at the scene of her crime, based on the fact that not only was murder in such a public place a very risky proposition, but also that no blood had been spilled anywhere near her body. Based on the sheer number of very precise wounds that had been inflicted upon her, Elizabeth had been murdered in a secure place somewhere else within the city—but where?

Because she liked to dress in black, journalists began referring to the dead woman as the Black Dalia, a play on the title of a popular movie, *The Blue Dahlia*. The nickname stuck. As the years turned to decades, investigators sifted through and discarded a mountain of false leads and dead ends. Finally, the Dahlia investigation became a cold case, and remained that way until a viable suspect finally emerged. Almost sixty years after the murder, a retired LAPD detective named Steve Hodel came forward with his suspicion that Hodel's own father, Dr. George Hodel, had murdered Elizabeth Short back in 1947. The trauma inflicted upon her body was almost surgical in its precision—and George Hodel had been a surgeon. Shortly after the murder, George Hodel left the

United States, emigrating to the Philippines. He died in 1999 and was never tried for the brutal killing.

Known colloquially as the Black Dahlia House, the 1940s home of Dr. George Hodel was designed by pioneering architect Frank Lloyd Wright in 1926. Visually distinctive because of its Mayan style, the house is a dark, gothic-themed place that would not look out of place in a horror movie. Some believe that George Hodel tortured and murdered Elizabeth Short in the basement—and that there may have been others in addition.

Patti was invited to visit the house and psychically read it. The intense spiritual darkness she picked up on disgusted and repulsed her, as few other things in her life ever have. She recalls that the malevolent force in the house followed her home. The house of a witch tends to be warded and protected to the nth degree, particularly when something extremely dark is in play. It's the equivalent of a spiritual home security system...and suddenly, after she returned from the Black Dahlia House, that system no longer worked.

An unseen something violently slammed Patti back in her chair, so forcefully that a visit to the emergency department revealed torn cartilage in her chest. It required a major effort on her part to banish what Patti believes was demonic interference and restore her home to normal.

"Was this dark energy there in the house because of what George Hodel is believed to have done," I ask, "or did he do what he did *because* of its influence?" In addition to the multiple murder hypothesis, there were accounts of drug-fueled orgies taking place at the house during Hodel's tenure. Police put Hodel under investigation due to the claims of abusive behavior on his part. He became increasingly erratic while living in the house. The question is—why?

"That's the chicken and the egg question," she smiles. "Which came first? I believe that there was something so dark and sadomasochistic within him that he somehow fused with this dark power. This was far more than just a case of dark, cranky ghosts."

Patti is convinced that whatever infests the Black Dahlia House is demonic.

"Anything truly demonic is more than just scary," Patti tells me. "It affects your physical, emotional, and mental health. I don't know what his personal beliefs were, but maybe he sold his soul to the Devil."

Ah yes, that old chestnut. The story has been handed down through antiquity, from generation to generation: the concept that one can sign over their immortal soul to the powers of darkness in exchange for fame, riches, sex, or whatever else they might desire. The tales usually involve a contract written in the blood of the signatory. It's an age-old cautionary tale that we have all heard in some form or another—but is it actually possible?

Surprisingly, it turns out that Patti has some experience in this area, as she once appeared in a documentary film in which the star, a musician, would attempt to sell their soul to Satan…for real. Patti's role was to hold a séance in which she would attempt to make contact with the spirits of those since departed who had made this nefarious pact in the past. Presumably, they were now languishing in Hell, or wherever it is that the Lord of Darkness resides.

"The results of the séance were very clear," Patti says. "Don't do it! DON'T DO IT! That's exactly what I told him [the protagonist] and the rest of the production, all on camera. They chose to go ahead anyway. He wrote a blood oath on goatskin parchment, agreeing to sell his soul in exchange for fame or fortune. The next step was for us to go out into the desert to an abandoned grain silo in order to perform the actual ceremony. We set up special candles for the protection of everybody else on the crew. They all started going out, until all but one had been extinguished."

Patti sensed a low, ominous rumbling, growing increasingly more forceful. *Oh crap, this is really going to happen*, she realized. A black mirror had been set up to allow the Devil an entry point onto this plane of existence.

"At the very last minute, he got a hammer and smashed the mirror," she recalls. That derailed the exchange before it could be completed. After deciding not to seal the deal, it was recommended that the musician burn the piece of parchment containing his contract with the Devil. "It took multiple attempts to set this thing alight. Once it caught fire, we threw it in the corner of this silo and left it to burn. Later on, when we checked on the parchment, one side of it was charred, but the other side was completely legible."

Despite their best efforts to burn it up, the written contract was still in existence. To Patti's knowledge, it remains in the musician's possession to this day. I'm sure he safeguards it with his life.

"This is all so much bigger than some guy in a red Devil suit," Patti goes on. "It's all about action and reaction, cause and effect. If you're willing to do a certain thing, for your own benefit, then boy are you going to pay for it!"

In other words, Patti believes that there are dark things out there in the spiritual realm, and anybody who is disposed to making a pact with them can do so...at a very high price. For our convenience, we label these things demons.

"It's a form of energy," she explains. "A dark, evil energy that we put horns on and try to personify."

This force is intelligent, interactive, and dark in nature. Many other witches and mediums hold similar beliefs.

"Demons are real," she concludes. "We as people want to think they're exciting and fun, but they aren't. Far from it. Dabbling with the negative can have very real consequences. For one thing, they don't have a moral code. They'll lie to you."

Once we've said our goodbyes, I ponder some of the points the Good Witch made. A theme is beginning to emerge among many of the interviewees I've spoken to on my search for demons: they believe in the concept of the demonic, but not in the literal horns and cloven hooves sense. In many ways, what they're describing is more insidious. It reminds me of the *Star Wars* movies and the dark side of the Force, capable of employing guile and seduction to taint those who seek to master it for their own purposes.

It's time for me to talk to someone who has spent decades peering into the darkness themselves in an attempt to find his own answers.

nineteen
HEY JUDE

Dave Schrader wears many hats within the paranormal field. He is well known for his work on television, fronting shows such as *The Holzer Files*, *The Curse of Lizzie Borden*, and *Ghosts of Devil's Perch*, to name just three. He has worked as a researcher and guested on numerous other shows and also hosts the popular podcast *The Paranormal 60* and has a wealth of experience investigating claims of ghosts and hauntings, having actively researched them for eighteen years. Surely, if *anybody* has experienced an encounter with the demonic, it would be somebody like Dave.

It's safe to say that he's a believer in the paranormal realm. From the age of two, Dave was visited by the ghost of his grandmother. The Illinois home he grew up in was haunted. When he was twelve, Dave saw what he's convinced was Bigfoot in Alabama, and in 2006, he sighted a UFO. His life has been anything but boring.

Despite this, Dave considers himself to be a "skeptical believer."

"I know that strange things happen more often than people think," Dave explains, "but even when something like that happens to me, I have to break it down, dissect it, and try to understand what exactly took place…to figure out whether it was a trick of the brain, a misunderstanding, or something genuinely paranormal."

He grew up Lutheran, and now classifies himself as being spiritual rather than religious, having a strong faith but no longer attending church. When it comes to the matter of demons, he is very open to the possibility of their existence.

Something Dave once said stuck firmly in my brain. When somebody tells him that they think they are dealing with a demon, he shakes his head and replies, "The most important word you just said is *think*." By this, he means that if somebody truly has fallen afoul of demonic forces, there is no equivocation, no mistaking it. A genuine demon wreaks havoc on the lives of those with whom it comes into contact. Nobody *thinks* they have a demon, he clarifies; when they really do, the signs and consequences are unmistakable.

"Out of the thousands of cases people have brought to me for assessment, once we take the time to deescalate and consider them, very few have turned out to be demonic in nature. Often, these were either not hauntings at all, or were hauntings that were misidentified and influenced by what the people involved had seen on TV and in the movies."

What are some of the things that were mistaken for demons?

"Most often, aggressive human spirits. I approach these cases by trying to determine what it is exactly that makes the people involved believe they're dealing with a demon. That answer is frequently *fear*. When we're able to help people realize that what they're most afraid of isn't necessarily what they're actually confronted with, it allows them to take a deep breath and better come to terms with the situation…once they refocus, they often realize that the reality isn't as terrifying as they once thought."

Reassessing and reframing things in a more positive way can be a good strategy in many aspects of life, particularly when we're deeply afraid of something. For those who believe in them, few things are capable of creating terror to the extent that demons can. Sometimes, troublesome human spirits can capitalize on that fear for their own amusement.

"How many of us played with a Ouija board at a party or sleepover when we were growing up?" Dave asks rhetorically. "I guarantee you that when I'm dead, I'll be the grandpa ghost who drops in at my grandkid's first Ouija session and give them a few good, healthy scares. That doesn't make me a demon, or evil—it just makes me a smartass ghost."

Note to self: make sure that all of Dave's grandkids get a copy of this book. Forewarned is forearmed, as they say.

Behind the humor is a great point. Plenty of living human beings like to mess with others, whether it be their friends or complete strangers. Why would we assume they'd change after they are dead?

In many of the cases Dave has investigated, the events that terrified people could just as easily be seen as mischievous and prank-sterish rather than evil.

"Now, I'm not dismissing them all," Dave clarifies. "There *were* cases that had demonic connotations. Some of them absolutely broke people down. On a *Holzer Files* episode named 'The Devil in Texas,' Dr. Hans Holzer dealt with a very prominent dark entity that was severely affecting a family. They reported thousands of bugs dropping out of thin air, as soon as they turned the light off in a room. Once the lights were turned back on, it was found that all the bugs were dead—not just dead, but apparently dead for *years*. This happened repeatedly.

"Threatening notes would also appear from nowhere, detailing secrets and weaknesses of family members that could be used against them. It tragically drove one person to take his own life. That case was taken as far as it could go, and then I was contacted by a lady from Missouri who was struggling with something very similar…at first glance. Once we actually met her in person, it became apparent that what we were dealing with was somebody who had been mentally and physically abused repeatedly throughout her life. This trauma had made her the focus for a type of anarchic poltergeist energy that flared up when she was upset, causing scratches to appear on her skin. She blamed an external force, but as investigators, we came to believe this energy actually originated within her. Once we helped her empower herself, the quality of her life improved dramatically…to the point where she is now helping others who are experiencing similar ordeals cope with and resolve them."

Dave and his colleagues brought in a priest to bless her and perform a deliverance (a method of expelling evil spirits and demons). The minister who carried out the ritual believed there was indeed something negative attached to her, though he stopped short of identifying it as a demon.

"It's remarkable what harm we humans can do to ourselves when we're walking in a place of fear," Dave muses. "I believe that we can create and manifest horrible side effects. That's not to say that good and evil don't exist. They most assuredly do, as represented by God and the Devil…two coexisting beings that are polar opposites."

In Dave's view, however, evil is embodied not by a horned overlord of Hell, but by heinous acts carried out by human beings, such as the three individuals who murdered one of his dear friends and her children in cold blood.

"Some might call that a demonic act, that they were influenced by evil. In my mind, they're horrible humans who did some *really* bad things."

Does the term *evil* fit this tragedy? Absolutely. Yet it's not something attributable to malign supernatural entities. This is evil wearing a human face, as it overwhelmingly seems to do.

"I would *rather* believe that a demon or the Devil forced those three people to murder my friend and her kids. It would be much more comforting, not to mention convenient, for me to think that…but the reality, that the guilty parties were three utterly barbaric human beings, is so much uglier, and harder to accept."

If it seems as though Dave is skeptical that negative forces of a paranormal nature actually exist, however, he's quick to disabuse me of that notion.

"I've often wondered why those kinds of energies seem to flock to asylums, jails, and abandoned hospitals," he goes on. "A few years back, I was enjoying a drink with my good friend Misty, and I asked her that very question. She very carefully peeled the label off the beer bottle she was holding and told me, *Let's say that this bottle is the best of who we are. It's what elevates on up to the next spiritual level once we die. This label is what's left behind: the garbage. Pettiness, rage, anger, jealousy…and the animalistic instincts we all have. It's territorial, and once our higher self is gone, this stuff stays behind on Earth in a place that was familiar to it. There are other beings there of a similarly negative nature. Like attracts like, so they flock together, developing a pack mentality."*

This may explain the primal, aggressive interactions many visitors have in such places. Loud knocks and thumps. EVPs and direct voices yelling profanities and screaming at the living to *GET OUT!* and *LEAVE!* If provoked, even unintentionally, there is a risk of scratching, shoving, and more serious physical injury. These are unquestionably aggressive phenomena—it's debatable as to just how intelligent they may or may not be—but Dave raises the insightful point of whether they should be seen as evil, or simply the toxic dregs that are left behind in the wake of so many human lives. We all have our trauma and our emotional baggage. What if the byproducts of that are left behind once we die, unceremoniously dumped at the place of our passing with no more thought than an old mattress being abandoned at the side of the road?

"When I wash my car, the dirt that I rinse off it isn't evil," he tells me. "That dirt leaves my driveway stained and filthy. Perhaps it's analogous to what we sometimes think of as demonic hauntings. Some of these...let's call them *fractals* seem capable of learning and developing over time, to the point where sometimes paranormal investigators can communicate with them."

The point Dave's making here is very clear. In the paranormal field, many of the entities that behave animalistically and with belligerence are mislabeled as being demons, when it's every bit as likely they are simply aggressive human spirits or the psychic residue of human life trauma. But it's also bigger than that. We live in a time when some of the greatest demons we face are fear, loneliness, doubt, and isolation—days in which good people are being broken down by a seemingly uncaring society and a world that's beyond their ability to control. The good news, he points out, is that we all have tools at our disposal with which to exorcise such demons: tools such as kindness, compassion, and empathy. The willingness to reach out and lift up somebody who is suffering. To give a voice to those who feel unseen or unheard. If we did more of this during somebody's physical lifetime, imagine how fewer aggressive hauntings there would be...and, if one believes in the literal existence of demons, how much less vulnerable would somebody be to demonic oppression and possession if they felt emotionally secure and appreciated? Significantly less, I suspect.

In an ideal world, paranormal investigators who are working on potentially demonic cases would carefully consider all aspects before arriving at the best solution for each client.

"In reality," Dave sighs, "what often happens is that after a short 'investigation,' an EVP is recorded of someone or something growling. Based on that, the client is told that they're dealing with a demonic infestation, and they're sent down a very specific path... which is quite often the *wrong* path."

"Dave, do you truly believe in the existence of the demonic?" I ask. His demeanor turns grave.

"I do. I truly believe that the Devil is at work, and that the best trick he ever pulled was to make us think that he doesn't exist...but I also think that the Devil is in *all of us*. He manifests in our actions when we don't keep our baser instincts and urges in check. That can result in very real, very palpable evil. Much like the old story about the two wolves, one of darkness and one of light, whichever side of our nature wins out tends to be the one we feed the most. That's why compassion, kindness and love are so important."

In Dave's philosophy, the best way to cast out demons isn't with a prayer book and a ritual. It's by caring for our fellow human beings and keeping our own darker impulses under control.

"As hard as it is," he concludes, "do not walk in a place of fear. That applies whether you're setting foot in a haunted location, or going to work, or parenting your children. What might at first seem terrifying often appears that way because it's a great unknown to us. Let me finish up by sharing how I learned the lesson."

As a teenager, Dave was trying to win the affections of a girl by accompanying her to a home for children with special needs, where she volunteered. Not knowing what to expect, Dave was led into the room where a young boy named Jude lived.

"I had never seen anything as scary, as horrifying in my entire life up to that point," Dave recalls, his voice cracking with emotion. "Jude was developmentally disabled. He had a hunched back, and his face was deformed, so much so that he looked—for lack of a better word—terrifying to me. I was there to help with physical therapy, which basically meant playing with him. As I stood in front of Jude and looked at him, I was shuddering, trying not to physically recoil at his appearance. Remember, I was just a boy myself back then. Then he reached out a little clawlike hand to me, through the bars of his crib.

"It took every bit of strength I had not to pull back and run out of that room."

Ah, he wants to hold hands with you! Jude's caregiver said. Refusing to turn and flee, Dave instead went down on his knees and slowly reached out, allowing the little boy's hand to curl around his own finger…

…and that's when it happened.

Jude's face lit up in a million-dollar smile, suffused with joy and love at having made that most basic and primal of connections with another human being. Sometimes, a single touch is worth more than a thousand words, as Dave Schrader learned that day at the side of the little boy's crib.

Then, the child began to sing. Because of his physical condition, his voice was broken and a little difficult to understand, but there was no mistaking the song.

It was *Hey Jude* by The Beatles.

"All of that fear instantly fell away," Dave recalls. He's polite enough not to acknowledge the fact that I have tears running down my face now. "It had been replaced by recognition of the true beauty that really defined who and what Jude was. No matter what he looked like on the outside, he truly was a beautiful soul within, and that hit me square in the face right then."

It's a lesson Dave carries around with him to this day.

"When you push past the superficial, when you reach out to someone even if they seem difficult or frightening...that's when life becomes truly meaningful. I've never forgotten that feeling of holding Jude's hand and what it awoke in me. He and I became buddies, and it's no exaggeration to say that he changed my life with his friendship. If I had given in to the urge to run out of there, I would have missed out on so much."

As, I am sure, would Jude.

As for Dave Schrader, he has managed to teach me something about defeating our demons, but I had no idea that the lesson would turn out to be this: giving in to our demons, and the fear associated with them, can be the most damaging thing of all.

CONCLUSION

It's been a long and eventful road since I first set out in search of demons. I've learned so much, had my eyes opened to many fascinating viewpoints and perspectives ranging from the skeptical to the all-in believer and everything in between.

When I started making public my intention to write this book, a number of people in the paranormal and theological communities reached out to warn me that it could entail some personal jeopardy. To borrow a phrase, when you show an interest in the demonic, there's a chance it will show an interest in you.

I'm not sure what I think about that, but after more than three years spent researching and writing the book, I certainly do wonder.

The evening after I returned from my research trip to Iowa, I sat down to begin writing that particular chapter of this book. It was the first thing I wrote, apart from the introduction. Ten minutes after I started writing, I lost internet connectivity—not just to my laptop, but to *everything*. Not only was my home Wi-Fi network down, but so was the cable TV stream. That meant I couldn't write. I typically save my work to an online file storage system, where I also keep digitized versions of the reams of research documents that underpin the writing process of each book I put out.

With no work getting done, I went about the rest of the evening, periodically checking the status on the router. The amber LED obstinately refused to turn green. By midnight, I gave up. It was still out of service at eight o'clock the following morning, and stayed that way throughout the day until four in the afternoon, when my doorbell rang. I opened the door to a technician from the cable company, who was nicely going from house to house making sure that everybody's internet was back up.

"I've never seen anything like it in all my years on the job," he told me, shaking his head and whispering conspiratorially that one of the fiber-optic network nodes had spontaneously caught fire late last night, for no obvious reason the engineers could see. Although this was summertime, and the weather had been warm, infrastructure equipment like this is designed to deal with heat. It should not catch fire and burn so intensely that it melts the actual glass itself.

Thanking the man for his time, I closed the door and found myself wondering whether this was a simple coincidence, or something more. Was this a "curse of *The Exorcist*" situation, or something similar?

Fast-forward three days, and I'm heading to my day job in the medical field. No sooner have I walked in the door than I'm approached by a member of staff I've never met before, a nurse who has heard about my reputation as a paranormal investigator through the grapevine and wants to ask my opinion about a photograph she has just taken. Setting down my bag, I accept her phone and look at a series of pictures of her daughter, taken in an idyllic countryside setting. She's sitting on a swing, enjoying a sunny afternoon. In five of the pictures, there's nothing abnormal whatsoever. The sixth is a different story. Swiping with my fingers to zoom in, I'm at a complete loss to explain why the face of a young girl has been somehow replaced with that of a screaming ghoul that looks—and I really hate to use the word—*demonic*. The girl's mother is credible, insofar as she doesn't want any publicity, isn't trying to sell the picture or cash in on it somehow. There's no obvious benefit to her Photoshopping the image or manipulating it in any way. Of course, it's possible that what we're both puzzling over is digital corruption or an artifact on the file. However, the fact the anomaly is localized exactly over her daughter's face is something she finds particularly disturbing.

Once again, I'm forced to ask myself whether this is a coincidence, a mere technical glitch, or something more.

With my search for demons now drawing to a close, I have some time to look back and reflect on what I've learned. It has been a strange and winding road, and I made every effort to gather as many different perspectives on the topic as I could. I spent nights in houses said to be infested with demons; participated in a talking board session in an attempt to contact the Zozo demon; made myself the subject of an exorcism ritual; and even laid my hands on the handwritten notes from the infamous St. Louis exorcism of 1949. Yet there's one thing I didn't do.

Attempt to actually summon a demon.

Although there are rituals intended to call demons into our world, the literature of demonology tells us that it's rarely, if ever, a good idea to do so. As we learned from the section of this book covering the Monroe House, it's all too easy for the entity to slip the proverbial leash and run amok, causing havoc in the lives of all those involved.

I gave this a lot of thought. To my knowledge, there is no objective evidence that demons can truly be summoned at all. There's no video footage of a demon manifesting in a cloud of sulfurous black smoke, or anything akin to it, that I'm aware of. All the claims regarding the successful summoning of demons are anecdotal.

And yet...

I have to consider the possibility that this is a very real and potentially harmful phenomenon. My high-speed tire blowout shortly after leaving the site of a demonic haunting has made me wonder just how much risk is involved with getting *too* hands-on. After all, it's one thing to go see lions and tigers at the zoo...and another thing entirely to unlock their cage and invite one to come eat you.

As my quest draws to a close, I have to acknowledge it's been a wild ride, but I remain undecided about the objective reality of demons. I have come to respect the perspectives of those who believe, those who do not, and those who, like me, still sit on the fence.

In writing this book, and making the journey that underpins it, it was never my intent to turn skeptics into believers, or believers into skeptics. My goal was always this: to immerse myself in the subject and form my own opinion. If you happen to believe in demons, I have not proven you right or wrong. The same holds true for the skeptic.

I will, however, close by saying this. Call it superstition, call it fear, maybe even call it a warning from the spiritual side of my consciousness that acts like Spider-Man's spider sense, tingling at the approach of danger—it feels like a bad idea to push my luck any further than I already have.

To borrow a phrase from the philosopher Friedrich Nietzsche, sometimes, when you stare into the abyss, the abyss stares back. I'm done staring into this particular abyss. I just can't shake the feeling that something is lurking in its deep, dark depths.

Could it be that something is staring right back?

ACKNOWLEDGMENTS

This, more than any other book I have written, took a village. If you enjoyed *In Search of Demons* and found anything of value in it, these are the people who deserve the credit. Any fault lies solely with the author. I would like to extend my heartfelt gratitude to the following people, without whom this book would not have been possible:

Michelle Belanger for writing a phenomenal foreword.

Laura, for supporting a moody writer who kept using the phrase "I'm on a deadline!"

The following friends and contributors who generously gave their time and expertise to help shine a light on this complex subject: Jesse and Seth Alne; Frank Anderson; Jeff Belanger; Karen A. Dahlman; MJ Dickson; Darren Evans; Jason Hawes; Steve Higgins; Johnny Houser; Becca Knight; Dr. Travis Langley; Dr. Joseph Laycock; Dr. Donald Molnar; Robert Murch; Greg Myers; Patti Negri; Dr. Ciaran O'Keeffe; Sandy Oates; Bryan Oullette; Rob Gray and Sarah Stream; Aaron Sagers; Dave Schrader; Aiden Sinclair; Erin and Mike Taylor; Troy Taylor.

Acknowledgments

The memory of Rosemary Ellen Guiley, who continues to inspire writers and paranormal enthusiasts.

Jason and Linda Fellon, for sharing a nightmarish drive to a slightly less scary location.

Josh Heard, for sending me on the road to Earling.

Lisa Krick.

Eddie and Pam Norris.

BIBLIOGRAPHY

Allen, Thomas B. *Possessed: The True Story of an Exorcism*. Lincoln, NE: iUniverse.com, 2000.

Belanger, Jeff. *Fright Before Christmas: Surviving Krampus and Other Yuletide Monsters, Witches, and Ghosts*. Newburyport, MA: New Page Books, 2023.

Belanger, Michelle A. *The Dictionary of Demons: Names of the Damned*. Woodbury, MN: Llewellyn Publications, 2021.

Brisbane, Arthur S. "Violent Deaths Plague Old 'Exorcist' Haunts." *Washington Post*. May 5, 1985. https://www
.washingtonpost.com/archive/politics/1985/05/06/violent
-deaths-plague-old-exorcist-haunts/4f734eaf-2239-4ad1-827f
-1e9580ce7db6/.

Dahlman, Karen A. *The Spirit of Alchemy*. Carefree, AZ: Creative Visions Publications, 2015.

Estep, Richard. *A Nightmare in Villisca: Investigating the Haunted Axe Murder House*. Independently published, 2020.

———. *On Dark Ground: Investigating the Haunted Monroe House*. Independently published, 2021.

Bibliography

Evans, Darren, and Rosemary Ellen Guiley. *The Zozo Phenomenon.* New Milford, CT: Visionary Living, 2016.

Gibson, Marley, Patrick Burns, and Dave Schrader. *The Other Side: A Teen's Guide to Ghost Hunting and the Paranormal.* Boston: Houghton Mifflin Harcourt, 2009.

Higgins, Steve. *The Rational Demonologist's Handbook.* Independently published, 2023.

Huxley, Aldous. *The Devils of Loudun.* New York: Harper Perennial, 2009.

James, Bill, and Rachel McCarthy James. *The Man from the Train: The Solving of a Century-Old Serial Killer Mystery.* New York: Simon & Schuster, 2017.

Laycock, Joseph P. *Penguin Book of Exorcisms.* London: Penguin Books, 2021.

Laycock, J. "The Secret History of the 'Earling Exorcism.'" In *The Social Scientific Study of Exorcism in Christianity* 3 (2020). https://doi.org/10.1007/978-3-030-43173-0_2.

Martin, Malachi. *Hostage to the Devil: The Possession and Exorcism of Five Contemporary Americans.* New York: Quality Paperback Book Club, 2000.

Opsasnick, Mark. *The Real Story Behind the Exorcist: A Study of the Haunted Boy and Other True-Life Horror Legends from Around the Nation's Capital.* Philadelphia, PA: Xlibris Corp., 2007.

Scott, Marvin, and Dan Rather. *As I Saw It: A Reporter's Intrepid Journey.* New York: Beaufort Books, 2017.

Taylor, Troy. *The Devil Came to St. Louis: Uncensored True Story of the 1949 Exorcism.* Jacksonville, IL: An American Hauntings Ink Book, 2021.

Vogl, Carl, and Celestine Kapsner. *Begone Satan!: A Soul-Stirring Account of Diabolical Possession.* Hong Kong: Catholic Truth Society, 1935.

Williamson, George Hunt, and Alfred C. Bailey. *The Saucers Speak! A Documentary Report of Interstellar Communication by Radiotelegraphy*. Mokelumne Hill, CA: Health Research, n.d.

Connecting with the Contributors

Frank L. Anderson: www.wisconsinology.com

Jeff Belanger: www.jeffbelanger.com

Michelle Belanger: www.michellebelanger.com

Karen A. Dahlman: www.karenadahlman.com

MJ Dickson: www.patreon.com/mjdickson

Jason Hawes: www.the-atlantic-paranormal.society.com

Steve Higgins: www.higgypop.com.

Dr. Travis Langley: www.travislangley.info

Dr. Joseph Laycock: https://faculty.txst.edu/profile/1922193

Robert Murch and The Talking Board Historical Society: www
.tbhs.org

Dr. Ciaran O'Keeffe: https://theschoolofparapsychology.ecwid
.com/

Patti Negri: www.pattinegri.com

Bryan Oullette: www.nicholean.org

Aaron Sagers: www.aaronsagers.com

Dave Schrader: www.paranormal60.com

Aiden Sinclair: www.aidensinclairsunderground.com

Troy Taylor: www.americanhauntingsink.com

To Write to the Author

If you wish to contact the author or would like more information about this book, please write to the author in care of Llewellyn Worldwide Ltd. and we will forward your request. Both the author and the publisher appreciate hearing from you and learning of your enjoyment of this book and how it has helped you. Llewellyn Worldwide Ltd. cannot guarantee that every letter written to the author can be answered, but all will be forwarded. Please write to:

Richard Estep
℅ Llewellyn Worldwide
2143 Wooddale Drive
Woodbury, MN 55125-2989

Please enclose a self-addressed stamped envelope for reply,
or $1.00 to cover costs. If outside the U.S.A., enclose
an international postal reply coupon.

Many of Llewellyn's authors have websites with additional information and resources. For more information, please visit our website at http://www.llewellyn.com.